CW01457227

An Illustrated History of the
WOODHEAD ROUTE

An
Illustrated History
of the
WOODHEAD ROUTE

Alan Whitehouse

OPC

An imprint of
Ian Allan Publishing

An Illustrated History of the Woodhead Route
Alan Whitehouse

First published 2010

ISBN 978 0 86093 635 0

All rights reserved. No part of this book may be reproduced or transmitted in any form or by any means, electronic or mechanical, including photocopying, recording, scanning or by any information storage and retrieval system, on the internet or elsewhere, without permission from the Publisher in writing.

© Alan Whitehouse 2010

Published by Oxford Publishing Co

an imprint of Ian Allan Publishing Ltd, Hersham, Surrey KT12 4RG.
Printed in England by Ian Allan Printing Ltd, Hersham, Surrey KT12 4RG.

Visit the Ian Allan Publishing website at www.ianallanpublishing.com

Distributed in the United States of America and Canada by BookMasters Distribution Services.

Code 1007/B1

Copyright
Illegal copying and selling of publications deprives authors, publishers and booksellers of income, without which there would be no investment in new publications. Unauthorised versions of publications are also likely to be inferior in quality and contain incorrect information. You can help by reporting copyright infringements and acts of piracy to the Publisher or the UK Copyright Service.

Mixed Sources
Product group from well-managed forests and other controlled sources
www.fsc.org Cert no. SGS-COC-005526
© 1996 Forest Stewardship Council
FSC

Front cover: **A pair of Class 76 locomotives passing West Silkstone Junction, beginning the descent of the Worsborough Bank with a train of empty MGR wagons. The locomotives will have collected the train from Godley Junction and will take it to Wath Exchange sidings. West Silkstone was where the MSW system diverged from the Penistone-Barnsley line, which can be seen to the right.** *Les Nixon*

Back cover: **A pair of Class 76s head a train of loaded MGR wagons west through Longdendale towards Torside level crossing. The train is destined for Fiddler's Ferry Power Station near Warrington. The electric locomotives will take it as far as Mottram, where diesel power will be substituted.** *Les Nixon*

Title page: **An early Great Central Railway train crosses Owlerton Viaduct on the outskirts of Sheffield. The view today is highly industrialised. The train itself consists of a Class '8B' 'Atlantic' hauling a GCR Brake Composite and two vehicles dating from MS&LR days.** *Great Central Railway Society, courtesy of John Quick*

Half title: **Huddersfield Junction, Penistone, in all its electrification glory. Electric services have not yet started on the main line, though, for this is April 1954 and the 'J11' 'Pom-Pom' is working a road-learning special, doubtless for Darnall drivers to familiarise themselves with the new colour-light signalling.** *E. R. Morten*

> *To Liz*
> *For the support, the IT support and the tea*

WOODHEAD NEW TUNNEL

LENGTH, 3 MILES ·66 YARDS

OPENED BY

THE RT. HON. ALAN LENNOX-BOYD P.C. M.P.

MINISTER OF TRANSPORT AND CIVIL AVIATION

THURSDAY 3RD JUNE 1954

J I.CAMPBELL M.I.C.E. CIVIL ENGINEER, EASTERN REGION BRITISH RAILWAYS
SIR WILLIAM HALCROW & PARTNERS M.M.I.C.E. CONSULTING ENGINEERS
BALFOUR BEATTY & COMPANY LIMITED. CIVIL ENGINEERING CONTRACTORS

Contents

Manchester – Sheffield – Wath Electrification track plans

Foreword

by Frank Paterson, former General Manager, British Rail Eastern Region

The Woodhead line has evoked powerful reactions among many groups of people over the last 150 years, and Alan describes and illustrates the growth and decline superbly.

In the 1840s entrepreneurs of Sheffield and Manchester recognised the commercial opportunities of transporting Yorkshire coal to the growing industries in Lancashire. The 3-mile Woodhead Tunnel through the Pennines was then acknowledged internationally as an exemplar of British engineering skills.

By the end of the century the growth in demand for coal needed more efficient working methods and these were initiated and developed under the sponsorship of Sir Sam Fay, General Manager of the Great Central Railway. The train crews who worked the range of steam locomotives under unbelievable conditions through the tunnels had tremendous loyalty to the route.

In 1938 the LNER introduced electrification as a means of improving the economics of one of the most intensively used routes in the whole UK rail network, but the 1939–45 war interrupted progress. After the war British Railways engineered a brand-new 3-mile Woodhead Tunnel and full electrification was implemented on 14 September 1954 with the proud boast that it was 'Britain's First All Electric Main Line'.

Then in the space of 27 years came the transition from a national showcase to an unwanted liability.

As General Manager of the Eastern Region of British Railways from 1978 it became my responsibility to oversee the successful closure of the Manchester–Penistone–Sheffield–Wath route, known in short as 'MSW'.

British Rail was, as ever, under intense government pressure to reduce costs. In 1977 we had agreed with government that the Rail Freight business should operate profitably. Part of the strategy to achieve this was the closure of the MSW. The incentive was that achievement of the profit target would release funds for investment, and high on our priority list was electrification. But to the general public there was an apparent contradiction – we were seeking to develop an electrified

network and at the same time proposing to close a line that had been electrified only relatively recently.

Alan has done an excellent rational analysis of the reasons, but emotions aren't receptive to rational arguments. We recognised that a communications strategy was essential. The message had to be clear and consistent – there was surplus capacity on the four trans-Pennine routes and the closure of the Woodhead line gave the best financial return.

I recall a dress rehearsal for the first staff and public consultation meetings when I'd asked all the local managers to 'role play' as objectors. The Wath Area Manager and his team marched into the boardroom at the York headquarters wearing badges and carrying banners 'SAVE THE MSW'. A taste of things to come!

We announced our intentions on 21 October 1979. The reactions from the trade unions were structured and well organised, and produced resolutions from their National Conferences directing the leadership to resist closure. Local Authorities and other groups lobbied intensively. The heaviest workload was on the area and divisional management teams who had to satisfy the knowledgeable staff and local opinion-formers that the proposals made sense. Transparency wasn't a buzzword at that time, but all the facts were revealed and substantiated. The reality was that the coal movements that had created the original need for the MSW had largely disappeared. After nearly two years of consultation, negotiation and considerable brinkmanship, the last train ran through Woodhead Tunnel on 18 July 1981.

The MSW closure generated a tremendous amount of public reaction and national media cover. The commitment and perseverance of railway managers to achieve the objective did, however, register with our political masters. I'm convinced that this influenced the government subsequently to approve two electrification projects in East Anglia and finally, in 1985, the East Coast main line. That made the aggro of the MSW saga well worthwhile!

Introduction

Forty years since the passenger trains were withdrawn and almost 30 years since the line closed completely, the Woodhead line still attracts a huge amount of attention and interest.

Much has already been published about the line, so what is there left to say? Clearly the first task of a new history is to ensure that it overlaps as little as possible with anything that has been written previously. This task has been tackled in two ways.

First, it has been written as much from a social perspective as an economic one. The names, dates, facts and figures are all there – they have to be. But overlying this traditional history is an attempt to convey the thoughts and feelings of the people involved from the line's inception, construction and operation through to the final closure. We will hear from those who built it, who stood on

exposed footplates to run the trains across it in all weathers, and who rode the line to measure the performance of the steam and electric locomotives that plied it, as well as the thoughts of those who finally decided, however regretfully, that closure was the only realistic option.

Second, the closure itself. Published material to date has tended to skirt around the issue of why a recently electrified main line was stripped of its passenger services and, a decade later, closed completely. There have been claims of conspiracies, old scores being settled and straightforward incompetence on the part of those running the line. Here is an attempt to get to the truth, and for the first time some of the senior British Rail officials involved in the closure have broken their silence to speak about their part in the Woodhead line's demise. Some still wish to remain anonymous.

In his Foreword, the man ultimately responsible for that decision puts forward what might almost be seen as an 'anti-conspiracy' theory: that closing the line actually paved the way for bigger and better things on other parts of the rail network.

Indeed, a dispassionate analysis leads to the conclusion that the Woodhead line was not so much the victim of a vindictive and mendacious BR management, but rather of a general anti-railway climate fostered by a series of governments that saw only a limited future for rail transport.

Under these circumstances, BR was buffeted by events beyond its control. Woodhead's passenger services were lost in the wake of the Beeching era, when a stripped-down and streamlined railway performing a limited range of tasks was seen as the future. Complete closure came after a government decision that the social benefits of having freight on railways were not worth the cash subsidy required. So rail freight had to become profitable almost overnight. A freight-only railway was then clearly going to be vulnerable. As the former BR officer John Nelson remarked during the research of this book:

'Everyone has this nostalgic view. But there were momentous events taking place that were reshaping the social and industrial landscape and this was part of it.'

But there is equally no doubt that, having made the decision, BR built an impregnable closure case by making sure that all the facts fitted it. The bad news – the cost of converting the system to AC electrification, the cost of replacement locomotives and so on – was certainly played up, some would say shamelessly exaggerated, while the route's strategic potential was dismissed as an irrelevance. This might not be completely honourable, but it is also a long way from the conspiracy theories that have been aired in the past.

Aside from the text, other efforts have been made to bring a fresh aspect to the story of the route. The 'Woodhead Line' is defined here as the limits of the pioneering Manchester, Sheffield and Wath (MSW) electrification scheme. This project involved drawing up a comprehensive resignalling scheme from Manchester London Road to Rotherwood, east of Sheffield, and Wath Yard. Signal engineers from both the Eastern Region and the London Midland Region drew up a schematic plan covering every running line, loop, siding and junction. It was produced in two halves – the style changes at the Woodhead tunnel portal – and is reproduced here, it is believed, for the first time. Some editing has been necessary to make it fit – the original is some 90 feet long when pieced together! But it should still give an impression of the scale of the task facing the signal, electrification and civil engineers who reworked the route in the post-war years, turning it into a showcase railway. It will also assist in following the geography of the line.

Efforts have also been made to showcase photographs and other images that have been seen only rarely, or never, before. The hope is that some of them will either rekindle memories among those old enough to remember the line as it once was, or to stimulate further interest among those unlucky enough never to have seen it in action.

Curiously, for a line that closed almost three decades ago, the Woodhead route's future is still in a state of flux. There have been three distinct proposals to reopen it, while a fourth may be just around the corner. Few railways can claim the formation of a protest group to save a line of route so long after the last trains ran, but that is exactly what has happened here. As with so many things on the MSW, always expect the unexpected!

Alan Whitehouse
Holmfirth, April 2010

Acknowledgements

Few people write a factual book completely alone and this one is no exception. Many people have been generous with their time, expertise, photographs and memories. The individual photographers are named in the captions and I can only add my gratitude to those who dug deep in their files to find a few more little-known pictures.

Simon Foster deserves an honourable mention for taking the two halves of the resignalling plan, making it whole and adding the colour. Trevor Moseley and John Saxton kindly made the originals available. John Quick of the Great Central Railway Society, David Annable of The Woodhead Site website, Keith Long and Andrew Walker read the text, combing out the more obvious mistakes. The ones that remain are my own responsibility.

David Jackman of the Railway Correspondence and Travel Society was helpful in obtaining permission to quote from Part 10B of Locomotives of the LNER – it contains what is still the best account of the development and operation of both the EM1 and EM2 electric locomotives. Nick Pigott, Editor of *Railway Magazine*, and George Reeve of *British Railways Illustrated* both readily gave permission to quote from their magazines. Barbara Semmens was also agreeable that her late husband's work should be extensively quoted. The Stephenson Locomotive Society also allowed parts of Peter Semmens' analysis of declining coal traffic across the Pennines to be reproduced here. The publishers Harper Collins gave permission to quote from Prof. W.A. Tuplin's *Great Central Steam*. Julie Brown at Arriva Plc was helpful in arranging permission to reproduce an impression of their proposed Woodhead Line Class 180 DMU.

Frank Paterson, John Nelson and Malcolm Morris were good enough to spend time recalling their part in the route's closure, providing valuable insights into official thinking at the time. Others who wish to remain anonymous have also been helpful in this area. David Ward, formerly of Dutch Railways, drafted an account of his part in that organisation's failed attempt to buy some of the fleet of Class 76 locomotives after closure. He was also good enough to answer supplementary questions via e-mail.

Others who have assisted in various ways include Alan Butcher of Ian Allan, Les Nixon, Chris Hogg, Chris Nettleton of the Gresley Society and, finally, my editor at Ian Allan, Peter Waller, who generously turned the Ian Allan Library upside down searching for pictures while I was temporarily disabled. My thanks to them all, and to anyone else who has been inadvertently left off this list.

This leaves one uncredited source: George Potts' book, *Bankers and Pilots*, was published by D. Bradford Barton, a company no longer in existence. Extensive inquiries have failed to establish who may now hold the copyright. If any reader can assist, it would be appreciated if they could make contact via the publisher so that this omission can be corrected in a future edition.

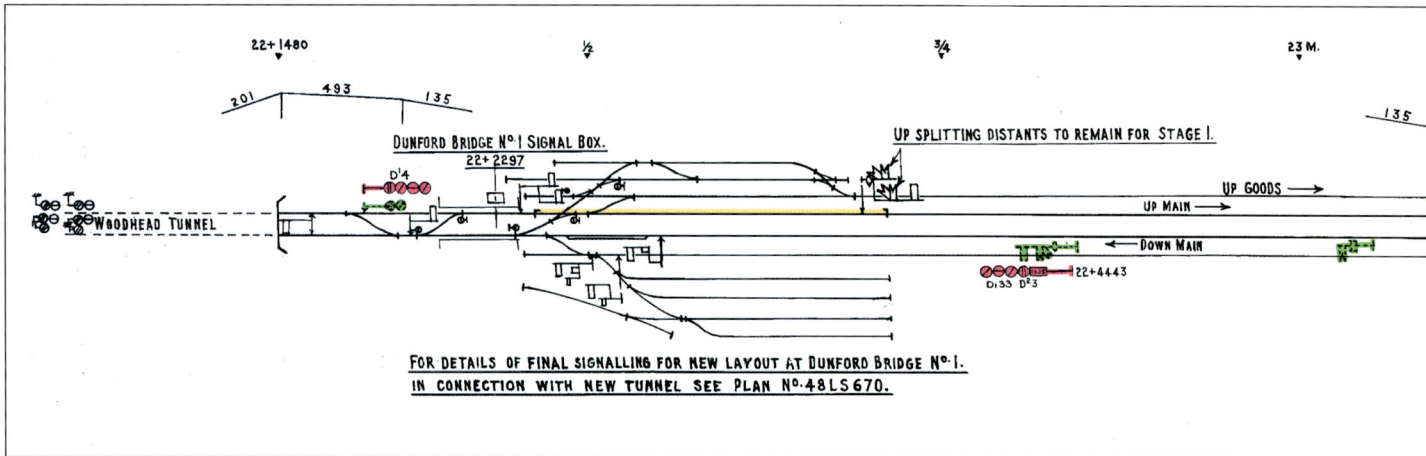

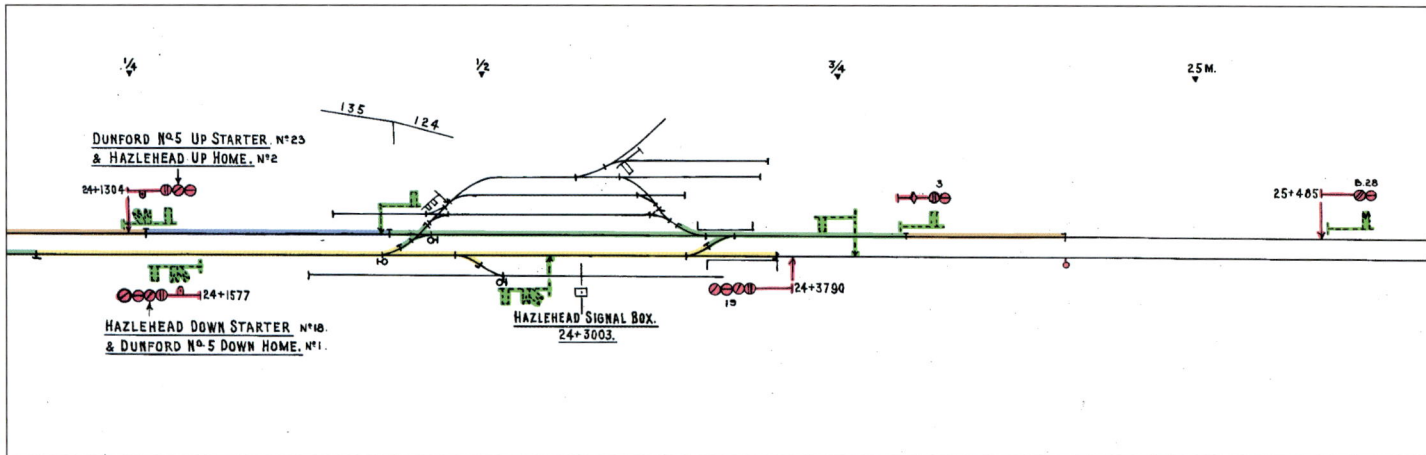

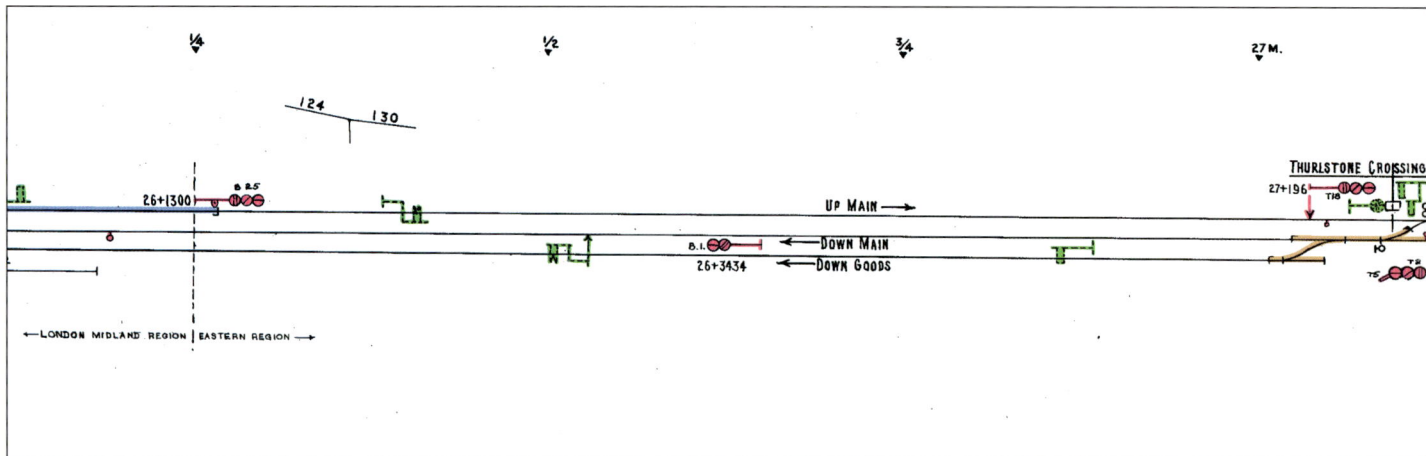

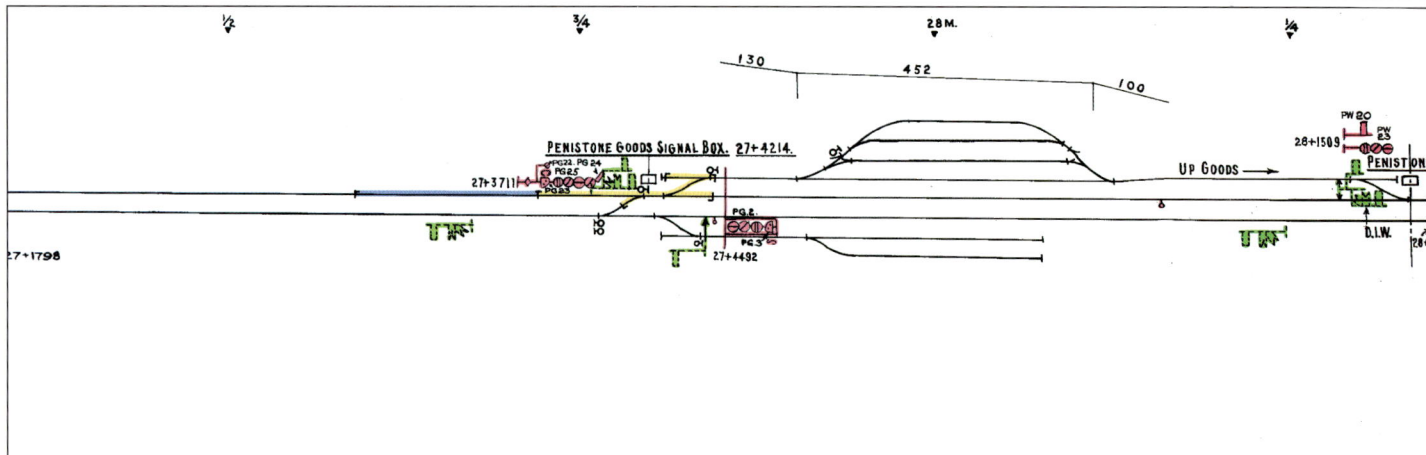

Panel 1 (top):

¼   ½   ¾   24 M.

135

15
27
28

No.2 SIGNAL BOX.

23+5159   18
16
17

DUNFORD No.5 SIGNAL BOX.
24+275.

23+3758   Ds 24

01

23+1676

7   2   10

29
31

D21   Ds 4   23+4301

Panel 2:

½   ¾   26 M.   ¼

124

26

25+4231

BULLHOUSE COLLIERY SIGNAL BOX. 25+5082

26+1300

25+1664

25+3676
5

01

26+410

3
12

← LONDON MIDLAND REGION | E

Panel 3:

¼   ½   ¾   28 M.

130   452   100

PENISTONE GOODS SIGNAL BOX. 27+4214.

PG22. PG 24
PG25
PG23

27+3711
1F
01

UP GOODS

27+1798

00

PG.2
PG.3

27+4492

Panel 4 (bottom):

½   ¾   29 M.   ¼

100

166

TO WATH

15 M.P.H. →

HJ 33.13.
HJ11A
HJ16
HJ1B

.P.H. →

28+3002

HJ49   BJ48

29+1188

BJ4.

NO BLOCK

28+2616
HJ2

28+3373

UP GOODS No.1. →

28+5212

BJ35

29+1120

NO BLOCK

(+1772)

HJ12.
HJ61

28+4035

DOWN GOODS No.1 →
UP MAIN →

BJ36

BJ12.

BJ9/10

← DOWN MAIN

29+864

→ TO SHEFFIELD

SSIVE BLOCK

DOWN GOODS No.2 →

WILLEY BRIDGE
DISTANT No.26

BARNSLEY JCN. SIGNAL BOX.

29+1120

HUDDERSFIELD JCN. SIGNAL BOX.

-40 M.P.H.

28+2916.

HJ62

29+540.

483 YDS.

HJ66
HJ64/65 HJ67

28+3560.

BJ14   BJ13   29+175

HJ 54
HJ 59   HJ 56
HJ60

28+3074

FOR DETAILS OF COMPLETE SIGNALLING
AT BARNSLEY JUNCTION SEE PLAN No. 50 LS.687 B.

9

'A triumph of art over nature'

The first day of October 1838 dawned fine, dry and clear, something that was by no means a guaranteed occurrence at that time of year in the unpredictable surroundings of the Pennine hills. The weather was doubtless appreciated by Lord Wharncliffe and his two sons as they picked their way on horseback over the summit and descended to a patch of boggy ground close to the River Etherow.

The Etherow is not one of Britain's best-known rivers, and here it is no more than a stream tumbling enthusiastically into Longdendale. At this point it turns sharply, falling away from a steep slope that seems to extend well into the sky.

This was to be the western portal of the Woodhead Tunnel, centrepiece of a new railway linking Manchester with Sheffield – and beyond – carrying passengers at comparatively breakneck speed across the often inhospitable moorland.

Wharncliffe was Chairman of the nascent Sheffield, Ashton-under-Lyne & Manchester Railway. He paused at a small collection of tents and marquees set up to provide refreshments for the company's guests, then walked a little further down the hill, took a spade and drove it into the peaty soil, turning the first sod of the new railway. A procession of other directors followed, each wielding the spade. Some were more expert than others, causing the ladies of the party a little amusement as they watched from a nearby knoll. Finally, the line's engineer, Charles Vignoles, stepped up and took the spade himself. The SA&M had been started.

That Victorian staple, a cold collation, was served. We can easily imagine the conversation: talk of difficulties to be encountered, fortunes to be made and alliances with other railway companies to be forged. As the sky began to darken, the party broke up and went its separate ways.

Another seven years and more would elapse before the first trains ran over the Pennines. But even getting this far had not been easy. There had been trade between South Yorkshire and Lancashire for centuries, but the Pennines remained an obstinate physical barrier to any attempts to speed up the three-day journey between the two places. In the early 1800s canals linked them, but offered few time advantages.

In 1813 a canal engineer, William Chapman, proposed a tramway to link Sheffield and Manchester. He had recently taken out patents on designs for a steam locomotive and pivoted bogie. His scheme would use six inclined planes, three on each side of the summit. Interestingly, he was not concerned with carting coal from the coalfields of the east to the industries of the west, but instead saw a market moving limestone in the opposite direction, calculating that his engines could shift around 600 tons per day. However, he rather spoiled his case by proposing not a rail but a canal tunnel under the summit. It would have meant lengthy and costly transhipment – twice – on every trip, and the idea was not pursued.

But the idea of a Sheffield–Manchester link would not go away. In 1824 the canal idea was revived again and was swiftly followed by five more proposals using a variety of routes: Edale, Castleton and, rather improbably, Penistone. But a year later the Cromford & High Peak Railway opened for business. At a stroke it killed off any thoughts of a waterway link. The C&HPR demonstrated beyond doubt that railways were faster, even if you had to keep stopping to haul wagons up and down inclined planes – steeply graded sections – that steam locomotives could never hope to handle. The C&HPR used inclined planes at gradients of 1 in 8 and 1 in 9, powered by stationary steam engines. Initially the intervening sections were operated with horses, though later the Hopton Incline – 1 in 14 – would be operated by conventional steam locomotives.

At about the same time, Henry Sanderson, a Sheffield-based surveyor, emerged as the leading campaigner for a link between Manchester and Sheffield. Within a few years he would go head-to-head with George Stephenson over the best route. But in 1826 he issued a 92-page pamphlet proposing a route via Edale with two tunnels, one half a mile long, the second 1¾ miles. There would be five inclined planes, and the route from Sheffield Canal Basin to Chapel Milton, where a junction would be made with the Peak Forest Railway, would be 22 miles.

No great distance away, the Liverpool & Manchester Railway obtained its Act the same year and opened in 1829. The Railway Age had well and truly begun. But the Pennine ridge appeared as impassable as ever. The following year, however, the Sheffield & Manchester Railway prospectus was issued and a few months later, in 1831, Sanderson crossed swords with Stephenson over how the proposed line could best be built. Stephenson came up with a scheme involving a total of 6½ miles of tunnelling. Sanderson's counter-proposal suggested a route from Sheffield to Penistone, Woodhead and Glossop Dale to Stockport, then Manchester. It would be worked by locomotives throughout. Inclined planes were now as old hat as canals, he reckoned.

But Stephenson's scheme, inclined planes and all, was the one that was pushed forward and here is a minor mystery. Stephenson was the champion of the self-contained locomotive. Almost single-handedly he had turned around opinion at the Liverpool & Manchester company, persuading unconvinced directors that locomotives, not horses, were the way ahead. Why abandon that view now?

The clue may be in Stephenson's whole outlook on railways and difficult terrain. Seven years later, in 1838, at the opening of the Sheffield & Rotherham Railway, Stephenson declared that Rotherham was the only route out of Sheffield and defied anyone to build a route westwards. This was unusually defeatist talk. Had he taken on too much? Were other projects more pressing, leading him to talk down the prospects for a Sheffield–Manchester link? We shall never know, but by 1833 Stephenson's plans were in trouble. Sanderson had effectively exposed the scheme's weaknesses, and at a special meeting called on 5 June to decide whether or not to go ahead, he once again tore into Stephenson's proposals, and the Sheffield & Manchester Railway was abandoned.

Sanderson himself became more and more convinced that a route from Sheffield via Deepcar and Langsett was the way to go, reaching Woodhead, then down Longdendale to Hadfield, Mottram, Godley and Stockport.

But for now the idea of a Manchester–Sheffield railway link went firmly onto the back burner and it was not until 1836 that a new company – the Sheffield, Ashton-under-Lyne & Manchester Railway – was set up. Here we see yet another variation of the possible route for such a scheme: this one would leave a station in Store Street, Manchester, and run via Gorton, Ashton, Hyde, Glossop and Woodhead to Thurlstone, Penistone, Wortley and finally to Sheffield.

The eminent engineers Charles Vignoles and Joseph Locke were involved, together with a selection of the great and good from both sides of the Pennines. By the end of the year rapid progress had been made. A 'tweaked' route running via Guide Bridge was proposed and a longer tunnel – 3 miles rather than 2 – was proposed. The whole route would be workable by locomotives. It would stretch for a little over 40 miles, city centre to city centre.

There is a feeling here of a route chosen as a 'means to an end', rather like the later Settle & Carlisle proposals in which the goal was simply to link two centres; serving communities between the two was seen as having little if any priority. The decision to bypass Glossop – building instead a three-quarter-mile branch line, an operational inconvenience to this day – is evidence of the thinking. Something similar happened with Ashton, where a branch from Guide Bridge was proposed instead of the original direct route.

By now, Britain was at the height of Railway Mania. The SA&M Railway Bill was one of a batch of 118 presented to Parliament. Charles Vignoles claimed that the locomotives of the day would be capable of a journey time of 2½ hours, while lengthening the proposed Woodhead Tunnel from 2 miles to 3, thereby reducing its summit to 943 feet above sea level, would mean that the line had no gradient steeper then 1 in 120.

But it was Joseph Locke who finally put his finger on what this new railway would be all about. Not only would it be of '…great mercantile importance, destined to form a direct thoroughfare between the East and West seas', but it would also be extraordinarily well placed:

'The great, I may say greatest unworked coalfield in England is contiguous to the line and since this field must have an outlet to the Eastern sea by the Humber, it amounts to a certainty that a communication between this line and the Humber will in no distant period be made.'

Flowery language perhaps, but Locke had tapped into what would be the guiding vision of the successor companies to own the Woodhead route: in effect, Manchester, Sheffield and now Lincolnshire!

The Parliamentary Bill met with little opposition. A deal was agreed whereby it would meet the Manchester & Birmingham Railway's line at Ardwick, a mile or so from Manchester city centre, and from there run into a joint terminus at Store Street.

Work began almost immediately, sinking test shafts along the line of what would become the Woodhead Tunnel. Vignoles then ordered a drift tunnel, large enough for two men to work in, to be driven along the proposed alignment. This would be enlarged to form the single-line running tunnel envisaged by the SA&M proposals. It was estimated that the complete railway would cost £700,000.

It has often been said that the Woodhead Line resembled nothing so much as the gable end of a house - and this gradient profile shows the difficulties faced by loco crew with sustained gradients in each direction. The map gives an idea of the line's strategic value.

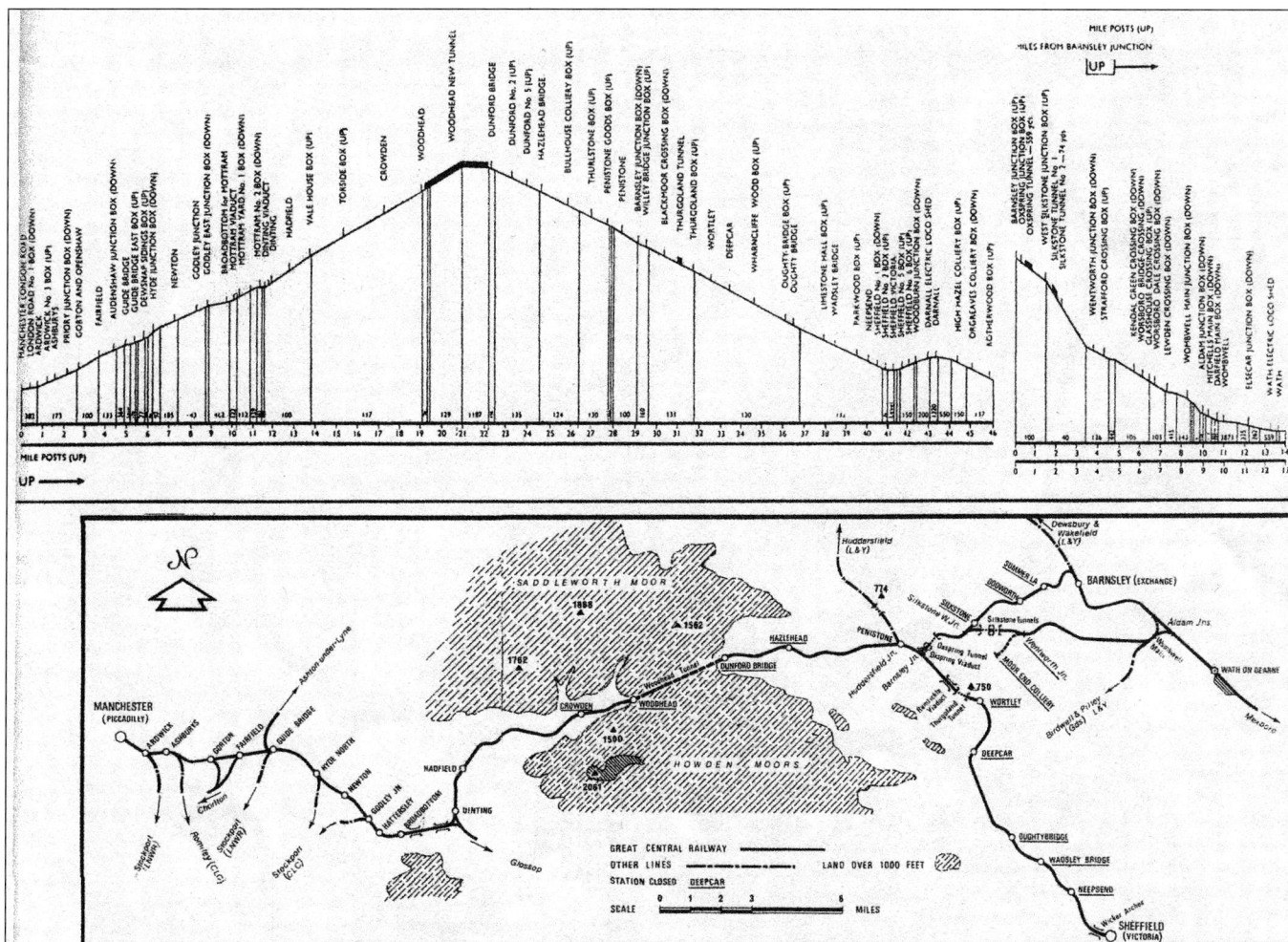

Right: **An early-20th-century view of Manchester London Road. The view today is changed out of all recognition apart from the ramp access from street level to the station.** *John Quick collection*

Below: **At the other end of the line, an early MS&LR locomotive pauses at Neepsend, on the outskirts of Sheffield.** *Great Central Railway Society*

Then, on that clear October day in 1838, construction work proper began. By 1839 the whole line of route had been staked out and contracts to build it had been let. Perhaps inspired by Locke's vision, approaches were made to the Liverpool & Manchester Railway to create an end-on junction to allow through-running between the two lines. Alas, the idea was rejected, or Manchester city centre might have appeared very different and yet another set of operating problems, still present, might have been avoided.

Building a railway line across a great physical barrier like the Pennines brought its own problems. In 1839 the directors – drawn, naturally, from both sides of the hills – agreed to meet at an Inn at Salters Brook, out in the wilds, about halfway between the two cities. As an inducement to attend board meetings, £32 was placed on the table at the start of each meeting and each director who turned up before 11am was entitled to take £2 for his trouble. Any cash remaining was divided pro rata.

And now the problems began. There was a falling out with Charles Vignoles towards the end of that year. By January 1840 Locke had been confidentially approached and agreed to take on the job of engineer. Within months, Wharncliffe himself had resigned following a row with his fellow directors. But progress was being made and by the end of the year the first rails and chairs were on order.

But others were making progress too. The Leeds & Manchester Railway had been pushing ahead with its own line and in March 1841 the Summit Tunnel was completed. By using the L&M to Normanton, the North Midland Railway's line to Rotherham Masborough, then the Sheffield & Rotherham Railway's route, it was now possible to travel between Manchester and Sheffield by rail. Three years later, in February 1844, a journey was described in the *Sheffield & Rotherham Independent* newspaper that began at 4.45pm and ended at 12.30am. It appeared under the headline 'Brisk travelling'!

However, in 1841 the SA&M started to look like a proper railway company. Track was being laid and Engine Driver No 1 was appointed, an enthusiastic young chap called Richard Peacock, who would go on to become Superintendent of the Line, and then leave to co-found Beyer, Peacock, just across the tracks from Gorton Works. The company of Beyer, Peacock would in the fullness of time supply the Woodhead line's future owner, the London & North Eastern Railway, with Britain's largest steam locomotive, the Class 'U1' Beyer-Garratt, which was used as a banking engine on a section of the Penistone–Wath route. As we shall see, if things had worked out differently a whole class of these locomotives might have been built to haul coal over the Woodhead route.

At last, in November 1841, the first trains began running. The railway was complete only from Store Street to Godley Toll Bar, some 8¼ miles away. The directors had a private trip and an inspection was made by Sir F. Smith, the Board of Trade's Inspector of Railways. He must have been satisfied with what he saw because on 17 November the first public train left Store Street at 8.00am. There were just three locomotives and 14 carriages available, but the SA&M railway was in business.

Operation over the single line was simple: when a service arrived at one of the terminals, another train was sent off in the opposite direction. Police, or early signalmen, were stationed along the route with flags and lamps. There were no fixed signals and no block working. But the new line appears to have been a hit, carrying 17,400 passengers in its first 17 days.

Left: **A panoramic view of Woodhead station with a down express headed by what may be a 'Sir Sam Fay' Class 4-6-0 locomotive.**

between Manchester and Woodhead. It took 70 minutes to complete the journey. The Woodhead Tunnel was more than half complete by now, with 3,250 yards ready for tracklaying. Just another 2,050 yards to go! The following year a single-track branch into Glossop was opened from the junction at Dinting and the station there now took this name.

At the same time the Sheffield–Dunford section was also nearing completion. Seven stations – Dunford, Penistone, Wortley, Deepcar, Oughty Bridge (the village itself is named Oughtibridge), Wadsley Bridge and Sheffield – were provided. This section was opened without formalities on 14 July.

This now left the small matter of completing the 3 miles of tunnel between Dunford Bridge and Woodhead. Even today this would be a major undertaking. Then, it was civil engineering on a breathtaking scale.

The next three years saw the rails extended slowly eastwards. January 1842 saw instructions issued to double the line (though not at Woodhead, where a single-track tunnel was still thought to be adequate). In December the line reached Broadbottom. Two weeks later, on Christmas Eve, the next section to Dinting (then named Glossop) was cleared for traffic. Horse-drawn road coaches took passengers on to Sheffield.

The line was now a long scar of construction work running right along the Etherow Valley, and the route had been set out along the Don Valley from Dunford Bridge down to Sheffield. Right in the middle, gangs of tunnellers were at work up to 200 yards beneath the Pennines digging the first Woodhead Tunnel.

Commercial traffic was also beginning to make itself felt. In addition to all those passengers, the first colliery branch on the route opened in 1842, running to Dunkirk Colliery near Dewsnap.

The potential connectivity of the line was also being explored. In 1843 plans were put forward for a Barnsley Junction Railway, leaving the SA&M at Penistone and running eastwards through Barnsley itself and on to Royston on the North Midland Railway.

The line from Dinting to Woodhead opened in August 1844 with a service of five trains per day

Above: **Wortley station is seen in a classic Biltcliffe photograph. This is one of the less-photographed locations and the station itself was an early casualty, closing in the 1950s.** *Peter Sunderland collection*

Left: **Deepcar station early in the 20th century. MS&LR architecture is obvious.** *Biltcliffe, Peter Sunderland collection*

A rare view of a Great Central train on the exotically named Romtickle Viaduct, Thurgoland, near Wortley. It is believed to date from 1900 and shows a Pollitt Class '11A' 4-4-0 on a down train. Note the early French grey and brown livery of the coaching stock. *John Quick collection*

The original plan had been for a twin-track tunnel, but economies forced on the project almost from the start meant that it was scaled back to be a single-track bore. There are clues that the SA&M directors knew that they were creating a future bottleneck: enough land was bought to add a second tunnel later.

The major problem was housing and feeding the huge workforce needed to complete the tunnel out in the wilds between Woodhead and Dunford Bridge. The nearest settlement of any size was Penistone, a full 7 miles from Dunford Bridge. The SA&M management acquired government-surplus military field tents for the summer of 1838 until more permanent buildings could be erected. Four miles of cart roads were constructed to link the various work sites. Workers' cottages followed, together with stables for the many horses and stores. It was autumn 1839, more than a year later, before these preliminary works were finished and full attention could be given to the tunnel itself.

It was a complex piece of engineering, on a rising gradient of 1 in 201 from west to east until just a few yards from the east portal at Dunford Bridge, where the summit was breasted and the line began to fall. The geology was complex too, with strata of millstone grit, shale and sandstone to be dealt with. Five ventilation shafts, each 8 feet in diameter, were to be sunk.

Tunnelling teams began work at each end and, as the ventilation shafts reached their required depth, teams began working outwards from them to link up with each other. It is a remarkable footnote that when all these headings broke through to link with each other, there was never an error of more than 3 inches.

There was a social as well as an engineering story to the Woodhead Tunnel. At the peak of construction work, more than 1,500 navvies, specialist tunnellers and labourers were working on the 3-mile site, though a more typical figure was between 400 and 500. The men were paid generous wages to tempt them to life in what could be violently inhospitable surroundings, living in what were regarded as primitive conditions even by the standards of the day.

Even so, the project was plagued by labour shortages and it is unsurprising that 26 men died building the tunnel. The work was slow and dangerous, partly because of the huge volumes of rock to be shifted, which had to be blasted apart with gunpowder – they used 157 tons of the stuff – and partly because of problems with water entering the works as underground springs were accidentally tapped.

But finally, on 22 December 1845, the first Woodhead Tunnel was complete. The SA&M had created the longest railway tunnel in the country at 3 miles 22 yards.

The smoky hole itself: a view thought to date from 1910, and which may be a Biltcliffe picture, showing the tunnel portals at Woodhead. Of interest is the original, castellated station building. It is winter: both the chimneys and the 'fire devil' at the water column are pouring out smoke. *John Quick collection*

Left: **The classic Biltcliffe view of Hazlehead station, near Dunford Bridge, one of the most remote on the line, serving a collection of farmsteads and isolated cottages.**
Peter Sunderland collection

Above and left: **Two views of Dunford Bridge, one showing the remote nature of this moorland community, the second showing the railway making its presence felt with station, goods yard and the start of the extensive coal sorting sidings.**
Both Biltcliffe, Peter Sunderland collection

15

The company seems to have had an inkling of the operating problems that a lengthy tunnel on a rising gradient would cause. At one stage plans to operate it using atmospheric traction – rather like Brunel's ill-fated Devon scheme – were floated. Joseph Locke was even asked to report on the experiences of the Dublin & Kingstown Railway, which opened in 1843 using a similar system. But Locke was unconvinced and came down in favour of steam traction.

Now public anxieties about using the tunnel had to be addressed. A telegraph system – a primitive form of block working – was installed, operated by station clerks at Woodhead and Dunford Bridge. A pilot engine had to be attached to every train to minimise the risk of passengers becoming stranded in the subterranean gloom, choking on smoke and fumes, because of a locomotive failure. This was an era when there were still many public anxieties about travelling on railways at all, let alone through a 3-mile tunnel in the middle of nowhere.

But these worries could be set aside on 22 December 1845, when the formal opening took place. More than 20 years since the first stirrings and more than 7 years after the first ground had been broken, at 10.05am a 20-coach special train hauled by two locomotives left Bridgehouses station. Flags flew, and the band of the Sheffield Yeomanry played. Contemporary accounts describe the countryside as being deep under snow. This first service took 10 minutes to pass through Woodhead Tunnel. It is easy to imagine the inward sighs of relief from engineers and directors that at last the railway was complete – and the inward sighs of relief from passengers, who spontaneously gave three cheers as they emerged safely through the Woodhead portal into Longdendale. Manchester was safely reached by 12.15pm.

A day of speeches, eating and drinking followed. The party made the return trip a little over an hour later, pausing to admire some of the more impressive engineering works, and to pick up more guests from intermediate stations. Public opinion seemed to be firmly behind the new railway and its courageous promoters. The *Sheffield Iris* called the Woodhead Tunnel, 'A triumph of art over nature and may be pronounced the greatest engineering work of the kind which has yet been consummated'. Praise indeed.

The Sheffield, Ashton-under-Lyne & Manchester Railway was complete and open for business. Deals had been done and alliances cemented that would allow the line to prosper by feeding traffic into and out of other routes. The seemingly impossible Pennine barrier had been breached. The future must have appeared bright almost beyond belief.

In the first few years of the new railway's existence, there was no shortage of ideas and schemes for lines that would feed into and out of what was, virtually from day one, a strategic piece of railway. Branches to almost every conceivable town within striking distance were drawn up. Wakefield, Pontefract, Newark, New Mills and Buxton all, apparently, simply had to be connected to the Woodhead line.

Most of these schemes came to nothing, like so many other Railway Mania-inspired ideas. However, one that did bear fruit was a plan for a line from Sheffield to Grimsby. The details fall outside the scope of this book, but as early as September 1845, just three months before its own line was fully opened, SA&M directors met their opposite numbers at the Sheffield & Lincolnshire Junction Railway and the Great Grimsby & Sheffield Junction Railway.

When both these schemes were complete, a continuous line from Manchester via Sheffield to the North Sea coast would exist, fulfilling the vision expressed by Locke even before work on the Woodhead line had even begun.

A grand scheme to amalgamate all three railways was put together as a way of freezing out potential rivals, and the newly formed Manchester, Sheffield & Lincolnshire Railway held its first board meeting on 6 January 1847. While the Woodhead line was only one part of the new railway, it was very much the pivotal part, allowing trains not only to reach Manchester from the North Sea coast, but later from Manchester to London, when the MS&LR transformed itself again into the Great Central Railway. It also triggered the decision to begin work on a short extension east of Bridgehouses station to make the physical connection between the three lines, establishing along the way the new Sheffield Victoria station.

But for all its strategic value, the Woodhead line always had a shaky financial existence. Conquering the Pennines did not come cheap and, from an original estimate by Charles Vignoles

A pair of vintage MS&LR locomotives: No 216 was a Charles Sacre design built by Sharp Stewart, while No 223 was built in 1867 at the Atlas Works in Manchester. *Ian Allan Library*

Early pictures of the route to Wath are rare. In this Biltcliffe picture, a Class 8A 0-8-0 'Tiny' locomotive crosses Oxspring Viaduct, running light. *Peter Sunderland collection*

of £106,000, Woodhead Tunnel actually cost more than £200,000. And there was worse financial news. The single-track tunnel quickly turned into the bottleneck that it had always promised to be: 3 miles of single track in the centre of a 40-mile double-track main line, requiring special provisions to work it. A second track was urgently needed, and in 1847 work began on the second tunnel, also single-track.

This was to carry the up line, so was built to the north of the existing tunnel and connected to it by opening out the 25 niches or manholes built into the tunnel wall to give maintenance staff a safe refuge if caught in the tunnel by a passing train. These niches became small cross-passages linking the two bores.

Again, a workforce had to be assembled out in the Pennine wilds, but this time, as well as industrial accidents, disease struck – a cholera outbreak claimed 28 victims at the Woodhead end. Almost five years after work began, the second tunnel opened in February 1852.

A year earlier, Bridgehouses station in Sheffield was abandoned in favour of the new Victoria station, which was closer to the city centre and was carried about 40 feet above street level on a series of arches. Bridgehouses became a goods depot, with coal drops, hydraulic cranes and a siding for potato traffic, from which locomotives were forbidden. A century or more later this anonymous piece of track would be immortalised in the BBC TV documentary *Engines Must Not Enter The Potato Siding*.

At this stage, the second arm of the Woodhead line, the branch from Penistone to Wath, had been given little or no thought. True, work had progressed on the line from Penistone to Barnsley. The original scheme for a direct route to Royston to join the North Midland (later Midland Railway) main line between Sheffield and Leeds came to nothing. A link was built later, but it never carried the direct passenger trains originally envisaged.

Instead, in 1851, work began on a line that left Penistone at Barnsley Junction, passing through Oxspring and crossing a viaduct before plunging into a tunnel to emerge near Silkstone, on a falling gradient through Dodworth, tapping several collieries along the way. Work then paused for a while to allow the engineers to think long and hard about the best way of driving a line into Barnsley.

The MS&LR line from Penistone was opened for goods working as far as Dodworth in May 1854, and passenger workings commenced in July of the same year. By November 1855 passenger workings had reached a temporary terminus at Summer Lane. From this point onwards the topography became very difficult, with the line descending into Barnsley on gradients of up to 1 in 50. Although only a short distance, the size of the cutting required was such that it took a further two years to complete the final stretch. Goods working to the

Barnsley Junction, Penistone. The view is undated, but note the 'MS&LR' on the locomotive tank sides and the wagon coupled to it, suggesting that it was taken before, or not long after, the change of name to 'Great Central'. *Biltcliffe, Peter Sunderland collection*

MS&LR depot at Regent Street, later renamed Barnsley Central (Goods), began straight away, but although an Act of 1853 had authorised the MS&LR to connect its branch with the existing Lancashire & Yorkshire Railway station at Barnsley, there was a lengthy dispute over the signalling of the new junction, forcing Summer Lane to remain the effective passenger terminus. The situation was eventually resolved, and on 1 December 1859 passenger trains began working from Penistone into Barnsley station and from there over South Yorkshire Railway tracks to Mexborough and Doncaster.

Barnsley's railway history is complex and falls outside the story of the Woodhead line, but the MS&LR and later the Great Central and LNER found themselves sharing two stations in the town with the Midland and Lancashire & Yorkshire railways, with access to the South Yorkshire Railway's routes to both Doncaster and Sheffield. And it was the SYR that held the key to the final development of the Woodhead line.

The SYR reached Wath via a single-track line from Doncaster. Its purpose was pure and simple: to feed coal from the burgeoning mining industry of the Dearne Valley into the Great Northern Railway at Doncaster for onward transport. It was set up in 1846 and the line was built in several stages to Mexborough, then on to Elsecar to serve a string of new coal mines, including some of those of Earl Fitzwilliam, the first chairman of the company. Barnsley, as we have seen, was reached in 1851. This gave the continuous run from Doncaster and Mexborough to Barnsley, Penistone and the Woodhead line, allowing valuable coal traffic to be tapped along the Dearne Valley.

Just as important to the SYR's fortunes was a lengthy branch built from Aldam Junction, on the outskirts of Wombwell, and

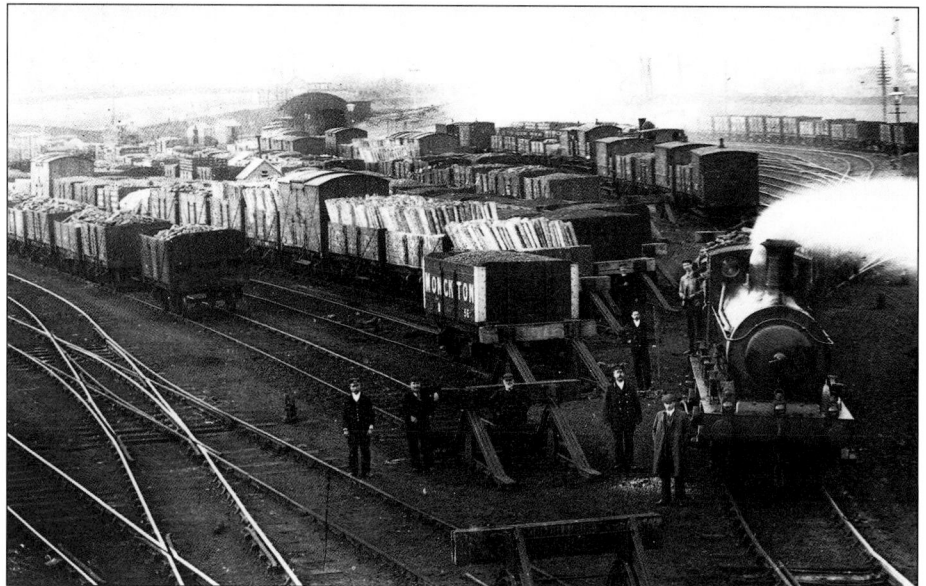

Right: **Another view of Barnsley Junction. There is a Monckton Colliery private-owner wagon on view, but the sheer variety of traffic being handled is striking, including many wagons loaded with wooden pit props.** *Biltcliffe, Peter Sunderland collection*

Below: **This is Penistone station with what appears to be a Robinson 4-4-0 at the head of a passenger train and one of the ubiquitous 0-6-2 tank engines on a coal train.** *Biltcliffe, Peter Sunderland collection*

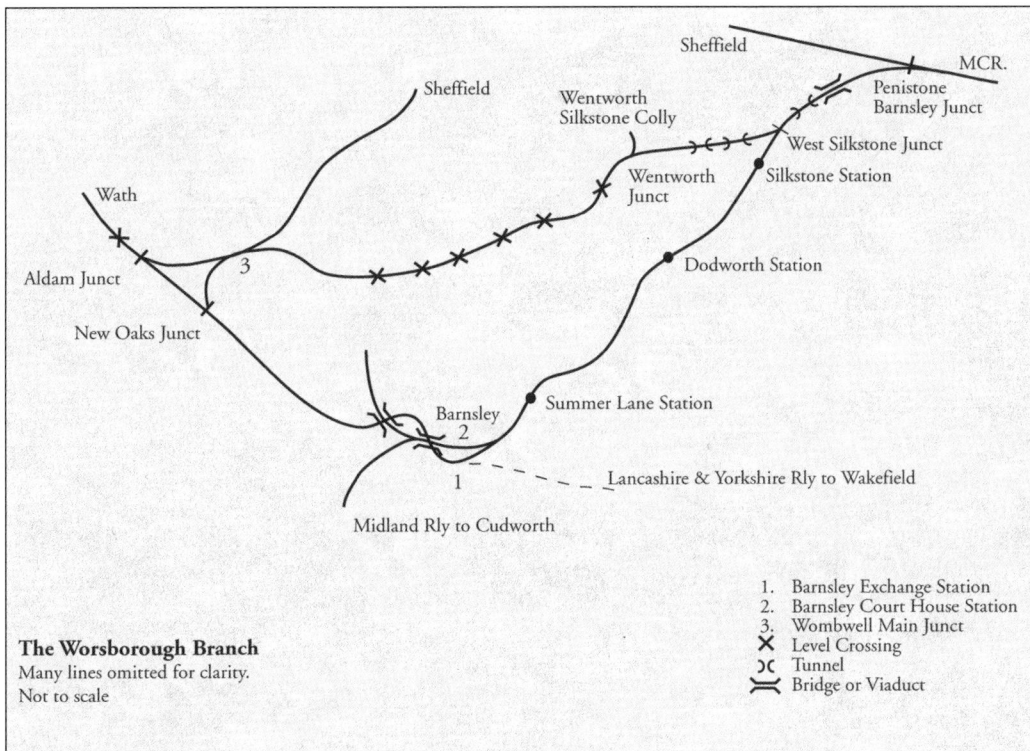

The route of the Wath Branch. It was built to bypass the congested routes around Barnsley by extending a colliery branch that ran from Aldam Junction to the area around Wentworth Junction to meet the Barnsley-Penistone main line at West Silkstone Junction.

The Worsborough Branch
Many lines omitted for clarity.
Not to scale

1. Barnsley Exchange Station
2. Barnsley Court House Station
3. Wombwell Main Junct
X Level Crossing
)(Tunnel
⋈ Bridge or Viaduct

along Worsborough Dale, where it served around a dozen collieries. A high-quality coal had been discovered here in the 1830s; it burned fiercely, gave off a great deal of heat but left behind only a tiny quantity of ash. It was ideal for many industrial purposes.

It was quickly in demand and was transported away from a clutch of small mines by tramway and barge along an arm of the Dearne & Dove Canal. A full-size railway inevitably followed and this ultimately ran from Aldam Junction to Moor End, about a mile from the village of Silkstone Common – through which the Penistone–Barnsley line passed.

The South Yorkshire Railway had always led a colourful existence. When its other main line, between Barnsley and Sheffield, was diverted away from a planned tunnel, the hapless contractors, who had built all but the portals, had to sue to recover their money. In another incident, coaches broke away from a locomotive and began running away. The only passenger, a market trader named Walker, jumped for his life and broke a leg as he landed heavily on the trackside. He also had to sue when the SYR refused him compensation, offering the defence that notices in each carriage clearly stated that passengers must not try to leave them while the train was in motion! Walker won his case.

By 1864 the SYR's board decided to give up the unequal struggle and agreed to a partial amalgamation with the MS&LR. A full takeover was complete by 1874. By this time the Worsborough branch had been doubled to cope with increasing coal production, and the MS&LR board was increasingly pondering the problem of getting coal out of the Dearne Valley and up to Penistone to cross the Pennines to the ever-expanding industries of Lancashire and Merseyside. In particular, Barnsley was becoming a serious bottleneck.

A glance at the map showed a potential solution. The collieries at Moor End were 2 miles from a potential junction with the Penistone–Barnsley line just beyond Silkstone. Bridge the gap and Barnsley could be bypassed by turning off the main line at Aldam Junction and running along the Worsborough branch to a new extension to run into the Penistone line at West Silkstone Junction.

The route took around four years to complete, opening in August 1880 – a long time for such a short length of railway. But this was another line on a difficult alignment, sharply curved, heavily graded – this time at 1 in 40 – and with two tunnels. It was a heavy price to pay to bypass Barnsley, but it was the only practical route on offer.

The line was always something of a byway, rarely photographed even after electrification. It was also an assemblage of railway oddities: at one point there were five level crossings within the space of 3 miles. At the foot of the new extension sat Wentworth Junction, which was officially – and for footplate crew promotion purposes – a loco shed, even though its only building was a small brick shed used for signing on and storing oil and other consumables.

Finally, there was the gradient itself. Officially 1 in 40, there was a short stretch, caused it is said by mining subsidence, that was at approximately 1 in 37. It would bring operating problems that would cause generations of enginemen to curse – problems that would remain until the final closure.

As the veteran chronicler of locomotive performance, Peter Semmens, put it, 'The whole line from Wath and Sheffield to Manchester was thus an operational problem of the greatest magnitude.'

But at last the Woodhead system was complete. The main line pierced the barrier of the Pennine hills, linking Yorkshire coal with Lancashire industry. The branch from Penistone to the Dearne Valley (for Wath had yet to achieve railway fame) tapped coal from scores of highly productive collieries.

It also linked two great cities with a transport system that shrank the 40 miles that separated them and ended the idea that in winter you might choose not to travel at all for fear of becoming stranded or worse. The Manchester, Sheffield & Lincolnshire Railway was now in a commanding position. But it would also face financial and operational problems that would never be completely resolved.

2

Wath and Mottram

The Woodhead line may have been an engineering marvel, but the directors and officers of the Sheffield, Ashton-under-Lyne & Manchester Railway quickly realised that, in operational terms at least, they had created something of a monster.

The basic problems were twofold: gradients and curves. A glance at the gradient profile shows the extent of the problem; it has been said that the Woodhead line resembles nothing so much as the gable end of a house. From both directions there are lengthy climbs to the summit with plenty of 1 in 100 and 1 in 120 to tax the relatively low-powered locomotives of the day.

There were also plenty of curves as the line of route closely followed the natural contours, seeking the easiest possible climb. They were not particularly severe, but enough to prevent any thoughts of taking a run at any of the inclines, and certainly enough to discourage any thoughts of racing downhill to make

up for time expended on the climb. This was not a racetrack railway and it was never going to be.

All these issues were made worse by the difficulties of combining relatively fast-moving passenger services with the lumbering, unfitted heavy coal trains, which could not move any faster than 20–25mph, partly because of the power of the available locomotives, but also because of the difficulty of stopping such a train of unbraked wagons once it reached a downhill stretch.

By the time the line was open, the development of the South Yorkshire coalfield was in full spate and traffic grew at an alarming, if welcome, rate. The capacity issues quickly made themselves felt, but the SA&M's initial reaction was to try to muddle through. Building the line had been more expensive than anticipated – hence the decision to build only a single-bore tunnel at Woodhead – and cash for improvements was tight.

The priority was the second tunnel at Woodhead, but even with this open the route was becoming slowly more congested, and it was not really until Great Central days that any concerted effort was made to tackle the issue. Getting the coal over Woodhead became something of a personal issue for the GCR's recently appointed General Manager, Sam – later Sir Sam – Fay.

He instituted the system of 'single' and 'double' loads over the route – trains of either 30 or 60 loaded wagons – which were given different amounts of banking assistance from extra locomotives. At the same time, his new Chief Mechanical Engineer, John Robinson, turned his mind to a new generation of locomotives better equipped to deal with the physical problems of the Woodhead line.

Above: **Tank engines operated most of the Sheffield–Penistone local trains, but in this 1937 view a 'D9' Class 4-4-0 locomotive, originally built to haul Marylebone expresses, is in charge.** *C. B. Harley*

Right: **Classic power for the Sheffield–Penistone stopper in the shape of Class 'C13' 4-4-2T No 6065, seen near Wortley in 1933.** *E. R. Morten*

Above: **The legendary railway photographer Gordon Tidey visited the Woodhead line in 1927. Among his pictures was this view of Robinson Class 'B3' war memorial engine *Valour* on a Cleethorpes–Manchester express. Robinson's 4-6-0 classes were more often to be found on the Cleethorpes route than on the main line to London.**
H. Gordon Tidey

Middle: **This view of a Robinson 2-8-0 heading up Longdendale towards Woodhead is worth including just for the sheer variety – and sheer length – of the goods train it is hauling. It is undated but some time in the 1930s would be a good guess. *IAL***

Left: **A fine view of a member of Robinson's largest 4-6-0 class, 'B7' No 1360, as she grinds her way up the 1 in 120 gradient with a Class A freight in June 1948.** *Austin Brackenbury/IAL*

Right: **Still wearing wartime black livery, Class 'B7' No 5467 pauses at Guide Bridge with the 10.30am Manchester–Scarborough train in September 1945.** *H. C. Casserley*

Below: **Meanwhile, at the other end of the station, one of the familiar 'Atlantic' tanks is ready to leave with a Hadfield– Manchester local. The line to Stockport veers off to the left.** *H. C. Casserley*

Bottom: **Robinson's 'Director' class locos were versatile engines, so it is no surprise to see one pictured at Guide Bridge in the early 1950s. This example is No 62665 *Ypres*.** *G. Parrish/IAL*

A traffic survey at Guide Bridge, taken in July 1900, gives a feel for the scale of the problem. This showed that every 24 hours, the two tracks handled 252 up (ie eastbound) trains and 265 down trains. Even today, with modern signalling methods, that would be a remarkable number. When the Manchester– Sheffield–Wath electrification scheme was complete, the commemorative poster issued by the British Railways Board thought it worth boasting that 'there are operated about 100 trains each way every 24 hours'.

Part of the problem was the way the coal traffic was worked. In a system that harked back to the earliest pioneering days of the railways, colliery companies owned and maintained their own fleets of 'house wagons'. These private-owner vehicles had to be registered with the Railway Clearing House (RCH) – a sort of central administration office – but after that had been done they enjoyed full access rights on the rail network. They must have made a colourful sight: the bright yellow of Barrow Barnsley; the pale blue of Monk Bretton Collieries; the red oxide and elaborately shaded lettering of Denaby or Stanton & Staveley.

But they foisted onto the railway an incredibly inefficient way of working. Wagons would leave the collieries bound for a range of destinations. They would need to be rough-sorted, then remarshalled again to create trains bound for the same destination. When each train over the Woodhead line reached the Manchester area, it would have to be broken down, taking wagons from each colliery for a range of destinations – the industries of Lancashire, or the Merseyside docks for export to Ireland, for example – and remarshalling them yet again into complete trains.

Guide Bridge again, this time with 'C14' 4-4-2 No 67447 on a service to Hayfield. Identical trains worked to Glossop and Hadfield. *G. Parrish/IAL*

disintegrating after a rough shunt, depositing their coal across the 'four foot'. More delay, more expense.

The first in a series of radical steps to combat the problem was taken just yards from the tunnel mouth at Dunford Bridge, where extensive sorting sidings were laid out. Their only function was to pick out wagons and rearrange them into trains that could be dispatched to the same place. It grew into a sizeable installation. Dunford Bridge ultimately boasted five signal boxes, two of them entirely devoted to working the sorting sidings. Locomotive facilities, including a turntable, were provided, partly because of the sidings, and partly to service the banking engines that worked from Wath and Sheffield, giving the loaded coal trains a 20-mile push to get them to the summit.

A clutch of traditional railway terraced cottages was incongruously planted on the moorland, looking down on the new complex, to house the signalmen and shunters who worked around the clock and through most of the weekend too to keep the traffic moving. The community at Townhead survives to this day.

The same process happened in reverse with the empties. Groups of wagons arrived back in no coherent order and would need to be sorted into groups for individual collieries or a tight geographic area. Once back in South Yorkshire, each wagon had to go back to its owning colliery. It was hugely wasteful of manpower and locomotives.

In addition, the wagons themselves were built down to a price rather than up to a standard. The basic RCH 10-ton wagon had no brakes other than a handbrake acting on two of the four wheels. It would have a basic five- or seven-plank wooden body and axle boxes lubricated by grease – not the modern automotive grease but a rather cruder substance. They were also indifferently maintained and run into the ground, sometimes almost literally. There are several recorded accounts of colliery wagons simply

Hazlehead itself had a tiny passenger station and goods sidings, mostly for dealing with traffic from the Hepworth Iron Co's works, which had its own private branch line. The gated entrance can be seen behind a Class 'O4' on the daily pick-up goods. *Roger Goldthorpe*

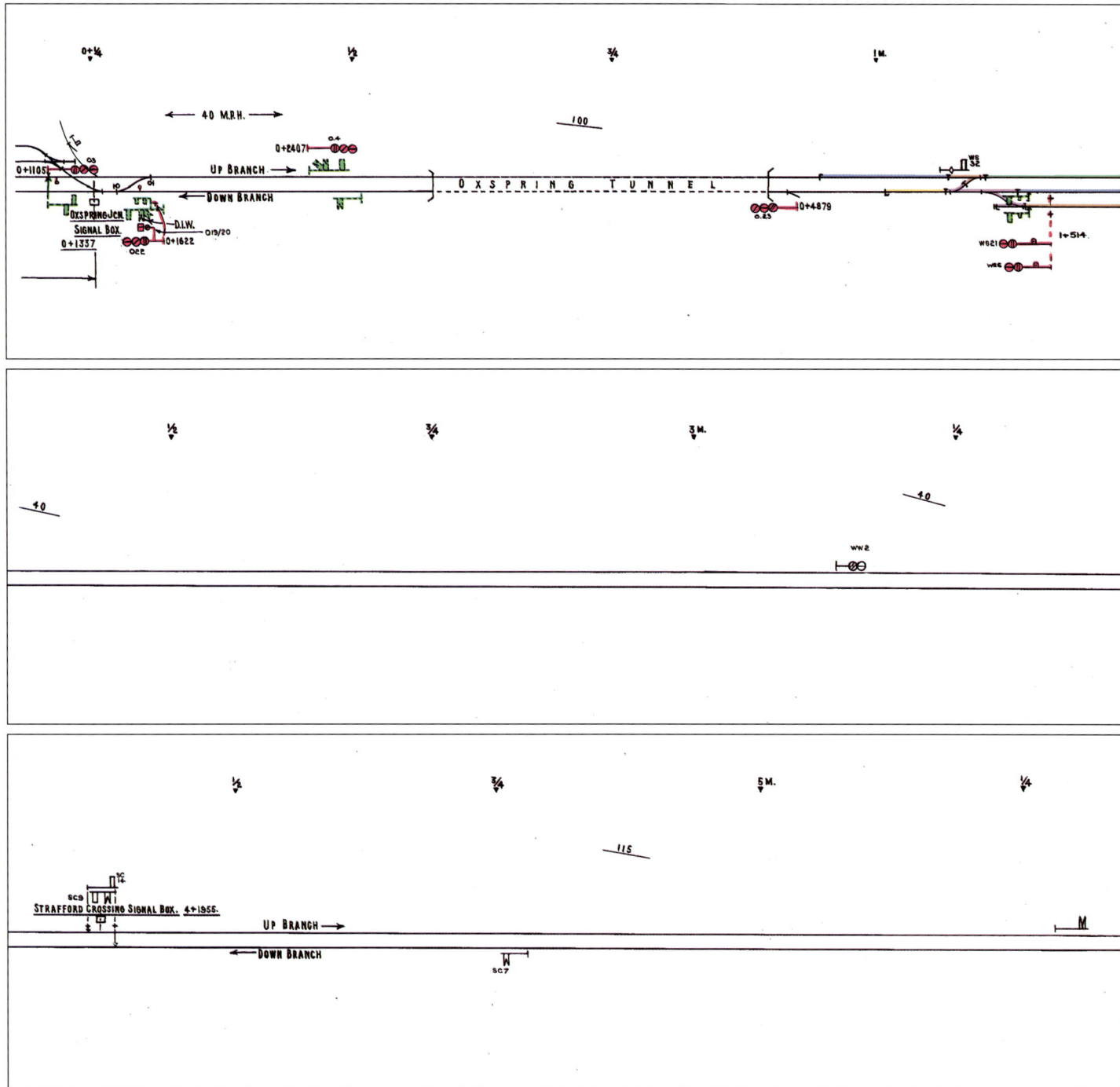

0+¼

½

¾

1 M.

← 40 M.P.H. →

100

0+2407

0.4

Up Branch →

0+1105

Down Branch →

OXSPRING TUNNEL

0+4879

0.23

WS 52

Oxspring Jcn.
Signal Box
0+1337

D.I.W.

013/20

0+1622

022

W621

1+514

W86

½

¾

3 M.

¼

40

40

WW2

½

¾

5 M.

¼

115

SC9

12
12

STRAFFORD CROSSING SIGNAL BOX. 4+1955.

Up Branch →

← Down Branch

M

W
SC7

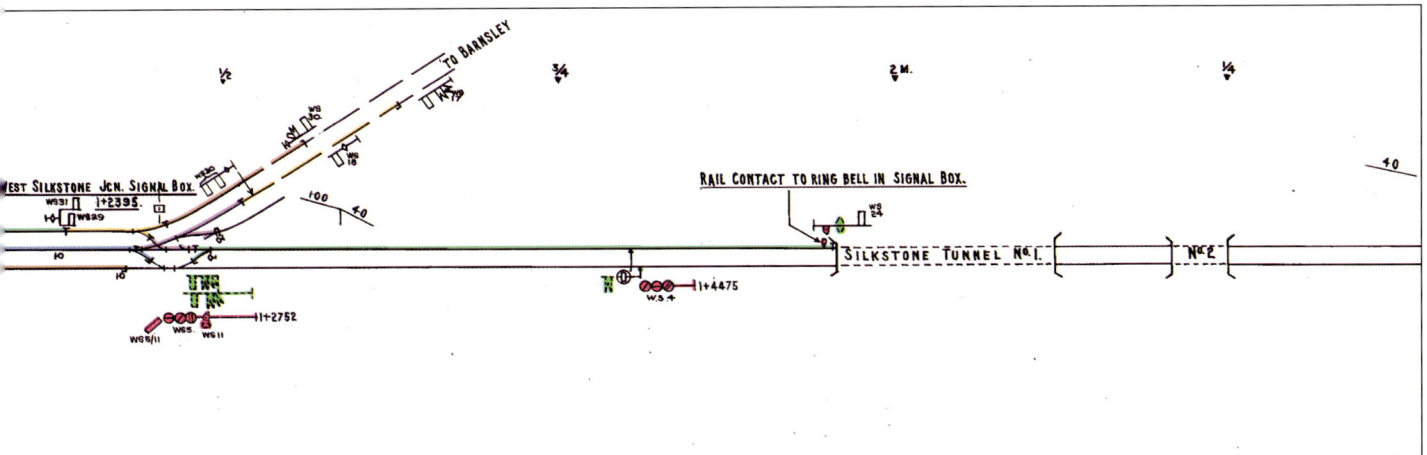

WEST SILKSTONE JCN. SIGNAL BOX.

TO BARNSLEY

RAIL CONTACT TO RING BELL IN SIGNAL BOX.

SILKSTONE TUNNEL Nº 1.   Nº 2.

½   ¾   2 M.   ¼   40

WS31   1+2395.   100   40   WS34   1+4475   WS11   1+2752

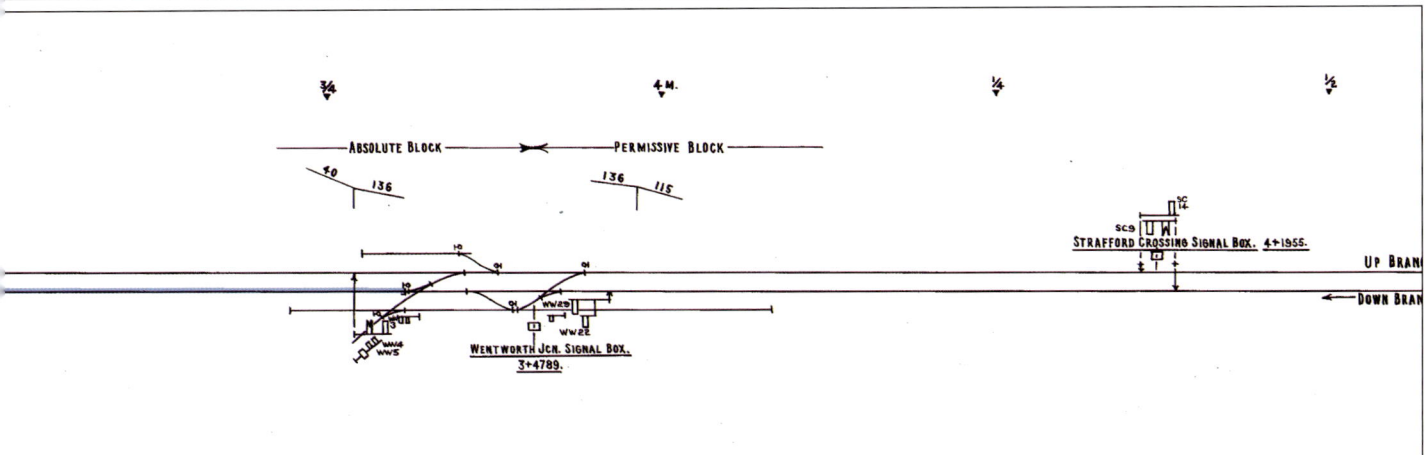

¾   4 M.   ¼   ½

◄ ABSOLUTE BLOCK ►◄ PERMISSIVE BLOCK ►

40   136   136   115

STRAFFORD CROSSING SIGNAL BOX.   4+1955.   UP BRANCH

WENTWORTH JCN. SIGNAL BOX.
3+4789.   DOWN BRANCH

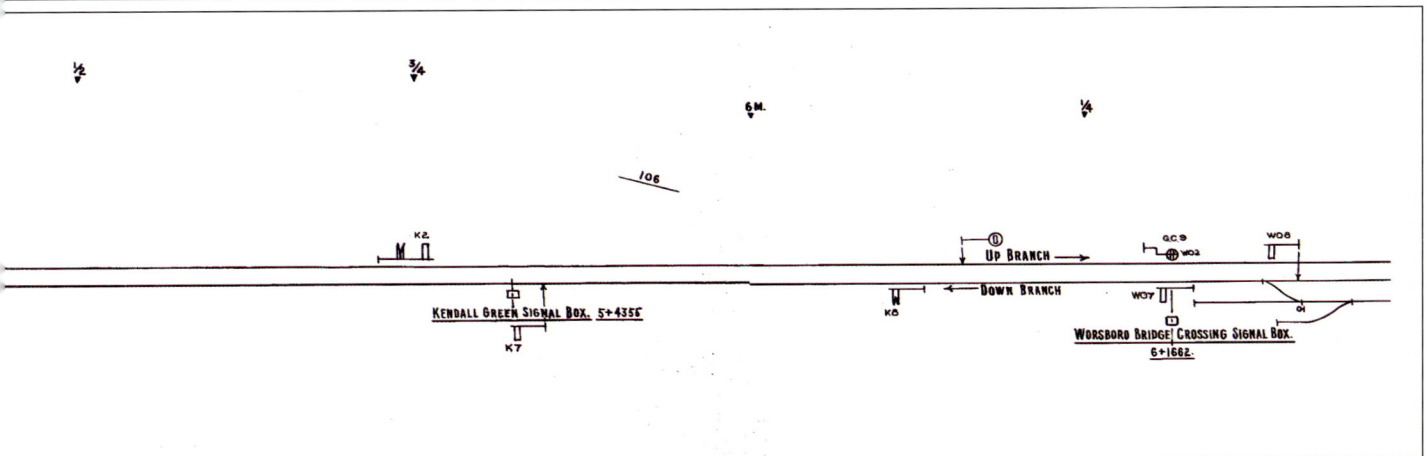

½   ¾   6 M.   ¼

106

K2   UP BRANCH ►   GC9   WO2   WO8

KENDALL GREEN SIGNAL BOX. 5+4355   K8   ◄ DOWN BRANCH   WO7

K7   WORSBORO BRIDGE CROSSING SIGNAL BOX.
6+1662.

This tackled one of the problems, but the real difficulty was that as soon as new capacity was provided, it was swallowed up by new traffic. What was needed was additional track capacity. This came first with a short loop at Woodhead itself, which allowed trains of coal empties to be sidelined in favour of faster or more important traffic through the tunnel. It was followed two years later by a similar loop on the eastern side at Wadsley Bridge, on the outskirts of Sheffield.

These capacity improvements now came thick and fast. The Woodhead loop was extended through Longdendale to connect with an existing siding at Torside, creating an up-line running loop some 3¾ miles long. A companion for the down line was already in the pipeline, creating a four-track railway from Woodhead to Torside Crossing. This meant rebuilding Crowden station and, in true Great Central style, it was reconstructed on the island platform principle, opening in 1908. In the same year Sheffield Victoria itself had to be rebuilt with a new frontage to accommodate a down goods loop.

In the same period two more loops were added in the Sheffield area, and part of the line from Ardwick – where the

Right: **Leaving the Manchester suburbs behind, Class 'O2' 2-8-0 No 63983 passes Crowden station in July 1949, with Nos 63945 and 63966 in tow. Great Northern locomotives were far from strangers on the Woodhead line, but three in a row is unusual!** *P. J. Lynch/IAL*

Right: **Heading west down the valley with a varied goods working, this ex-North Eastern Railway Class 'Q6' has reached the end of the goods line at Torside Crossing and is making its way out onto the main line. The picture was taken in June 1951.** *E. R. Morten*

Right: **At the same location about 15 years earlier, a Robinson Class 'Q4' 0-8-0 has been given a run on the main line.** *E. R. Morten*

Above: **A classic view of the 'North Country Continental' train with Class 'B17' No 2805 *Burnham Thorpe* in charge. The train is heading east, close to Torside Crossing. Note the Westinghouse pump for operating the Great Eastern Section air brakes.** *E. R. Morten*

Middle: **It was followed by this complete contrast – an 'O4' plodding up to the summit with a string of coal empties in tow.** *E. R. Morten*

Left: **This 'C4' picture is definitely post-war, taken in 1947 when the last 20 or so engines were put out to grass on the Lincolnshire lines, so this appearance at Sheffield Victoria, with No 2915 wearing express passenger headlamps, would have been unusual.** *H. C. Casserley*

Right: **One of the later 'B17s', by this time known as 'Footballers', No 61660** *Hull City,* **at Sheffield Victoria on a Liverpool Central–Parkestone Quay express in July 1950.** *IAL*

Below: **An ex-ROD engine, now Class 'O4/3', No 63781, pounds westward with a mixed freight near Godley East Junction.** *J. Davenport/IAL*

Great Central diverged from what had now become the London & North Western Railway – to Hyde Junction was quadrupled. In addition, extensive sidings were laid in around Dewsnap and Guide Bridge to assist with the endless shunting and sorting of coal wagons.

The end result was a three- or four-track railway for much of its length, with most of the four-track section on the western side. At first glance this seems odd: after all, the loaded trains are climbing the eastern slope from South Yorkshire up to the tunnel mouth at Dunford Bridge. But getting a loaded coal train moving is only half the battle. Stopping it when necessary is equally difficult, so, even when running downhill, loaded trains still had to move slowly.

With brakes only on the locomotive and brake-van, crews learned to handle their trains cautiously. Indeed, S. C. Townroe, in his memoir *The Great Central As I Knew It,* recalls being 'severely rebuked' by a driver supervising him on a footplate trip for daring to open the regulator to restart a coal train from one of the loops. The weight of the train alone was quite sufficient to get it moving again at the required speed. And just in case

things did get out of hand, the finishing touch was a substantial sand drag at Valehouse to catch any overrunning heavy freights before they tangled with the suburban passenger trains from Hadfield to Manchester.

With the potential for increasing track capacity virtually exhausted, the Great Central turned to other methods of increasing the number of trains it could squeeze onto the line. One of these was Permissive Block signalling, which was applied to most of the loop lines and parts of the freight-only route to Wath. In essence, Permissive Block turns on its head the fundamental rule of signalling safety, that each train occupies its own section, or block, of track to the exclusion of all others, maintaining a safe braking distance between trains and, theoretically, at least, preventing collisions.

Permissive Block allows more than one train into each section, but only under carefully controlled conditions. The driver of the second train to enter an occupied section has to be verbally cautioned by the signalman before being allowed in. Special bell codes are exchanged between the two signal boxes involved. The train is then worked at reduced speed to allow it to stop before colliding with the rear of the train it is following.

The Great Central devised a special type of Permissive Block instrument that showed not only a 'Train on Line' indication, but, as the operating knob was turned, numbers for each successive train. The numbers went up to '6' and each time a new train was allowed in under caution, the knob was turned once again, then back as each train was cleared back by the signal box ahead.

It was an imperfect system. Loco crews would find themselves, in all weathers and at all times of day and night, gingerly inching along, anxiously looking for the tail lamps on a brake-van ahead, then quickly applying the brakes to stop before running into it. Permissive Block was also the cause – direct or indirect – of at least two accidents, both on the Worsborough branch.

Left: **A pair of Class 'C13' 4-4-2 tank engines wait with suburban services from Manchester London Road. The picture is undated, but must be from the early 1950s – the locomotives have the early BR crest applied. There is surprisingly little evidence of electrification work.** *Kenneth Field/IAL*

Below: **A careworn Class 'B7', No 1367, heads a westbound Class J train at Hyde Junction. None of the 'B7s' lasted long enough to be given a British Railways number.** *Peter Cookson*

Left: **Photographers rarely ventured along the Worsborough branch in steam days, except to see trains being worked up the bank itself. However, in this rare view a 'K3' 2-6-0 hauls what appears to be a steel train past Worsborough Goods, between Glasshouse Crossing and Worsborough Bridge Crossing in the 1950s. The 'K3s' were among the few Doncaster-built locos liked by Mexborough crews.** *Brian Almond*

Above: **At the bottom of the Worsborough Bank (some called it the Wentworth Bank), a 'J11' buffers up to a 'single load' coal train for the 2½-mile slog up to West Silkstone Junction in April 1947.**
H. C. Casserley

Middle: **At the front end of a similar single load, a Class 'Q4' 0-8-0 gets to grips with its train. The plume of smoke from the banker at the rear suggests that the work is not being split fairly! The locomotive is LNER No 3219 and the date is April 1947.**
H. C. Casserley

Right: **A single load climbing the bank behind Class 'J39' No 4745 in June 1947. The electrification gantries had been installed before the outbreak of war in 1939.** *Peter Cookson*

30

In 1911 a Board of Trade inquiry revealed how two trains of empties were allowed on the up line from West Silkstone Junction down the gradient towards Wath. The first train came to a halt and the second train ran into the back of it because of a mix-up over how many wagon brakes had to be pinned down to retard its progress. Sixty years later, a pair of Class 76 electric locomotives approaching Wentworth Junction on an MGR working on the down line collided with another pair standing on the same running line. The driver had not been cautioned when passing Kendall Green Crossing and assumed (rightly) that the line was clear.

Some of these congestion-busting measures smack of pure desperation. To tackle the problem of Woodhead Tunnel itself, a signal box was opened halfway along the up tunnel, controlling only that line. The idea was to cut in half the 3-mile block section

Below and right: **The Woodhead line saw few significant accidents and no fatalities in its later years. But one remarkable incident happened on the Worsborough branch when an MGR working ran into the banking locos at the rear of another MGR train being made up at Wentworth Junction. The first picture shows No E26022 being re-railed while in the second the severity of the impact on No E26025 is obvious. Remarkably, the loco was repaired and put back into service.** *Keith Long*

Above: **A single load on the move was impressive enough, but to see a full double load, worked by four locomotives, must have been an incredible sight. In this picture the train is about to enter Silkstone No 2 Tunnel, the first and shorter of the two tunnels on the climb to West Silkstone Junction. The unidentified locomotives are a Class 'O4' and a Class 'O1', the latter being a Thompson rebuild of the 'O4'.** *E. R. Morten*

Heading straight for the feared up-line tunnel at Woodhead is Robinson 'Atlantic' Class 'C4' No 5194 on a Sheffield-bound express in 1930. *R. K. Blencowe*

between Woodhead and Dunford Bridge. Trains would clear the new 1½-mile section in half the time, thus increasing capacity. The up line was selected because the summit of the line was almost at the Dunford Bridge end of the tunnel, so up trains were climbing most of the way through the tunnel working harder and generally moving more slowly than on the down line.

To someone sitting in a warm, well-lit signalling design office, this must have seemed like a good idea. To the men who actually had to work in the box, spending their working day in the smoky darkness of a single-bore tunnel, it was anything but.

Few details of this box survive. We do not even know precisely when it came into use, though it was certainly open for business by 1902. It was created by opening out one of the niches or manholes built into the side of the tunnel to give an escape route for permanent way or other staff caught in the tunnel by a passing train. Not surprisingly, it proved difficult to find enough signalmen to staff it. The working day was cut to 6 hours in an effort to find more volunteers, but even this was insufficient inducement and the box closed in 1909 – even though the Great Central had spent more than £2,000 installing new low-pressure pneumatic signals in the tunnel.

After the tunnel box was abandoned, little else was done to alleviate the Woodhead bottleneck and it became an operational

hindrance that lasted until the end of steam working. However, in 1912 another £12,000 was spent enlarging one of the up tunnel ventilation shafts from 8 to 16 feet in diameter. Did it bring any improvements to the hard-pressed engine crews, handkerchiefs pressed to their mouths as they braved the smoke and fumes? We simply do not know.

But the Great Central was nothing if not innovative and the next big improvement was to authorise the spending of £191,000 on a coal concentration yard at Wath. Then just an unremarkable village halfway between Barnsley and Doncaster, Wath was destined to become a major railway centre. George Dow, in his *Great Central*, tells us that it lay at almost the geographical centre of the South Yorkshire coalfield, with 45 collieries within striking distance.

It was thus the logical place to lay out a hump shunting yard where coal traffic could be brought together, or concentrated, for sorting into complete trains. This eliminated much of the shunting done at individual collieries and improved track capacity by ensuring that almost all train movements were of complete, full-length, ready-marshalled trains. This was a project on a heroic scale. There was not one yard but two, one for each direction, because the Great Central was not just in the business of heaving coal across the Pennines, but also in carrying it to the east coast for export.

The two yards took up 1¼ miles alongside the Barnsley to Doncaster main line between Elsecar Junction and Wath signal boxes. Trains entered on one of 15 reception sidings and the locomotive was uncoupled. Shunters then divided the train into individual groups, or 'cuts', of wagons, each destined for a different destination. The train was then slowly pushed over the shunting hump and each cut of wagons rolled down the other side on a slope of 1 in 40, lessening to 1 in 60, then 1 in 100, 200 and 300, then level, into the sorting sidings where they came to rest. There were 21

The Woodhead line and the Wath branch spawned some unusual motive power, including the Class 'S1' 0-8-4T hump shunters built by Robinson for Wath Yard. They were tried on other duties, including banking trains to Dunford Bridge. In this 1950 view, it is on its way for attention at Gorton Works. *IAL*

sorting sidings for each direction and complete trains were made up in them for onward dispatch.

In all, there were 36 miles of sidings and, according to *Great Central*, the yard was capable of handling 5,000 wagons every 24 hours, with just 36 staff employed on each 8-hour shift. It opened in 1907 and, with coal traffic still expanding – British coal production did not peak until 1913 – two years later it was equipped with low-pressure pneumatic signals, which cost another £17,000. Two cabins, one for each hump and its associated fan of sidings, controlled 80 signals and 58 turnouts and locking bars using simple push-buttons rather than having to heave heavy mechanical levers between each cut of wagons to direct them into the correct siding. Wath became the first power-operated yard in the country.

It was the last word in modernity and, writing in *The Railway Magazine* in 1908, J. T. Lawrence was clearly filled with admiration: '...standing at the summit and looking in either direction, the symmetry of the whole arrangement is visible, and fills one with admiration.'

The finishing touch would have been a mirror-image facility somewhere at the western end of the line to sort and route the empties back just as efficiently. The Great Central recognised

Left and below: **A pair of passenger workings near Mottram. The local train is hauled by one of the Class 'F1' 2-4-2 tanks, which were later replaced by the 'C13' and 'C14' types, while the Sheffield–Manchester express is hauled by a 'V2', No 4828, resplendent in apple green.** *R. Atkins & Bob Russell, both IAL*

The overhead line is conspicuous by its absence in this 1945 view of Woodburn Junction, with ex-Great Central 'B2' Class No 5428 *City of Liverpool* and 'D11' No 5501 *Mons* almost certainly heading for Darnall shed. *Howard Turner collection*

this but never had the cash to do anything about it, and it was left to the London & North Eastern Railway to pick up the baton and finish the job with a new gravity yard at Mottram.

Little has been written about the yard at Mottram, possibly because, by the time it was built, coal production was past its peak and it rarely operated at full capacity before the Second World War threw unprecedented strains on the whole network. Before it opened, sorting and marshalling had been carried out at sidings at Guide Bridge and Dewsnap, but they were cramped and inadequate for the job.

Jackson and Russell, writing in *The Great Central in LNER Days*, describe vividly the problems this created:

'Thus is was not unusual to find every single loop between Guide Bridge and Woodhead, if not indeed beyond, occupied by a coal train waiting to leapfrog for a short distance along the main line. So severe were the delays that at weekends the trains were often left standing in the loops with brakes pinned down, the engines being released and sent light to Gorton.'

During the week, it was far from unknown for a relief crew to be sent to a stationary train in some remote loop and spend their entire shift minding the footplate until they were also relieved, having moved not an inch. It was all wasteful and costly. The LNER recognised this but was prevented from doing anything by a lack of funds. The Mottram scheme was one of three – the others were Hull and March – approved as part of a major effort to clear freight bottlenecks.

The first problem was finding a suitable site for a new yard. Mottram was selected because it allowed the hump and sidings to be squeezed into a relatively flat site between the worst of the curves. Even so, it entailed diverting the existing main line for about three-quarters of a mile and buying a sizeable tract of land.

Mottram was roughly half the size of Wath – appropriate given that it was dealing with only one major traffic stream

rather than two. Eight reception sidings each held 80 wagons and fed into two groups of 10 sorting sidings. But there was no hump here: the natural slope of the site meant that the reception sidings stood on a gradient of 1 in 85. They were funnelled together into a single track where the gradient steepened to 1 in 30 before easing to 1 in 75 where the sorting sidings fanned out. The gradient eased again to 1 in 200, giving exactly the same effect as hump shunting. Each of the sorting sidings held 65 wagons, and they funnelled into a single track to give an outlet onto the main line at Mottram itself. Other sidings were provided for specialised traffic such as cattle, and an engine line ran through the complex.

The LNER provided a small block of office and mess accommodation for yard staff, and a small halt was opened on the main line to get them to and from work. Control was from an LNER-styled control tower, which closely resembled the signal boxes built as part of the widening or improvement projects such as those on the East Coast main line north of York. Like Wath Yard, this was also a power-operated installation, using compressed air to shift the points. Unlike Wath, a telephone link between the top of the gradient and the control tower allowed the shunter to uncouple wagons into 'cuts', then tell the controller into which siding they should be directed.

Mottram transformed the western end of the line just as Wath had transformed the eastern end. It marked the final development of the route until work began – only a year later – on the great electrification project.

3

Bigger engines – and the Garratt

What was it like to actually run such a demanding railway? And what was life like on the footplate, slogging up those gradients or gently easing 60-plus unbraked wagons full of coal down the western slope?

Woodhead was never a glamorous railway. Yet students of locomotive performance and photographers were drawn to it for virtually its entire life, and there is at least one recorded case of a career railwayman requesting a transfer to it, drawn by a combination of the operating challenges and the dramatic scenery.

Yet there are relatively few first-hand accounts of footplate work over the route. However, it is possible to piece together an idea of what life must have been like for loco crews by looking at a combination of the personal memoirs that do exist, and the accounts of those who rode the footplate as guests, recording locomotive performance and timings.

For many a young engineman, the first trip through the single-track bores of Woodhead Tunnel was an experience never forgotten, even if it was not their first footplate turn. In his account of life on the footplate, *Bankers and Pilots*, George Potts, who rose through the ranks at Mexborough shed, paints a vivid picture of his first trip as fireman of a down (Manchester-bound) passenger train, which he and his mate had been instructed to take over at short notice:

'I hadn't been through Woodhead Tunnel at speed before; the noise was indescribable, worsening by the second as we travelled further into the blackness. I noticed Percy [his mate] knocking the jet (blower) handle over just before he closed the regulator so as to take away the smoke from the chimney top and prevent the fire blowing back.

'We were going at a good rate because, after about a quarter of a mile the line drops, then about a quarter of a mile from the Woodhead end we depressed the treadle which works the gong to warn that Woodhead Distant signal is just ahead. As it happened to be off, there was no need to check our speed. I closed the damper to avoid blowing off and in another four minutes or less we were hurtling through Woodhead station doing 60mph.'

And that was the easy part! The locomotive was not working hard because the down tunnel is almost entirely on a downhill gradient. As George Potts describes a little later, working back home through the up tunnel was a completely different proposition. He is firing on a train of empties, heading back to Yorkshire:

'I kept the firebox well lined with coal so as to obviate much firing up through the tunnel. This was just over three miles long and on an up-grade for seven-eighths of the way, so you obviously wanted to minimise use of the shovel in there all you could. Being single-bore made it that much worse of course, and there was always enough smoke in there without adding any of

In addition to controlling access to the goods facilities, Penistone Goods box also operated refuge sidings, and the outlet onto the down main can be seen in this view of well-kept 'K3' No 61896 on a Saturday Sheffield–Manchester express in July 1952.
Kenneth Field/IAL

your own, from trains that had gone through earlier. Traffic was so frequent passing through that it never got a chance to clear.

'About a hundred yards from the entrance I put the shovel down and slipped the injector on at minimum, the steam gauge being then near enough on the red line. As we slammed into the single bore the noise was terrific, with a searingly hot exhaust of steam and smoke blasting back and swirling about the footplate. Albert [his driver] had got his handkerchief out to hold over his nose and mouth and I did likewise.

'As we went deeper into the tunnel the heat and fumes increased, a lot of it being from the loco that had gone through just before us. I was thankful that steam and water were satisfactory up to that point but I knew I should have to use the bent dart before too long. I had already got it down, resting on the tender end. The heat created by our exhaust seemed to get worse all the time. Eventually, pressure was falling back and I had to knock the injector off to maintain steam, so, tying my handkerchief around my mouth, I grabbed the dart to push the back end forward. The steam came round to 140 again. After another two minutes or so – which seemed more like an hour – we heard the gong sound and I put my head slightly out of the cab to try and sight the Distant signal. It was off when at last it came into view, but Albert had already eased the regulator when I shouted across "Right away!" He just nodded and closed the regulator while I put the injector back on maximum for as we came out into the daylight I could see only an inch or so in sight in the glass.'

And this was no epic one-off, but a daily routine for all footplate crew associated with the route. On that trip all went well, but later Potts cannot help reflecting:

'One thing I did recall was feeling a moment of panic at the thought of what would happen if the engine had started slipping in there… Both Albert and I were wringing wet with perspiration and the cab was wet with the condensation of the steam.'

He was justified in worrying. Locomotives often did begin to slip on the damp and greasy rails inside the tunnel. Some drivers opened the sanders and left them running all the way through as an insurance policy. Jackson and Russell, in *The Great Central in LNER Days*, tell us of one recorded instance of a passenger train getting into difficulties, then re-emerging backwards from the up tunnel mouth at Woodhead. The crew had become so disoriented by a combination of the violent movement of the slip, the darkness and swirling steam that they were moving backwards when they thought they were going forwards.

When seen from the more detached perspective of a footplate observer, the problems of working the line could be more graphic still. The veteran analyst of locomotive performance, Peter Semmens, knew the line intimately from the years immediately before electrification. Writing in *The Railway Magazine*, he describes a trip on board a passenger train from Sheffield Victoria to Manchester London Road behind a Thompson 'B1' Class 4-6-0 locomotive – a type that ruled the roost over Woodhead until electrification. The train consisted of eight bogies in the hands of a Sheffield Darnall crew. Here is the start of the run:

Right: **Another, unidentified, 'K3' 2-6-0 works tender-first over Dinting Viaduct in April 1954.** *E. R. Morten*

Right: **The almost inevitable 'B1', in this case No 61162, leaves Guide Bridge with the 9.30am Liverpool Central–Hull train on 17 November 1951.** *IAL*

Above: **An immaculate-looking 'B1', No 61179, heads a Sheffield–Manchester train near Torside. The picture is dated October 1953.** *Eric Oldham/IAL*

Middle: **It is May 1954 and steam's rule is about to come to an end, but 'B1' No 61092 puts up a spirited defence of steam power approaching Mottram on the afternoon Manchester–Marylebone express.** *W. A. Cockrill/IAL*

Left: **At the west end on Penistone station, 'B1' No 61228 restarts a Manchester express on 19 April 1954, just a few weeks before electric traction took over between Penistone and Manchester.** *E. R. Morten*

Right: **The York–Bournemouth working leaves Victoria for the south behind 'B1' No 61152 in September 1958. A few weeks later steam was replaced on this service by an EE Type 4 (later Class 40) diesel.** *Keith Pirt/IAL*

Middle: **Smartly turned-out 'B1' No 61161 is pictured on a Cleethorpes–Manchester London Road express at Willey Bridge Junction, near Penistone.** *Kenneth Field*

Below: **'B1' No 61162 is caught on a down special near Hazlehead.** *E. R. Morten*

Ashburys was a popular excursion destination for the tourist attractions of Belle Vue, but the service being handled by 'B1' No 61127 is more likely to be a regular Marylebone–Manchester express: the stock is almost all BR Mark 1, which would have been used only on front-line express services in the 1950s.
B. K. B. Green/IAL

'I had not previously travelled over this line and it was an eye-opener to find the locomotive being opened up to full regulator and 35 per cent cut-off not far beyond the platform end. This beat the boiler somewhat and the cut-off came back to 25 per cent. The pressure rallied from 200 to 215lb per sq in and we were doing 39mph at Oughty Bridge at the end of the 4 miles or so of 1 in 132.

'The cut-off was lengthened later to 28 per cent and we held 41mph on the long 1 in 120, although, in spite of heavy firing, the pressure had dropped to 195lb per sq in and the water to half a glass. We stopped in Penistone 21min 12sec from Sheffield after a final maximum of 43 on the easier gradients about Thurgoland Tunnel.'

After leaving Penistone, the train again reaches just over 40mph but is checked by signals at Dunford Bridge, spoiling the rest of the run. Undaunted, the writer made a second trip. This time a Gorton crew were in charge of another 'B1':

'My second westbound run later the same day was even more exciting. This time the load was appreciably heavier and the locomotive was in the charge of Driver Bowes of Gorton. In spite of an initial slip, the regulator was wide open after 200 yards, and the cut-off at 28 per cent. Boiler pressure dipped to 200lb per sq in briefly, but with considerable effort from our fireman, whose name I did not record, it rallied to 220lb per sq in by Wortley. With 30 per cent cut-off we accelerated to 37mph by the end of the 1 in 120 and were into Penistone in under 25½ minutes from Sheffield, dropping 2½ minutes on schedule.'

It is clear that the schedules were demanding, leaving little in reserve to compensate for a locomotive in poor condition, low-grade coal, bad weather or any one of the other misfortunes that could befall a footplate crew.

Nor was this a phenomenon new to the 1950s operation of the line. From the opening of its London Extension from Nottinghamshire to Marylebone, the Great Central had seen itself as in a fight for survival against two more powerful neighbours, the Midland Railway between London and Sheffield and both the Midland and the London & North Western Railway between London and Manchester. The Woodhead line was clearly central to the latter struggle. The GCR could never be the fastest route to Manchester, but it had to try as hard as it could.

So a great deal would depend on the qualities and abilities of the locomotives built for the route. The greatest single legacy in the locomotive field was provided by John Robinson, appointed as the GCR's Locomotive Engineer in 1900. His abilities and the determination of the recently appointed General Manager, Sam Fay, to turn the Great Central into a lean, commercial machine dictated much of what came next.

Part of Robinson's brief was effectively to overhaul the Great Central's locomotive stock. At the time some of it consisted of indifferent machines, and, oddly, for a railway so closely connected with heavy mineral haulage, there were no goods engines bigger than an 0-6-0 tender loco.

There can be few doubts that Robinson produced some real winners. Some of his designs, both passenger and freight, lasted almost until the end of steam and, even after electrification,

Dunford Bridge shows plenty of evidence of the forthcoming electrification: the new signal box and station are taking shape to the right. Overhead line equipment has been installed on the lines to the old tunnels to allow the change from electric to steam traction as part of Stage I of the scheme. It may be that Class 'O4' No 63716 has just taken over from an EM1 in this 1953 view.
John Quick collection

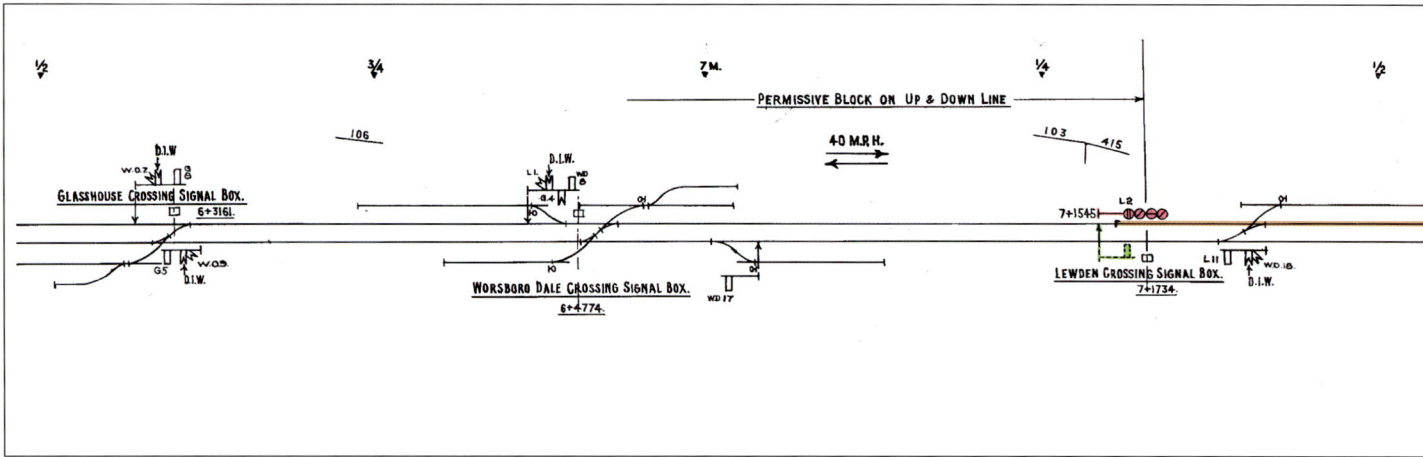

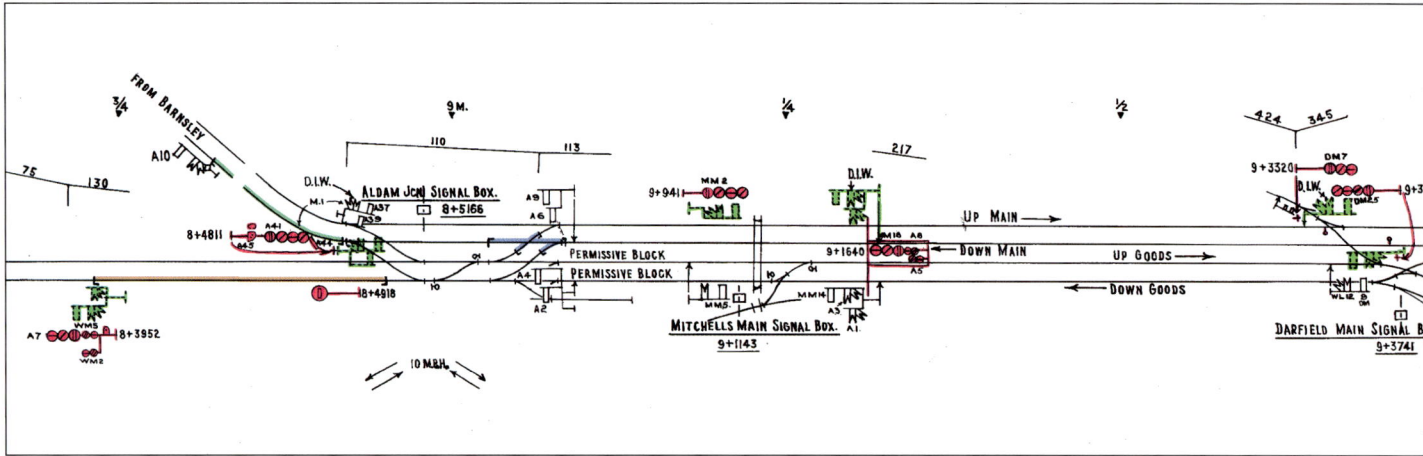

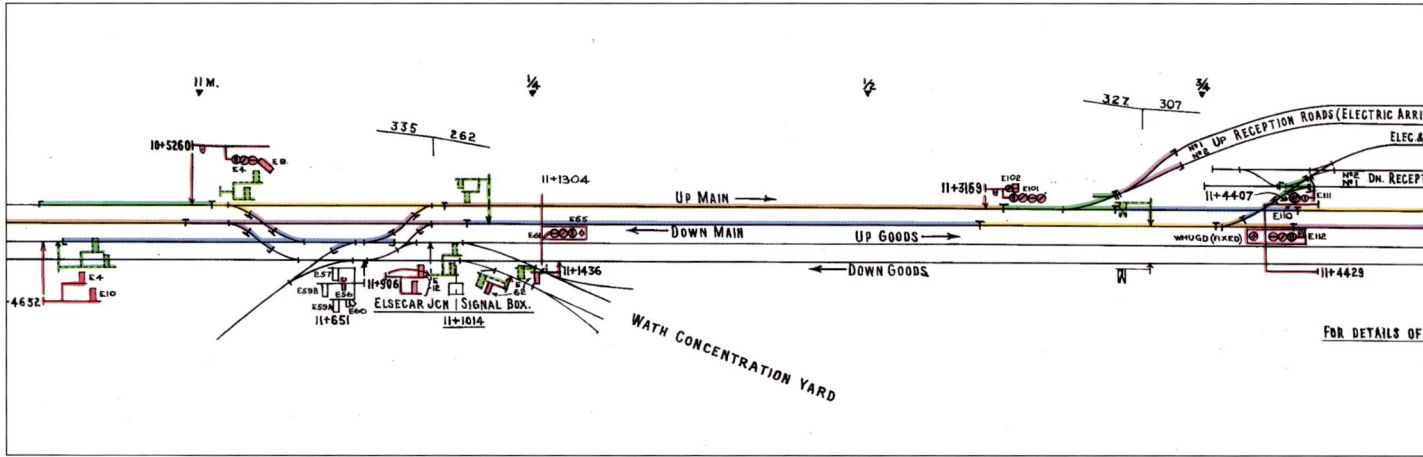

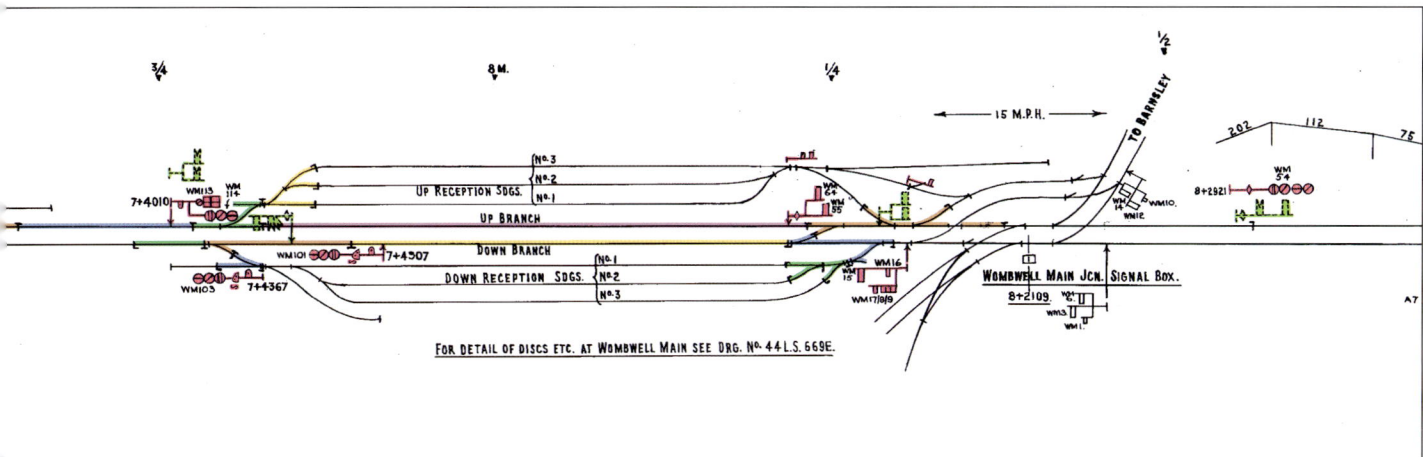

Top strip labels:

¾ 8 M. ¼ ½ ← 15 M.P.H. → TO BARNSLEY

202 112 75

UP RECEPTION SDGS. No.3 No.2 No.1

7+4010 WM113 WM 11+

UP BRANCH

WM 10. WM 12

8+2921 WM 34

DOWN BRANCH

WM101 7+4507

DOWN RECEPTION SDGS. No.1 No.2 No.3

WM103 7+4367 WM16 WM17/8/9

WOMBWELL MAIN JCN. SIGNAL BOX.

8+2109 WM13 WM12

A7

FOR DETAIL OF DISCS ETC. AT WOMBWELL MAIN SEE DRG. No. 44 L.S. 669E.

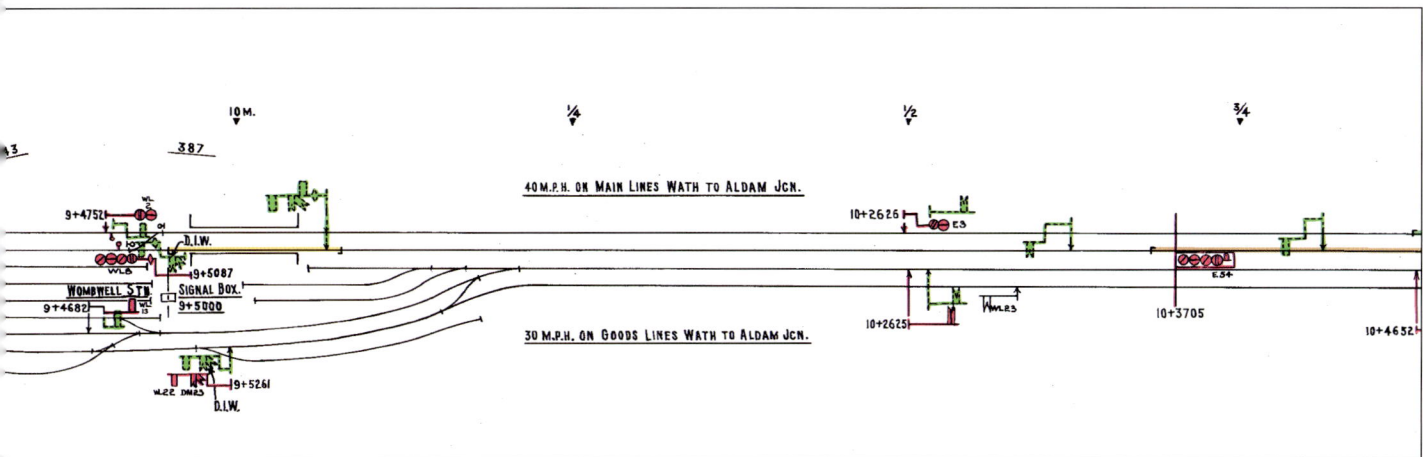

Middle strip labels:

10 M. ¼ ½ ¾

387

40 M.P.H. ON MAIN LINES WATH TO ALDAM JCN.

9+4752 WL5 No.2

10+2626 E3

D.I.W. 9+5087 WLB

E.54

WOMBWELL STN. SIGNAL BOX. 9+5000

9+4682 WL5 13

30 M.P.H. ON GOODS LINES WATH TO ALDAM JCN.

10+2625 WM.23

10+3705

10+4632

WL22 DM23 9+5261

D.I.W.

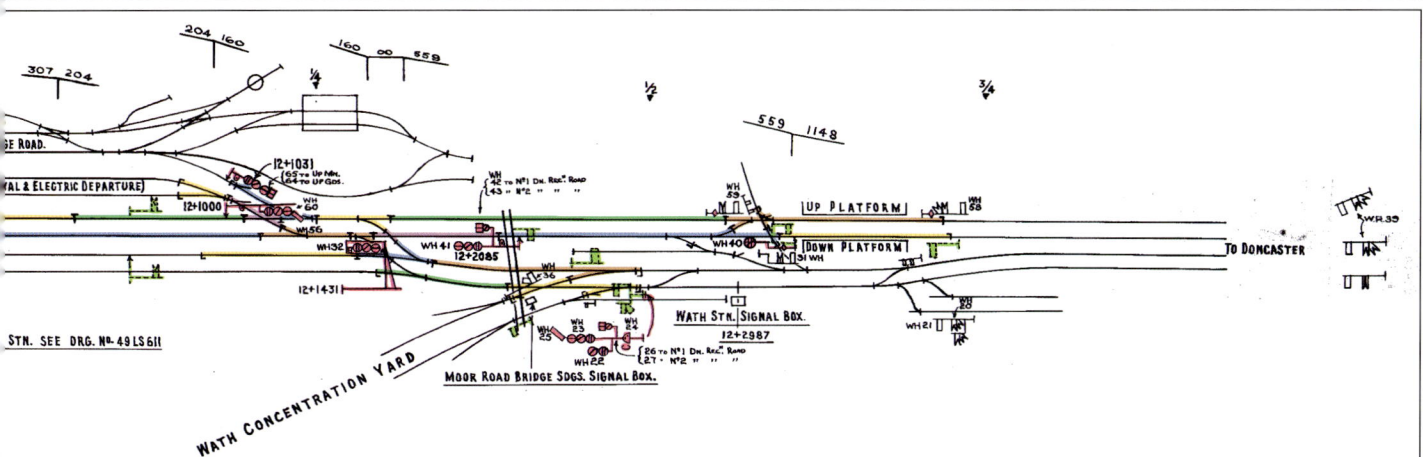

Bottom strip labels:

204 160 160 ∞ 559 ¼ ½ ¾

307 204

559 1148

GE ROAD.

12+1031 (63 to Up Mn. 64 to Up Gds.)

WH 42 No.1 Dn. Rec". Road WH 53

UP PLATFORM WM 58

VAL & ELECTRIC DEPARTURE)

12+1000 43 No.2 " "

WH 56 WR.33

WH32 WH 41 12+2085 WH 36 WH40 WH 51 WH DOWN PLATFORM TO DONCASTER

12+1431

WH 22 WATH STN. SIGNAL BOX.

WH 25 WH 24 12+2987 WH21

STN. SEE DRG. No. 49 LS 611

WATH CONCENTRATION YARD

MOOR ROAD BRIDGE SDGS. SIGNAL BOX. 26 to No.1 Dn. Rec". Road 27 No.2 " "

41

Right: **There's more evidence of the new order as rebuilt Class 'O4' No 63902 emerges from the down tunnel. Woodhead New Tunnel is taking shape in June 1951.** *E. R. Morten*

Below: **The view from inside the new bore: the down main signals have been cleared and Woodhead's old box can be seen in the distance.** *E. R. Morten*

local passenger services between Penistone and Sheffield could be seen ambling along beneath brand-new overhead line equipment – with a Robinson passenger tank at the head.

Even today, arguments rage about whether Robinson also produced a clutch of turkeys, locomotives that looked the part but could barely do the job. It is a criticism levelled particularly at his 4-6-0 classes, where the main plank of evidence seems to be that, because they were almost all built in small batches, none of them could have been the success that Gorton had hoped for.

This may be true, but there is also evidence – of a kind – that the Robinson engines were particularly suited to the demands of the line. George Potts certainly appeared to believe as much. This is his view of a Gresley-designed 'D49' Class 4-4-0 locomotive on a westbound passenger working over Woodhead:

'We were hurtling through Woodhead Station at 60mph or so, a lot too fast for this engine! She was loose between engine and tender and I'd never had such a rough ride in all my life... She was shuttling to and fro all over the road. I had really to cling to the handbrake when I went to close the water feed on the tender. After the bouncing we had had, I was glad to step back onto terra firma; my legs felt as though they were made of jelly.'

Fortunately his trip home was on board an ex-Great Central locomotive. Built a good 25 years before the 'D49', this one was clearly preferable. He and his mate are waiting to take it over at Guide Bridge:

'In about fifteen minutes, the light engine arrived, one of ours, a "B5" Fish (No 6067)... These 4-6-0s were lovely riding engines and going back up the bank it was a pleasure to sit there, admiring the scenery... A nice change from the shaking we'd had on the run down.'

And he was far from alone in his preferences. Jackson and Russell record an instance of a Gorton driver, Jimmy Rickards, simply refusing a new Gresley 'B17' 4-6-0 in the 1930s, demanding his faithful Robinson-designed 'Director' Class 'D11' instead. He took his protest to the point of booking off duty and going home!

Even Robinson's sternest critics could be won round. Professor W. A. Tuplin, whose book *Great Central Steam* dispassionately charts the perceived shortcomings of Robinson's designs, recounts an incident that shows a Robinson 'B7' Class 4-6-0 in a completely new light:

'It was observed on a wet Saturday afternoon in about 1946 at Penistone, that grim junction in the Pennines. A Sheffield–Manchester train of eight vehicles had made the usual stop at the station and the efforts of the Gresley "V2" to get away again were pitiable. Gresley regulators were hard hit by wartime types of maintenance and this did not help...

'Several refusals gave the driver a lot of exercise with the reversing gear besides much tugging and pushing on the regulator handle and even after the train was well on the move there were bouts of slipping as the "V2" clawed her way uncertainly up the curving 1 in 100.

'Immediately afterwards came a "B7" with 14 empty coaches and stopped at the platform end where the "V2" had stood. When the signal went "off", the driver released his brakes, set the regulator half open and left his driving position to open a tool-box and carry out some search inside it. The engine started immediately with no hint of a slip and moved

42

Left: **'B17' No 61643 *Champion Lodge* makes a rousing start from Victoria with the up 'North Country Continental'.** *Peter Cookson*

Middle: **A tired-looking 'D11' 'Improved Director', No 62660 *Butler-Henderson*, arrives at Sheffield Victoria with a stopping train in July 1958. By this time the 'Directors' were almost all in use only for the summer timetable. No 62660 was withdrawn in 1960 but happily was selected for preservation as part of the National Collection.** *Peter Sunderland*

Left: **A classic Sheffield transport scene with 'D11' No 62670 *Marne* shunting stock on the Wicker Arch while a Sheffield Corporation tram picks up passengers below. The picture is undated but has a late 1950s feel, when most of the 'Director' fleet had been concentrated on Darnall shed.** *Peter Sunderland*

43

Right: **Penistone had a short turntable, sited close to Huddersfield Junction box. Here it is being used by 'D11' No 62667 *Somme*. The picture is undated but is probably from 1954, when the loco was allocated to Mexborough for the summer season. It was kept in sparkling condition for use on specials and charter trains, filling in its time on Penistone–Doncaster locals.** *Kenneth Field*

Below: **A Manchester–Marylebone express, headed by a Gresley 'V2' 2-6-2, heads into Thurgoland Tunnel. The two tracks have been reduced to one in preparation for electrification.** *Kenneth Field*

those 14 coaches up the bank as positively as if on a mountain railway worked by rack and pinion. Moreover, it was quite evident that the driver was quite sure that she would.'

In this context, it is worth mentioning that it was well into the 1930s before the Robinson-designed 'Directors' and 'C4' class 'Atlantics' were displaced by Gresley's 'B17s'. And remarkably, both Robinson engines made a comeback when the initial batch of 'B17s' was found wanting. But it could not last, and both classes found themselves back on second-line duties as, first, the new 'Footballer' 'B17s' and, later, 'A3' class 'Pacifics' from the East Coast main line, together with 'Green Arrow' 'V2' class 2-6-2 locomotives, came to the fore.

The Second World War threw everything into a state of flux. Tuplin insists that he once saw a streamlined 'A4' class 'Pacific' working a freight over the Worsborough Branch. The final

flowering of top-link steam came with the Thompson 'B1' class, which quickly took over in the immediate post-war years. But it had already been decided that electrification was the way forward and the 'B1s' were merely a stop-gap.

As already described, the line was very much seen as a means to an end, rather than a communications link serving a string of communities. This meant that purely local passenger services were less prominent, consisting of a typical, haphazardly timetabled service between Sheffield and Penistone, and a more conventional suburban service between Manchester, Hadfield and Glossop.

By all accounts this was a typically LNER take-it-or-leave-it affair. Jackson and Russell paint a picture of ageing 'F1' class 2-4-2 tank engines hauling sets of seven or eight six-wheeled, gas-lit stock:

Above: **A pair of 'C13' 'Atlantic' tanks, working as Sheffield Victoria's station pilots, take a breather in September 1958. For locomotives close to the end of their working lives, they are in good external condition.** *Keith Pirt/IAL*

Left: **Another view of No 67439 taking water on the same date.** *Keith Pirt/IAL*

'Nor did the limited comfort derive purely from the design of the coaches: the less congenial Northern climate also had its effect during the winter, when it was common for passengers to be left shivering in poorly heated compartments while the trains were delayed by snow or fog or because the heavy main-line service had been disrupted.

It is not an encouragement to commute and, in fairness, relatively few people did in those days. The morning peak from Glossop, for example, consisted of just four departures for Manchester between 7.00am and 8.14am. A similar pattern could be observed in the return evening workings.'

By the mid-1930s push-pull working had been introduced on some services to avoid the time-consuming need to run the locomotive around its stock at each end of the journey. Modernisation of a kind came in the late 1930s when bogie vehicles were paired with 'C13' and 'C14' class 4-4-2 tank engines.

But modernity was never the watchword for either this service or the Sheffield–Penistone locals. The Manchester–Hadfield–Glossop service was electrified together

with the main line, but Sheffield–Penistone locals were steam-hauled to the end. They were axed, together with the Penistone–Barnsley passenger service, in 1959, causing several stations, including Oughty Bridge and Deepcar, to close.

Talk of passenger traffic with its stirring starts and on-time finishes, gleaming engines and state-of-the-art stock can sometimes blind those on the outside of the industry to the fact that railways were built primarily to carry freight. This was nowhere more true than on the Woodhead line. Far more effort in terms of men, machinery and money went into shifting freight virtually from day one until final closure in 1981.

Indeed, Robinson's first design for the Great Central was an 0-6-0 tender locomotive, a little bigger and a little more powerful than its predecessor, intended primarily for coal and goods traffic – the 'J11'. It appeared rapidly after his appointment, and Jackson and Russell speculate that the failure of Harry Pollitt (Robinson's predecessor) to come up with a better heavy goods engine was a major factor in the loss of confidence in him by the GCR board of directors.

Right: **Details are scant, but this train is almost certainly an excursion, which has probably arrived at Penistone via Barnsley. The steep gradients of the road to Penistone often demanded a pilot loco, a function being fulfilled here by 'C13' No 67411, assisting 'B16' No 61464.**
Kenneth Field/IAL

Middle: **It is April 1954 and electrification work at Manchester London Road is complete – although there is still some tidying up to do. Steam has far from disappeared though: this view shows three locomotives, including 'C14' No 67440.**
H. C. Casserley

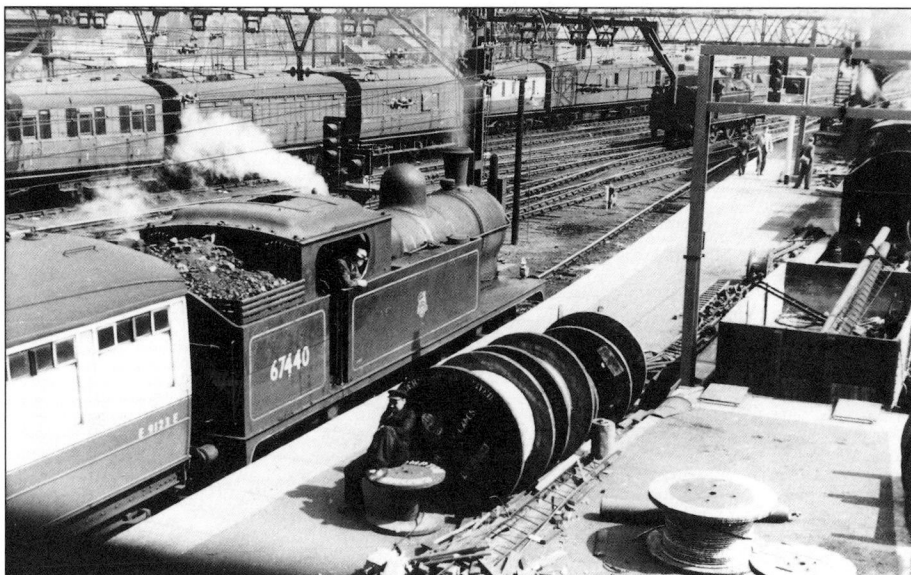

Below: **This Thompson 'L1' 2-6-4 tank makes a change from the Robinson motive power that still ruled the roost in the 1950s. No 67782 leaves Guide Bridge on a Macclesfield train in May 1959.**
C. W. Wood/IAL

Not all the Manchester suburbans were operated using tank engines. Here, 'J11' No 64435 has charge of a lengthy Hadfield–Manchester train, which includes two articulated sets. It is pictured in October 1953 leaving Mottram. *Eric Oldham/IAL*

Tuplin's analysis of the Great Central locomotive fleet is also instructive here: he tells us that between 1864 and 1899 the company built twice as many goods engines as passenger engines and twice as many tender engines as tank engines. The basic 0-6-0 tender engine accounted for 43 per cent of the stock. It is clear that something bigger was needed.

Robinson provided the company with the 'Q4' class 0-8-0, which was immediately put to work at Gorton, Neepsend (Sheffield) and Mexborough, the three sheds most closely associated with the Woodhead coal traffic. The larger 'O4' class 2-8-0 followed a few years later and quickly became the GCR's front-line 'heavy lifter'. The GCR built it in substantial numbers – more than 130 – for its own use, but the immortality of the 'O4' was assured when it was chosen by the British Army as its standard locomotive for the Railway Operating Division. More than 400 were turned out for service in the First World War and afterwards, and the newly formed LNER bought 273 of them, a decision that had a major impact both on the future of the Woodhead line itself, and on the LNER's future locomotive policy. The system was so effectively flooded with 'O4s' that, apart from a few small batches of the Gresley 'O2' design, no more eight-coupled goods locomotives were built by the company. In fact, when Thompson drew up his post-war modernisation plan, he intended not to build new eight-coupled freight engines, but to rebuild the faithful old 'O4s' instead. And this is exactly what happened, creating the Thompson O1 class.

The 'O4s' came ridiculously cheap – the final batch, acquired in 1925, cost just £1,500 each, a price far below their true worth. They effectively changed the course of railway history, for there is ample evidence that both Robinson and Gresley had been scheming out radical new locomotive designs, largely to keep pace with the Woodhead coal traffic.

Even on the main Sheffield–Manchester line, every 'double load' of 60 loaded coal wagons was piloted by a second engine from the start of its journey as far as Sheffield Victoria. Here the pilot went to the rear of the train and became a banking engine, assisting as far as Dunford Bridge before returning home to assist another train – a 40-plus-mile round trip that earned not a penny of revenue.

This sounds wasteful enough, but on the Wath arm of the system using two locomotives on each train was just the start. Up to four locomotives were needed to get a standard 'double load' up the 1 in 40 Worsborough Bank from Wentworth Junction to West Silkstone Junction. Two locomotives were needed all the way from Wath to Dunford. As well as being expensive, it was a complicated operation, as former railwayman the late Ron Fareham, writing in *British Railways Illustrated*, recalls:

'The correct procedure for a train leaving Wath Yard in 1908 with a double train of coal – I have yet to see it correctly described – was: the two engines (coupled together) would arrive, banker leading, from Mexborough shed. After coupling

The overhead line is in place, but the 'O4' class locos will be passing through Godley East Junction for more than another year. A typical (very) mixed freight is hauled by 'O4/8', with round-top Doncaster boiler, in March 1952. *IAL*

Right: **Class 'O4' No 63732 is on an up train of coal empties near Valehouse in February 1954. The left-hand track is the Down Goods line, which ended in a substantial sand-drag – the last line of defence against runaways from the line's summit at Woodhead.** *N. Fields/IAL*

Middle: **Class 'O4' No 63622 heads west with a loaded mineral train at Oughty Bridge in September 1954.** *Ian Pearsall/IAL*

to the train, the whole went forward to the next signal box – Wombwell Station. (The train was thus double-headed only for the first 2 miles). Here the banker was detached to go into a siding and the train drawn past. The banker then went behind the brake-van and exchanged whistles with the train engine; the train would then be on its way with an engine at each end. First stop would be Wentworth Junction where each engine obtained water (there were two water columns spaced so that the engines could be watered simultaneously). Another engine would attach at the front while the train engine got water. Whistles were exchanged and the train moved up to Wentworth Junction starting signal, which would be at danger. After the train stopped, a fourth engine would come up behind the train and exchange whistles. The two engines at the rear would not be coupled – and were not coupled to the train. The speed up the bank was very slow – such that one could get off and pick flowers and then get back on board!

'On arrival at West Silkstone Junction, the assisting two engines were removed and the train went forward with one at each end as far as the summit of the line at Dunford; the banker then returned light engine to Mexborough shed – 20 miles away!'

While there are no recorded accounts of loco crew actually picking posies, Fareham's description brings alive the problems of such a bottleneck. Everything happened slowly and everything needed a lot of resources in terms of locomotives and manpower. It would have been odd if Robinson had not turned his attention to potential solutions. We know that he came at the problem from two angles: first, he got out a scheme for a much larger mineral engine, a 2-10-2 type – in fact, there were two schemes because the Baldwin Locomotive Company

RIght: **Although electrification equipment is in place in this 1957 view, Rotherwood Exchange Sidings were actually laid to assist the war effort. Here Class 'O4' No 63889 arrives with a coke train. A 'B1' and another 'O4', No 63664, wait for their next workings.** *P. Ransome-Wallis/IAL*

48

Left: **A little west of Penistone, at Thurlstone, GCR-built 'O4/1' No 63707 slogs against the incline with a loaded coal train.** *Kenneth Field*

Below: **But the going is easier for ex-GNR 'Tango' 'O2' class No 63925 as it coasts downhill on an eastbound freight near Bullhouse.** *Kenneth Field*

Bottom: **On the Worsborough Bank 'O4' 2-8-0 No 3696 picks its way carefully down the 1 in 40 with an eastbound freight. Electrification gantries had been installed here before the Second World War began.** *H. C. Casserley*

in the United States produced its own design following a visit by Robinson. Second, he began looking at a better banking engine. He actually produced a design for an 0-10-2 tank engine, but both schemes came to nothing, being lost in the turmoil of the First World War.

Peter Semmens, again writing in *The Railway Magazine*, tells us that there were usually four 'O4' or 'Q4' class locomotives on banking duties at Wentworth Junction. But because they needed downtime for servicing and coaling, a fifth engine was usually sent out from Barnsley shed to ensure that four locomotives were continuously available. He also sampled freight working over the branch just before steam gave way to electric power. In this account he is on the footplate of an 'O4' acting as banker:

'Towards the top of the bank there were two tunnels, the first quite short, but the second somewhat longer. With up to four locomotives passing through on a single train, the atmosphere got pretty thick and one normally made use of a handkerchief to breathe through, especially on the rear locomotives. Although this filtered out most of the solid particles in the fumes, it could in no way remove any of the sulphur dioxide nor, for that matter, any of the carbon monoxide that might be around while the whole cab became filled with billowing steam.

'Firing was normally stopped before the locomotives entered the first tunnel, to minimise the emission of smoke, and the firehole doors were "cracked" open. As the cab slowly filled with exhaust fumes, streamers of steam-laden air would be sucked into the firehole as the locomotive blasted its way uphill, the thumps and crashes from the wheels below the floorboards keeping time with the blasts from the chimney. Slipping could occur and the leading banker would sometimes apply sand all the way through the tunnels for the benefit of both rear locomotives. It was always a great relief when we emerged into the

49

clear air again at the exit of the second tunnel, as the atmosphere was by that time approaching that of a Turkish bath with the temperature out of control.'

Semmens also noted that on many of the runs up the bank the driver would share the firing with his mate. Despite their joint efforts, it remained a slow and cumbersome business and there would often be a procession on trains waiting at Wentworth Junction for their turn up the bank.

In fact, prior to electrification there was only one development to try to ease the burden of banking up the incline, and that has been judged by almost everyone with knowledge of it as a failure – the unique 'U1' Class Beyer-Garratt locomotive. Now something of a legend, much of the story of this engine remains shrouded in mystery.

What is known with certainty is that Robinson had thought of taking two of his 'Q4' type 0-8-0 chassis and coupling them back-to-back. He was doubtless influenced by the Garratt locomotives then being built for export just across the tracks from Gorton at the Beyer, Peacock works. They were, in theory at least, a good idea. A large boiler could be slung between the two chassis with ample coal and water capacity. One set of engine crew could operate what was in effect two engines.

But once again the First World War intervened and no progress was made until after the Grouping, when the Garratt idea was revived. But now there was a new man in charge – Nigel Gresley. Gresley took the design forward, substituting two of his own three-cylinder 2-8-0 chassis, creating a 2-8-8-2 with Walschaerts valve-gear.

What is less clear is why the locomotive was built. Gresley reduced the order for two engines to one, which may suggest that no one had a clear purpose in mind. Jackson and Russell, in Volume 1 of *The Great Central in LNER Days*, put together a persuasive argument that the Garratt was never intended as a banker at all, but as a traffic engine. They suggest that its purpose might have been heavy coal hauls, certainly from Wath to Immingham Docks, possibly across the Woodhead line too:

'For the Woodhead service in particular the Garratt offered advantages that would have represented a marked improvement over previous types; the immense power of the machine would dispense with the use of banking engines on the heavy gradients, and on downhill sections the additional braking power would be invaluable; the fact that the Garratts did not need to be turned would help to simplify the problems of engine movements at

Gorton and Mexborough Locos, the two sheds that they would visit most frequently if used on the Woodhead service; and in the well-protected cab of the Garratt the crew would enjoy a greater degree of comfort. In addition the use of Garratts would mean the total number of engines employed on the mineral service could be reduced and fewer crews required; and also it would have been possible to speed up the mineral trains somewhat, on account of the extra power and braking capacity.'

The authors reach the conclusion that Robinson intended the two Garratts to be a pre-production batch to test the concept and iron out the flaws before ordering more for fleet service. It is a plausible argument that gains weight when it is remembered that the Great Central was at the forefront of innovation in the whole area of moving bulk traffic more efficiently; it experimented with high-capacity bogie coal wagons, an idea that foundered because the colliery companies would not invest in sidings and coal-loading screens to accommodate them, not because it was a bad idea. The company also revolutionised the export of coal with the Immingham Docks complex.

And there was one final, small but significant thing: the Garratt was built with vacuum train brakes – the pipes are clearly visible in pictures of it. Why equip an engine with train brakes when they will never be needed in ordinary service? As we have seen, bankers were not coupled to unfitted trains; they merely buffered up to the brake-van. It remains a mystery.

Opposite page and this page: **In April 1947 H. C. Casserley visited Wentworth Junction to capture Britain's most powerful steam locomotive in action. This selection of pictures shows the 'U1' 2-8-8-2 Beyer-Garratt still carrying its post-war LNER number 9999. It is pictured emerging from the bankers' siding to buffer up behind a westbound train; assisting a 'double load' freight together with a Class 'O4' (there will be two more locos at the head of the train); the view from the Garratt's footplate during the climb to West Silkstone Junction; the locomotive arriving back at Wentworth after a banking run; and standing on the ashpit during the hour's downtime allowed each shift for servicing.** *H. C. Casserley*

Above: **Electrification ousted the Beyer-Garratt – electric working meant that its days as a banker on the Worsborough Bank were over. It was tried briefly on more conventional workings and is seen here on a Class J freight at Hyde Junction in May 1954.** *Peter Cookson*

Right: **The climb from Wentworth Junction involved pleasant countryside – and two tunnels. Here a Class 'O4/3' 2-8-0 is at the head of a trip working, carrying coal from Wentworth Silkstone Colliery to Barnsley Junction. The date is July 1963 and the 'Mexborough Pacific' is approaching the first of the tunnels. It is being banked by an EM1 electric locomotive – perhaps that is why the safety valves are lifting!** *Peter Hogarth/IAL*

Whatever the thinking, the Garratt arrived at Gorton on 21 June 1925 and, after some trials on the main line, was sent to Mexborough as a Worsborough banker. Jackson and Russell speculate that the moment of truth came when the loco was first steamed and it was appreciated how difficult hand-firing such a large engine would be. At that point it became a case of finding a job, any job, for the behemoth.

The flood of war-surplus 'O4s' would also have helped seal the Garratt's fate. With more than enough conventional 2-8-0s on tap, why take a risk on unproven technology? Why spend yet more money on the mechanical stokers that would be

needed to use a fleet of Garratts on main-line duties? The reasoning no longer stacked up.

Moreover, it has to be said that the Garratt made a curious banking engine. Its 87-foot length and the need to operate it chimney-first up the bank to maintain a covering of water over the firebox crown-sheet meant that buffering up to a train at Wentworth Junction was a notoriously tricky operation: it is said that many guards chose to get down from their brake-vans, no matter what the weather, until the Garratt had safely made contact.

All in all, it was an ungainly beast. Steam very quickly began

Close to the same spot, but nearer rail level, the camera captures the tail end of a classic 'double load' coal train with an 'Austerity' and a Class 'O4' clearly working against the collar in an undated picture that must only shortly predate the start of electric services. *IAL*

leaking from the flexible couplings between the boiler and cylinders. The steam brake could be erratic because steam condensed in the long pipe runs. Like many a Doncaster product before it, the Garratt got a cool reception from the Mexborough and Barnsley crews who would operate it. Apart from its unsuitability for the job, firemen disliked it because they saw themselves as doing the work of two men. They had a point. Even management agreed that firing it was so arduous that firemen could not be rostered on the Garratt for two successive days: they had to fire a conventional locomotive instead.

Cleaners disliked it because, starting from cold, they would shovel coal for up to an hour just to give the firebars sufficient covering to light up. The Garratt returned to Mexborough shed each weekend for maintenance, and its firebox – quite capable of accommodating a card table and four folding chairs – was a favourite haunt of cleaners and fitters wanting to stay out of the chargehand's sight. Almost inevitably, George Potts found himself working on it. In this account, he has already worked

the locomotive from Mexborough to Wentworth Junction and has banked one train to West Silkstone Junction before returning to the bottom of the bank:

'For a change this was a mixed freight and not the usual load of coal. Just ahead of us the dolly swung off for us to go out on the main line and behind the train. I was now busy piling coal in as fast I could go for it was hardly believable how much fuel this monster loco consumed. It was rather like opening a window and throwing coal through it to the whole wide world, for there seemed no end to it!

'Our progress up the bank this time was a little faster due to the lighter load. As there were no intermediate signals between Wentworth and West Silkstone, Jack [his driver] told me to have a rest while he did a spell with the shovel. When it came to supplying six cylinders with steam, working hard up a 1 in 40 gradient, it was certainly hard work for the fireman. I was only too glad to have a breather, being wet through with perspiration. What a way to earn 10s 6d for a day's work, I remember

Gradually steam was subordinated to electric power and, after the full electric service began, was reduced to bringing trains to and from the electrified section. Here an ex-LMS 'Crab', No 42792, is performing exactly this task, taking over a Hull–Liverpool service at Guide Bridge. *Richard Parkes/IAL*

thinking. Jack sat down similarly exhausted, sweat running down his face.

'By then we were near the first tunnel, which as usual was full of smoke, and the heat in the cab and from our exhaust was really searing. The next tunnel was worse, being so much longer and with the smoke lingering due to lack of air from outside as it was a very humid day. Not ten minutes before, the cavalcade of three "O4s" and a "Crab" had gone through.'

He and his mate did another trip and suffered a burst water gauge glass before, thankfully, a Barnsley crew turned up to relieve them.

Another former LMS engine, 'Jubilee' No 45570 *New Zealand*, waits in the centre road at Victoria to take over a Manchester–Hull train from electric traction. *Peter Sunderland*

Understandably, Garratt duties became the most unpopular of the lot and the crews devised a means of disabling the beast to have it sent to Mexborough for repair; they discovered that closing the dampers and putting both injectors on caused the tubes to begin leaking – presumably because of the rapid cooling. This dodge resulted in an official investigation and a stern warning that the practice must cease.

In many ways the Garratt experience summed up the whole of the Woodhead experience in steam days: much of it was 'against the collar', a long slog up one gradient or another, followed by a cautious descent down the other side punctuated by tedious waiting in loops and sidings while more important traffic took precedence. For some crews, it was virtually their entire working life, summer and winter alike, in an open cab with few creature comforts.

However, in the mid-1930s came the first hint that it was all about to change.

4

'A giant refreshed'

Thoughts of electrification came early to at least one section of the Woodhead line. In 1910 the Great Central Railway's Electrical Engineer, C. W. Neele, proposed electrifying the Worsborough Bank to try to overcome the problems of using steam locomotives as bankers.

Neele and Robinson had recently returned from a fact-finding trip to the United States, where they were shown locomotives built by the General Electric Company for the Butte, Anaconda & Pacific Railroad. The BA&P used the locomotives in pairs, hauling heavy copper ore trains from mine to smelter. Fast forward 60 years, and this appears almost prophetic: pairs of engines working heavy mineral traffic.

Neele believed that something similar was the answer to the problem of getting heavy coal trains up the Worsborough Bank. He saw many similarities between the two lines. Few details of the idea survive and it is uncertain whether he proposed electrifying the whole branch from Wath Yard to Barnsley Junction, or just the incline itself. It matters little, because Robinson disagreed and that was enough to sway the Great Central board.

He was put off by the high capital cost of the locomotives – £12,000 each – and the additional expense of the overhead wiring and organising an electricity supply. Instead, he proposed his 0-10-2 banking tank, another idea that was abandoned. Indeed, it may have been, like the Great Eastern's 'Decapod', one of those locomotives that was never really intended to be built, but designed to prove a point: that steam could still do the job adequately and cheaply.

Elsewhere, however, the idea of using electricity to power railways was gaining ground. A handful of suburban services had been given over to electric traction and unit trains, rather than locomotives. The Mersey Railway had begun to run electric trains in 1903. The first stretch of what would become the Tyneside electrification, from Newcastle to Benton, opened in 1904. The following year the North Eastern Railway also began running electrically-powered goods trains, on the short Quayside branch, also in Newcastle.

The Quayside and North Tyne schemes gave the NER the confidence to try for something bigger and better. The company's Chief Mechanical Engineer, Vincent – later Sir Vincent – Raven also went to the United States to spend time looking at several electrified railroads, trying to quantify the benefits that electric traction could bring against the costs of installing the necessary equipment.

He returned home full of enthusiasm, envisaging nothing less than electrification of the North Eastern main line from York to Newcastle. But what was needed first was a pilot scheme to test the feasibility of working heavy trains hauled by locomotives, rather than the lightweight unit trains used on suburban electrification projects.

The choice fell on the Newport–Shildon line. In retrospect, it appears almost like a 'dry run' for the Manchester–Sheffield –Wath scheme of 25 years later: Newport–Shildon was relatively self-contained with heavy, well-defined traffic flows operating between two clear points on the system. It had significant gradients that hampered efficient steam working. And last but not

least, while acting as a 'pathfinder' scheme for the bigger York–Newcastle project, it would generate cost savings on the traffic worked electrically. Work began in June 1913.

An early decision was to adopt high-tension direct current using overhead contact wires. At the time, with little guidance to be drawn from elsewhere, this would not have been an automatic decision, but it played a major role in shaping future thinking. The locomotives would collect the current using two roof-mounted pantographs. A 'compound catenary' wiring system would be used, in which the actual contact wire was suspended from an 'auxiliary catenary' a few inches above it. This in turn was suspended from the main catenary wire strung from gantry to gantry – a system thought to give more stability. The gantries themselves would span the running lines as a portal with latticework uprights and a girder-type boom or crossbar, spaced every 300 feet on plain, straight track. Around curves and in areas of complex trackwork, spacings would be adjusted to suit the circumstances.

The system was split into a number of separate electrical sections to allow maintenance or repair work to be carried out locally without the need to switch off the entire system. But these sections were not centrally controlled; instead, levers mounted in nearby signal boxes were used to switch the current on and off. Signalmen operated them under orders from Control at Newport Yard.

To haul the trains a fleet of 10 locomotives was ordered. Weighing in at a little over 74 tons, they were designed to haul a 1,400-ton train at 25mph on level track, and to be able to restart the same train on a rising gradient of 1 in 300. This may sound unambitious, but the traffic would be almost entirely made up of full or empty coal trains, unfitted wagons that would not be allowed to travel any faster.

The locomotives were known as '0-4-4-0s' – it was not until much later that this became known as the Bo-Bo wheel arrangement – with four axles on two bogies, each axle powered by its own electric motor. The body was a centre-cab arrangement with a long bonnet at each end. One unusual feature was the decision to mount the buffing and drawgear on the bogies themselves, rather than the bodywork, which took none of the usual traction forces. Controllers were fitted at each end of the cab, and the Westinghouse air brakes, sanding gear and even the whistle were powered from an air compressor, which also generated the air to raise and lower the two pantographs. The locos were still crewed by two men, the erstwhile fireman being known as a 'helper'.

Electric working over the first stage began just over two years later in July 1915, while the complete system came into use in January of the following year.

The project was a huge technical success, with few problems in commissioning and later operating the new electric fleet. The locomotives behaved well and were consistently reliable. The only serious incident, involving a runaway loaded coal train colliding with a steam-hauled working, was a direct result of the driver being given inaccurate information about the weight of his train, rather than any defect with the locomotive.

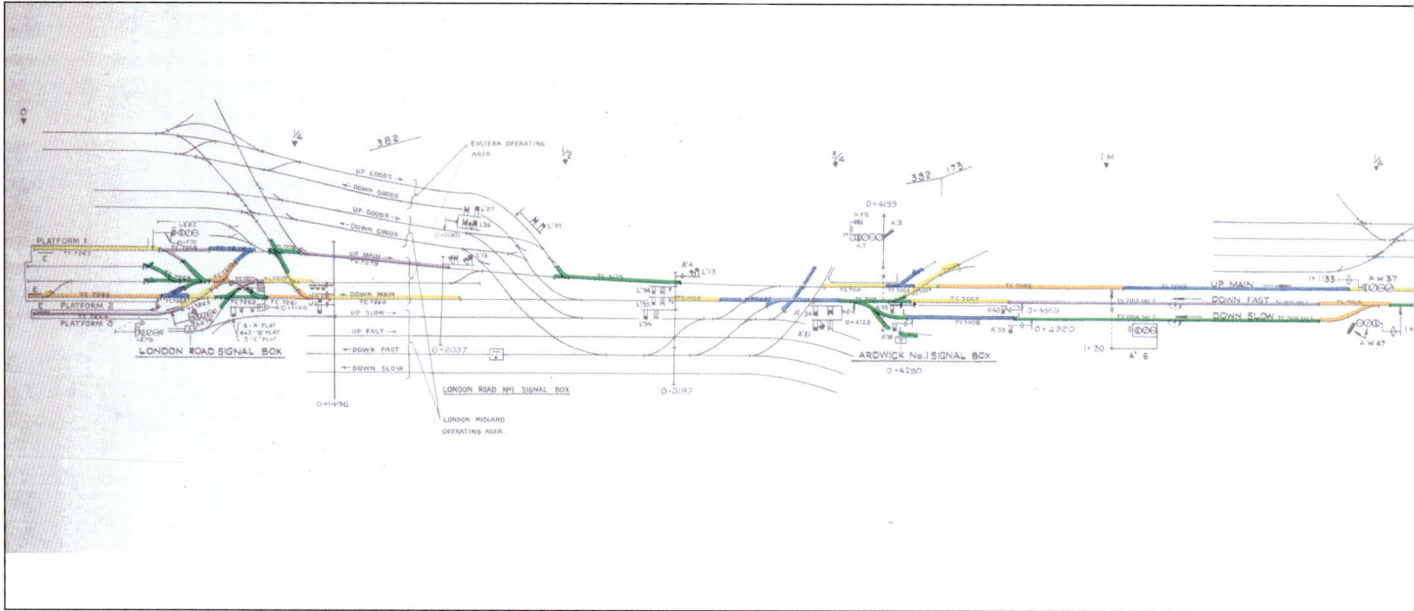

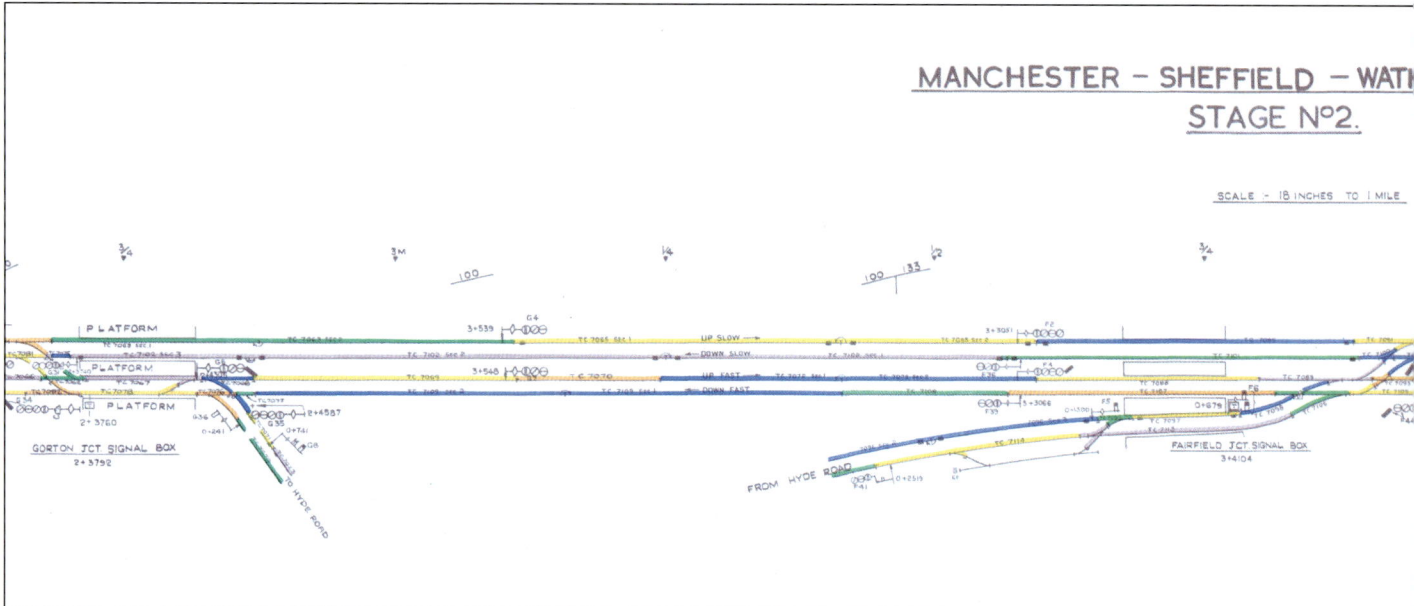

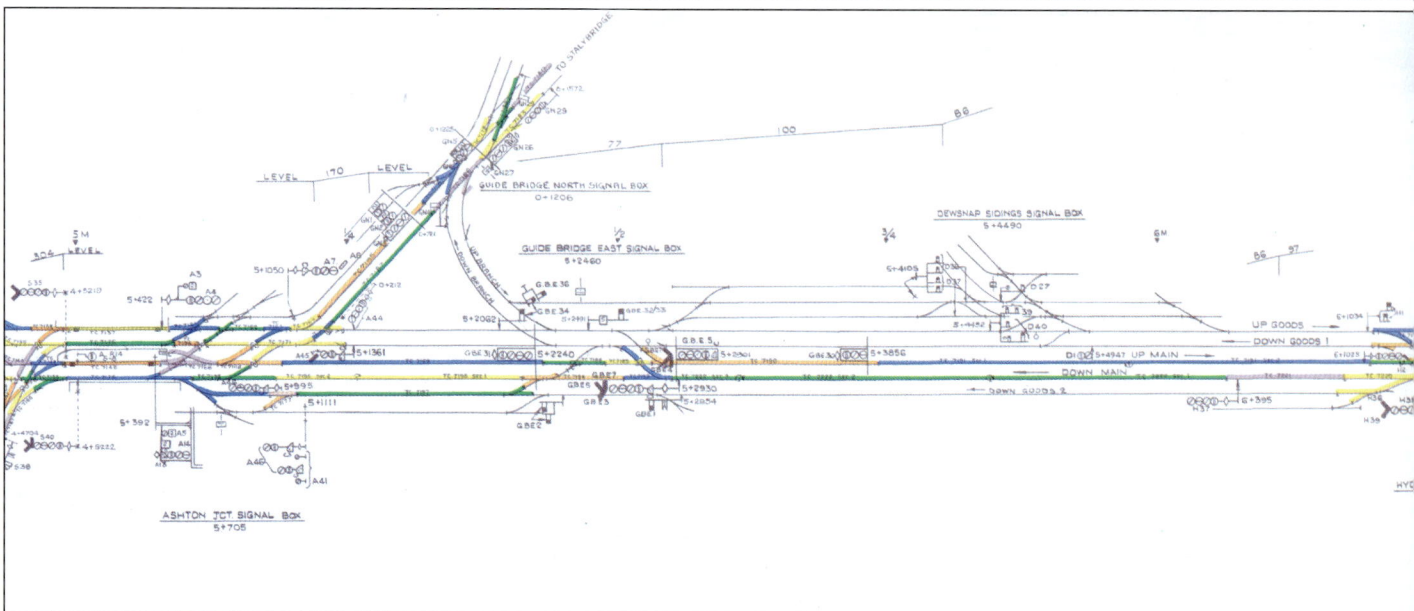

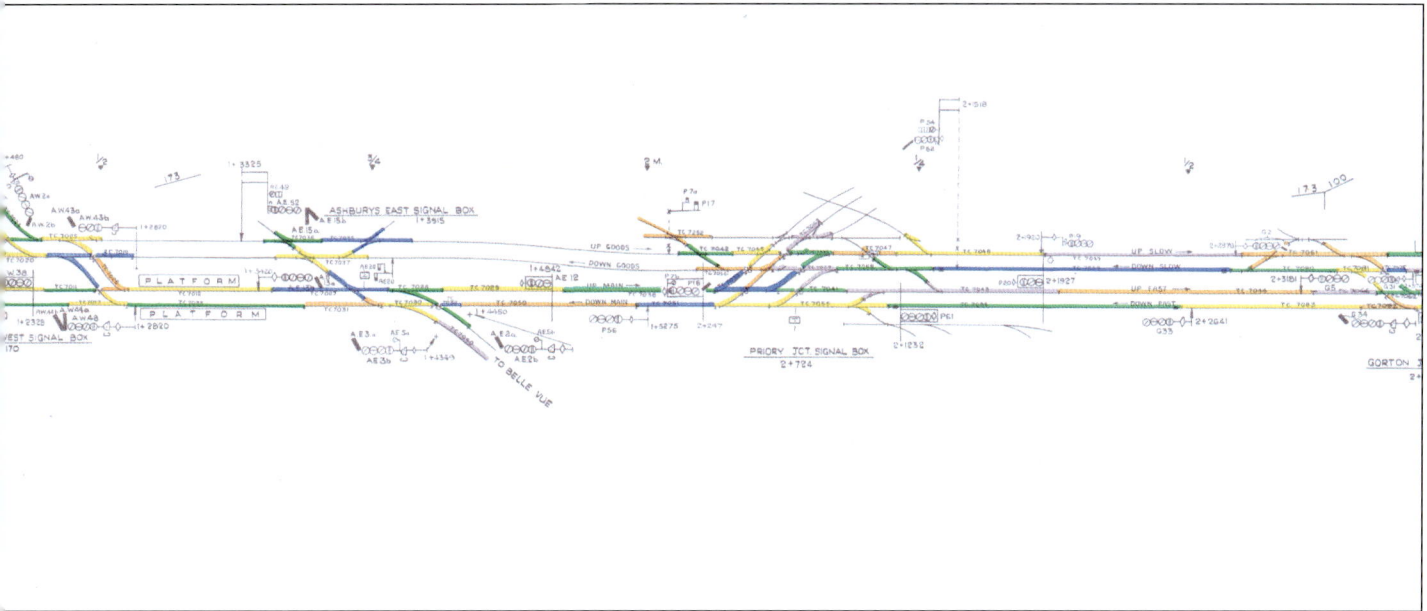

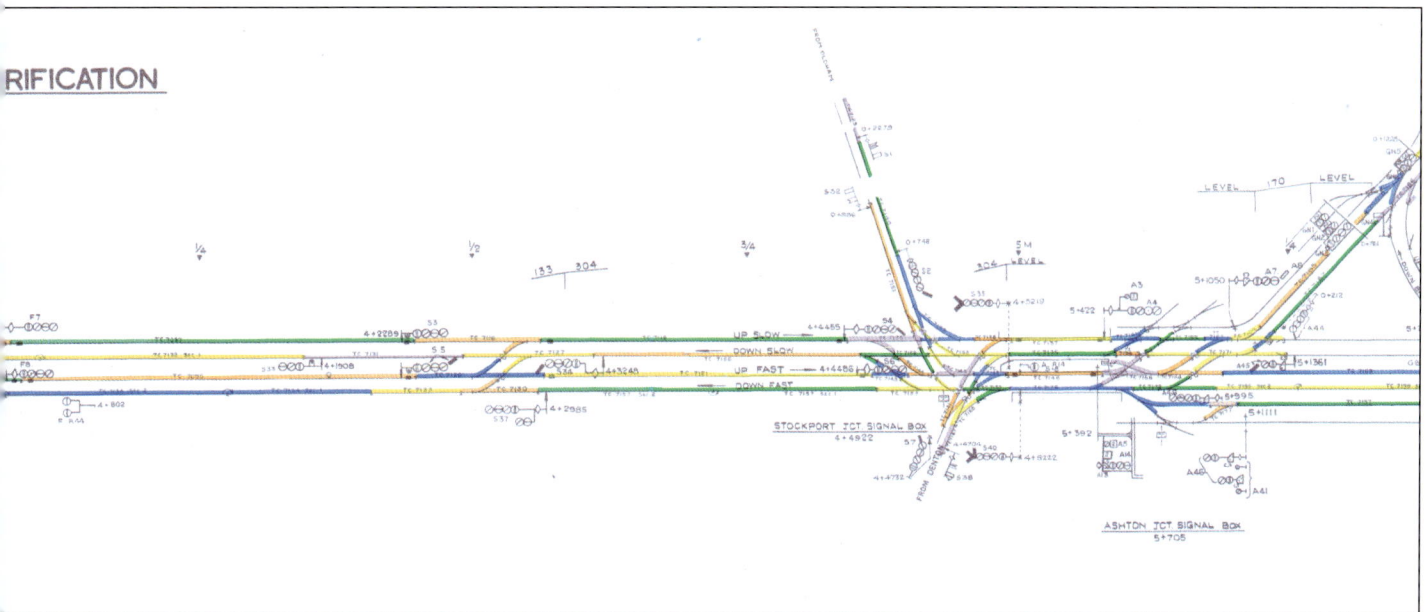

RIFICATION

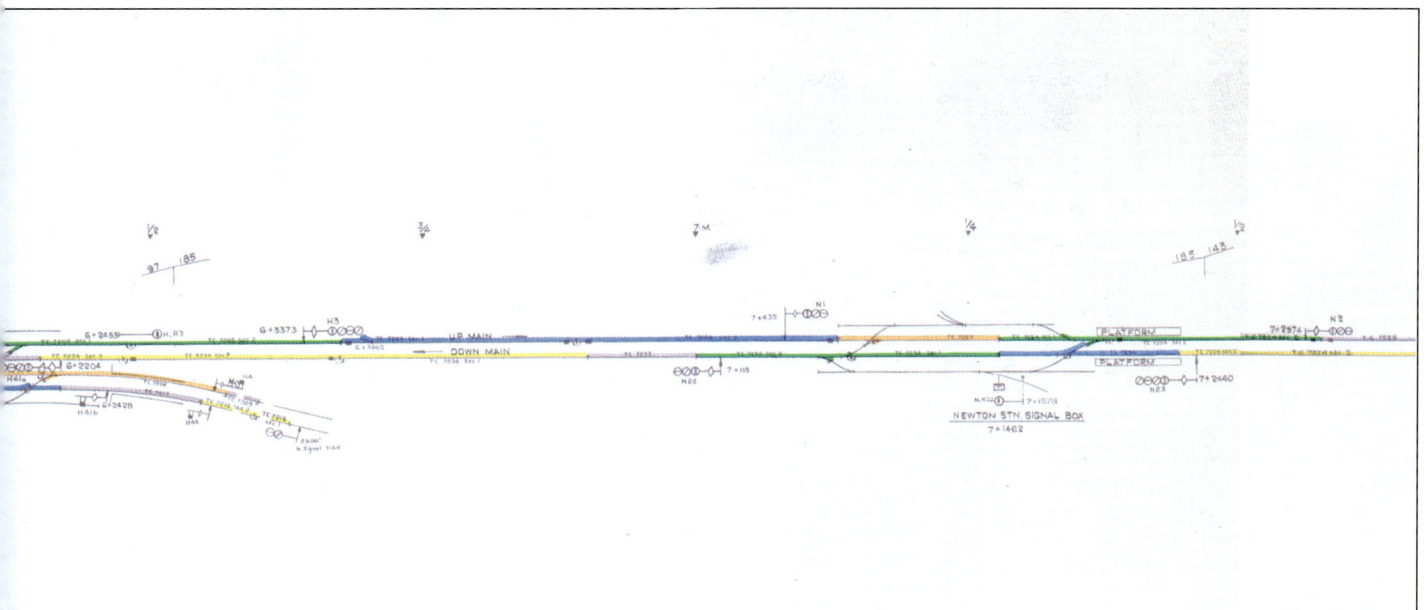

In 1922 trials were carried out with the NER dynamometer car and maximum train weights were increased to 1,400 tons – around 70 wagons – the theoretical maximum for the locomotives. Raven was able to claim that five of his electric locomotives could do the work of 13 steam engines. He gave a technical paper that made it clear that the next step was to push ahead with electrifying from York to Newcastle.

But there was a spanner in the works. Economic conditions in the 1920s were very different from before the First World War, and raising the huge amounts of money needed to install an electrification system before the advantages and economies could be reaped was becoming an insurmountable problem. It remains an issue to this day. Raven ordered the first of a fleet of electric express passenger locomotives; numbered, perhaps unluckily, No13, it was delivered but never turned a wheel in revenue service.

The Grouping of 1923, in which the North Eastern Railway became part of the London & North Eastern Railway (together with the Great Central Railway), also complicated issues, and the York–Newcastle project withered and died. There were problems, too, for the Newport–Shildon scheme. A success it may have been, and a genuine pathfinder for main-line electrification, but it was becoming severely affected by the economic conditions and changing traffic patterns. The nature of the South Durham coalfield was changing and that, combined with a lower demand for coal from manufacturing and heavy industry, was to have a major effect on the line's fortunes. From carrying 52 million ton-miles of coal in 1913, the route was handling just 7 million by 1930.

According to the Railway Correspondence & Travel Society's *Locomotives of the LNER*, although there were ten electric locomotives available, it was rare that more than two were needed on any given day. An argument about the price of electricity between the LNER and its supplier, coupled with the need to replace some of the overhead line equipment, spelled the end, and on 1 January 1935 Newport–Shildon reverted to steam haulage and its ten locomotives were put into store, still perfectly serviceable.

However, the idea of running electric trains was one that would not go completely away. A proposal to electrify the Woodhead line surfaced as early as 1926, and brief details have been given by George Dow and others. Jackson and Russell, in the first volume of *The Great Central in LNER Days*, refer to tests using an 'O5' class locomotive (a large-boilered version of the 'O4') between Dewsnap and Woodhead to determine what the design requirements would be for an electric locomotive.

With the prevailing economic forces, it is not surprising that the plan did not survive. But electrification was still not dead. In 1928 the LNER and LMS, joint owners of the Manchester South Junction & Altrincham Railway, agreed to electrify it, using the 1500v DC overhead system that had just been adopted as a national

standard. Electric trains began running in 1931, adding to the engineers' stock of knowledge.

Finally, in November 1936, the LNER board of directors announced that they were preparing not one, but two electrification schemes: the former Great Eastern suburban lines from Liverpool Street to Shenfield, and the Woodhead line. Both were triggered by the promise of substantial government grants as part of the New Works Programme, an economic initiative intended to create jobs by investing in major public projects.

The Woodhead scheme was the one that grabbed the attention because here, for the first time, was a proposal to create an all-electric railway on which every class of traffic from unfitted coal trains through to express passengers would be electrically hauled. The LNER's reasons for choosing Woodhead are unsurprising: it was said to be carrying more freight than any other trans-Pennine route, it was one of the most heavily trafficked routes on the network, and because of the 'geographical features' of the line – code for gradients and curves!

The first details also emerged, and the 1936 proposal was to electrify 75 route miles and 293 track miles of railway, taking in the following routes:

- The former GCR main line from Manchester London Road to Woodhouse, south of Sheffield

- The route from Penistone (Barnsley Junction) to Wath via the Worsborough branch

- The branch from Dinting to Glossop

- The branch from Guide Bridge to Dukinfield, on the route to Stalybridge

- The Oldham, Ashton and Guide Bridge branch from Guide Bridge to Ashton Moss South sidings

- The line from Manchester Central to Fairfield via Fallowfield, including the sidings at Trafford Park and Manchester Central.

It can be seen that this original project was more ambitious than the 'MSW' scheme that finally emerged in the 1950s, serving two of Manchester's principal stations and, significantly, the great industrial centre of Trafford Park.

It would use the – now national standard – 1,500v DC overhead line system of electrification, with changeover points

The Manchester South Junction & Altrincham electrification was completed in the 1930s, using unit trains for an intensive commuter service. One of the trains leaves London Road station for the viaduct section to Manchester Oxford Road. *Kenneth Field*

Left: **1500v DC EM2 No 27006 has just taken over the boat train to Harwich at Guide Bridge and is waiting for the 'right away'.** *Peter Sunderland*

Below: **As electrification work got under way, the new electric traction depots also began to take shape. These views show the Wath depot under construction and as it finally appeared in 1954 with No 26014 parked up for publicity pictures.** *A. C. Petty, EM2 Locomotive Society collection/John Quick collection*

from steam to electric, and vice versa, established for passenger services at Manchester Central, Guide Bridge, Godley, Sheffield Victoria and Woodhouse. For freight services the traction changes would take place at Trafford Park, Ashton Moss, Guide Bridge, Godley, Sheffield (Bernard Road), Woodhouse, Wombwell Main Junction and Wath.

A new locomotive shed, already planned for Sheffield Darnall (to replace the cramped and inadequate facilities at Neepsend) would become a joint steam/electric depot. Something similar would happen at Gorton running shed, where steam and electric power would co-exist side-by-side, while Wath would get a purpose-built all-electric shed.

The LNER reckoned that simply electrifying the Woodhead tunnels would boost capacity by 25 per cent, because all types of traffic could move more quickly with electric traction. It would eliminate the nuisance of smoke and steam lingering inside the up tunnel bore where locomotives were working hard virtually all the way through. And it would bring another significant benefit. The fumes produced by steam locomotives combined with the damp conditions inside the tunnels greatly increased corrosion of the rails. Standard bullhead rail, with a life of more than 15 years in the open air, lasted just over three years inside the tunnel. Eliminating steam working would not completely cure the problem – the damp would remain – but it was estimated that rail

life would be doubled, meaning fewer possessions for replacement work, which also reduced line capacity.

The proposals contained many other encouraging statistics. The 181 steam locomotives needed to maintain the current level of service over the route would be replaced by 88 electric units. The backbone of the fleet would be 69 mixed-traffic locomotives, with nine express passenger types and ten banking engines converted from the recently redundant Newport–Shildon locos. On average, each of the fleet would cover more than double the average steam locomotive mileage and would need less downtime for maintenance. A fleet of four six-car electric multiple units would cover the Manchester–Hadfield–Glossop suburban service.

Average speeds over the route would rise, partly thanks to the ability of electric traction to accelerate quickly. Express passenger trains averaging 40mph with steam traction would average 50mph with electric power. Express freights currently averaging 28mph would move at 40mph, while even unfitted coal and other mineral trains, presently averaging no more than 15mph, would rise to 22mph – an improvement of 40 per cent or so.

Top and middle: **The first component of the MSW system to be completed was the prototype locomotive, No 6701. Renumbered 6000 after the war, it was sent to Holland for testing on that country's 1,500v DC system. It is seen here at Hilversum in September 1947.** *LNER/IAL*

right: **One of the 'might have beens' of the MSW electrification was the plan to convert ten former Newport–Shildon locomotives into bankers for the Worsborough Bank. Only one locomotive was converted before the idea was abandoned. Instead of working in South Yorkshire, it was sent instead to Ilford as depot shunter. It is seen here, pristine at Ilford, in 1954.** *RAS Marketing*

Top and middle: **Two views of the production series EM1 locomotives under construction with the first, No 26001, at the fitting-out stage. The second picture shows an EM1 bodyshell undergoing electrical flash testing.**
Both Colin Marsden collection

Left: **The first few machines off the production line were sent to the Liverpool Street–Shenfield route, which had recently been electrified, for testing both on passenger and freight working. No 26002 is surrounded by officials and an admiring schoolboy while on a test freight train. Note that only the rear pantograph is raised. The intention had been to use only one pantograph in normal service, but operational experience with dirt and ice on the contact wire led to an early revision of the working instructions and both pantographs were then always raised.**
C. B. Herbert/IAL

Below: **A unit in passenger service rolls into Guide Bridge with a Manchester service in May 1960.** *Peter Sunderland*

These included better steam/electric changeover facilities at Sheffield Victoria; another look at where freight traction changes should take place; an investigation into colour light signalling on the main line (the original plan proposed few signalling changes); and, perhaps most fundamental of all, a re-examination of precisely how the line would be operated with electric traction. Pre-war thinking had been based around working 1,100-ton trains operating at timings only slightly better than steam schedules. Lodging turns for crews working between Wath and Mottram would still be needed.

Now the thinking shifted to operating lighter trains more quickly to bring benefits in train crew and locomotive utilisation. The plan was for 750-ton trains to operate unassisted from Rotherwood to Dunford Bridge, and 850-ton trains, assisted by a single banking engine, from Wath. As in steam days, trains climbing the western ramp to Woodhead would operate with a single locomotive.

The scheme was initially estimated to cost £2.5 million – a figure that had risen to slightly over £3 million by the time the outbreak of war brought its suspension.

Actions quickly followed the words. Design work on the overhead line structures was begun and in late 1938 or early 1939 – the precise date is uncertain – the first gantries, or portals, were erected along the length of Longdendale to the very mouth of the Woodhead tunnels and along parts of the Worsborough branch.

Work also began on the new Darnall depot and orders were placed with Metropolitan Vickers for 70 sets of electrical equipment for the mixed-traffic engines. The orders for the locomotives themselves, to be assembled at Doncaster Works in batches of ten, were placed in January 1939. But, with the project roughly 10 per cent complete, the Second World War intervened and brought work to a halt. One locomotive had been started and it was decided to complete it – the remaining orders were cancelled. A team of workmen was hurriedly dispatched to Longdendale to cover the garish red lead anti-corrosion finish on the portals with a coat of black paint – officialdom worried that they might be used as a marker by the Luftwaffe to target Manchester!

As early as mid-1944, when it was obvious that the war would be won, a committee was brought together to reappraise the MSW scheme. It was once again given a thumbs-up, but some changes to the original proposals were recommended.

Changes to the infrastructure were also proposed. The idea of creating an electric running shed within the steam shed at Gorton and Darnall was abandoned. Purpose-built sheds would be substituted, like the one planned for Wath. The Manchester depot would be built at Reddish and act as main base for the fleet, carrying out certain maintenance and repair work, with the locomotives visiting Gorton for heavy overhaul.

At Thurgoland plans to open out the existing tunnel to accommodate the overhead line equipment were abandoned because of problems with the rock formation. Instead, a new single-track tunnel would be driven alongside the existing one, creating two single-track bores. But the plan still envisaged the use of the two existing Woodhead tunnels.

The only cloud on the horizon was money: wartime inflation had greatly increased the cost of almost everything, and the revised estimate for the MSW project was now a little over £6 million, double the pre-war figure.

Work restarted in 1946 with the erection of more steelwork for the portals. A new signalling scheme was drawn up for the main line. This was expanded to include the replacement of some signals on the Wath branch, where the new overhead structures would interfere with drivers' sighting of semaphore arms.

The other major post-war decision was the future of the Woodhead tunnels themselves. Both were now 100 years old and had seen a hard life. The up tunnel, particularly, had been battered by steam locomotive exhausts as they worked up the gradient, weakening mortar joints and causing some of the stone lining to become dislodged.

Weekend possessions of one tunnel or the other had become an almost permanent fixture, recreating the bottleneck of the 1840s. Now, with concern about their condition growing, the Chief Civil Engineer was given two nine-month possessions running back-to-back to repair first one tunnel, then the other. But even as the work started it became clear that their condition was worse than first thought, and a report on their future stated that, even if they could be brought up to standard for electrification, the remedial work would need redoing within 10 years.

Considering the cost and scope of the scheme, it took remarkably little time to decide that the only realistic option was to build a new tunnel for the electric railway it was creating. It could be purpose-built for electric traction with generous clearances. The cost was put at £2.8 million, bringing the total for the MSW project up to almost exactly £9 million. Bringing the scheme forward was one of the last acts of the LNER before nationalisation.

The electrification equipment itself changed little from the pre-war plan. On plain line, steel portals would span up to four tracks, normally spaced at 210 feet apart (the 300 feet on the Newport–Shildon scheme had been found to be excessive), and they would be set into concrete bases. Register arms held the contact wire and auxiliary catenary in place while the main catenary was looped through pulleys mounted on the underside of the crossbeams.

For wider fans of sidings, in some areas of complex trackwork and at places where power was fed into the overhead line, lattice-type crossbeams were used, supported either on an 'A' frame-style upright, or by a pair of straight uprights – a style very similar to early AC electrification.

In areas prone to colliery subsidence – mostly the Wath branch – some way had to be found to make the system proof against the sinkage that would inevitably occur somewhere along the route. The answer was to extend the uprights and make the crossbeams moveable. If the mast base (or track) subsided, the crossbeam could be raised or lowered to maintain the correct contact wire height. This made some of the portals appear almost like giant rugby football goals.

A bewildering array of overhead support structures was eventually used. According to British Railways' own account, the 3,460 structures needed were built to no fewer than 500 different designs. Some were clearly necessary: the subsidence-proof portals are an obvious example and, further into the Dearne Valley, where the subsidence risk was greater, lattice towers were used with cross-catenaries strung between them across the four running lines and sundry sidings.

There were some other specialist applications, but it is difficult to escape the conclusion that the MSW was being used as a 'shop window' to showcase the variety of structures that could be made available. It may be, though no evidence has emerged, that these structures were being tested against the prospect of a rapid expansion of the electrified system, creating a set of off-the-shelf designs to cover most of the likely contingencies in any future project.

The contact wire itself was staggered by 18 inches from the centre line, to avoid wearing a groove in the current collector on the top of the locomotive pantographs. Normal operating height

Construction of the overhead equipment pushes forward. 'J39' No 64809 is in charge of a wiring train at Wharncliffe Wood near Sheffield in the summer of 1954. *Austin Brackenbury/IAL*

The complexity of the overhead wiring and the multiplicity of designs for the supports is evident in this official view looking into Wath Yard from Elsecar Junction. *IAL*

was 16 feet above rail level, but this could vary enormously. The pantographs could operate down to 13ft 9in above rail level – useful for getting the overhead line through tunnels and overbridges where replacement would be difficult and costly. At public level crossings, it was increased to 18 feet to give ample clearance for high road vehicles. A set of warning bells was installed at every crossing to prevent the contact wire being struck. These were simple but effective, consisting of a bar with bells mounted on it, slung above the road surface from two uprights on the approach to the crossing. If an overheight vehicle approached, it struck the crossbar and rang the bells.

Maximum contact wire height was 20 feet above rail level, a setting used in certain sidings and wherever a water column was sited. It is easy to forget that, for almost a decade, the Woodhead line electric locomotives operated alongside not diesel but steam locomotives. The latter still needed to take water frequently and the crew needed to clamber over the tender to push coal forward and use lengthy fire-irons that could all too easily come into contact with the 1500 volts flowing through the contact wire.

Special working instructions issued in the name of the British Transport Commission dealt with this issue at some length. Rule 22 states: 'It is forbidden to use any form of fire-irons or the slaker pipe while on or adjacent to the electrified lines.' This edict was followed up by Rule 23: 'It is forbidden to climb on the high points of locomotives for any purpose while on the electrified lines except

at those water columns where the height of the contact wire is 20 feet above rail level or the track is unwired.'

The electricity itself came to the system from the Central Electricity Generating Board into three substations at Gorton, Neepsend and Aldam Junction. From here, it was distributed to eight additional substations via a 33kV feeder cable. All substations were capable of converting the current from AC to DC and stepping it down to the 1500 volts required for traction. Additionally, a network of track sectioning cabins divided the MSW system into short electrical sections, so small areas could be isolated for

For a long period the new electrics worked alongside steam: this picture sums up the relationship splendidly as 'K3' No 61964 leaves Sheffield Victoria on a Lincoln train while No 26029 waits in the carriage sidings. The picture is dated August 1958 so the EM1, although not fitted with a train heat boiler, could have been rostered to work a service to Manchester. *Keith Pirt/IAL*

Left: **EM2 No 27005 has arrived at Victoria on an express passenger service. There is no date for this picture but it is unlikely to be high summer because the safety valve on the train heat boiler is sizzling nicely.** *Peter Cookson*

Below: **It was five years after electrification before main-line diesels became a common sight alongside the electrics. Here, EE Type 4 No D206 leaves with a York service. These locos were originally allocated to London services, so this may have been a filling-in turn. The date is June 1959.** *Peter Sunderland*

Left: **No 26024's pantographs are at full stretch as it works mineral empties east through Penistone. The contact wire height was 20 feet above rail level here to provide protection for steam crews watering their engines.** *Kenneth Field/IAL*

65

Right: **Steam had a long goodbye on the MSW, working alongside electric traction until the mid-1960s, so it is difficult to resist this shot of Standard Class 2 No 78014 in a bedraggled state under the wires at Guide Bridge in 1965.** *N. Gascoigne/IAL*

Below: **The crew of an ex-GCR 'J11' 'Pom-Pom' take an interest in the new order represented by EM2 No 27003 standing just outside Manchester London Road. It is August 1955, so the electrics are still a novelty.** *G. D. Parkes/IAL*

maintenance or repair work. All were unmanned, the system being operated from the Electric Control Station at Penistone.

Other infrastructure work included laying in exchange sidings. The pre-war proposals referred to 'nests of double-ended sidings' and this is exactly what was provided. At Rotherwood the work went ahead as part of the war effort. In places the facilities were modest; Wombwell Main Junction, for example, had just three loops laid alongside each running line. These were intended to capture traffic from the Barnsley direction and off the Midland main line at Cudworth, without the need to trip it all the way to Wath Yard, only to have to retrace its steps with electric traction.

Work also began on the three maintenance depots. The one planned for Wath caused particular problems, being right at the heart of the Dearne Valley, an area severely blighted by colliery subsidence. The structural engineers knew that subsidence would be a problem, but on what scale? They trampled the problem to death by designing a structure that could safely sink by up to 5 feet anywhere along its length. Any portion affected could then be jacked up to restore the integrity of the building. Inspection pits were built to be completely independent of the main structure and similarly designed to allow for sinkage. In the end, the east end of the building subsided by 3 feet, the west end by a mere 2ft 9in. But the depot fulfilled its designers' expectations: it was still standing when the line closed and went on to have a second career as home to a chemical recycling company.

At the same time resignalling was pushing ahead. From the original 'do nothing' proposals, the resignalling plan went through several re-evaluations. Initially, the plan for the main line was to replace all Distant signals with colour lights as well as some Home and Starter signals, where the arms would be obscured by new electrification structures.

Ultimately this evolved into a scheme to resignal the main line with three- and four-aspect colour light signals and to also replace some signals on the Wath branch, again principally for sighting reasons. This did not mean the end of traditional signalling because subsidiary signals in yards and sidings, as well as ground disc signals and points, remained mechanically controlled.

The MSW project came along just a few years too early to take advantage of the technological advances that allowed the long-distance remote signalling used in the 'power box' schemes from the late 1950s onwards. Had this technology been available earlier, it is quite possible that much of the main line, and the route to Wath, would have been centrally controlled from a panel at Penistone, which might have been co-located with the electric control panel. As it was, everything still had to be controlled locally, so the GCR-designed boxes survived – in many cases to the very end of the line's existence. Most of the new colour light signals were controlled not by push buttons or switches, but by mechanical levers, shorn of their connections and linked to electrical switchgear instead. It formed an intriguing blend of old and new. Indeed, at least one Manchester, Sheffield & Lincolnshire Railway box was still operational in 1981 (though open only as required), at Blackmoor Crossing, east of Penistone.

Some of the pioneering signalling work done by the Great Central Railway also survived in the shape of the pneumatic signalling equipment between Manchester London Road and Newton, and at Wath Yard. It was all adapted to suit the new scheme of things. In a few places, substantial alterations were needed: Wombwell Main, with its new exchange sidings, had a panel installed alongside the existing mechanical lever frame to operate signals and points at the far end of the sidings, which

Above: **One of the most advanced operational aspects of the MSW system was the use of regenerative braking. In addition to the normal benefits, it also meant that banking locos were effectively used twice, assisting with 'regen' on the Worsborough Bank where one locomotive would have been insufficient. Here Nos 26039 and 26042 approach Worsborough Bridge Crossing on the return to Wath Yard.** *P. J. Lynch/IAL*

Middle: **A less successful experiment was undertaken by No 27002, which for a time was fitted with experimental rotary windscreen wipers, as used on ships; they employed a circular rotating glass plate to throw water off the screen. The idea was not taken any further. The loco is pictured at Torside Crossing on an unusually short Manchester–Sheffield express in April 1964.** *John Morton/IAL*

Left: **The classic view of Wath shed, taken in 1969. By this time the shed itself had become a diesel depot, with the overhead line equipment removed. All electric loco maintenance was carried out at Reddish, with Wath acting as a stabling and signing-on point.** *Keith Long*

were too far away for mechanical controls. Thus the crew of an approaching trains would see traditional semaphore signalling for the path across this complex, five-way junction and into the exchange sidings, and colour light signals at the west end, giving authority to proceed along the Worsborough branch towards Penistone.

At Barnsley Junction a replacement 90-lever frame – which came from Potters Bar, where another resignalling scheme rendered it redundant – was installed to handle connections to the enhanced locomotive facilities. At Sheffield Victoria, No 3 box was swept away completely by an extension to the Up Goods line and replaced by a new structure on the opposite side of the track, while No 4 box was extended from 96 to 110 levers.

However, all these projects were small beer compared with what had now become the central task of creating the new Woodhead Tunnel. Preliminary work began in 1949. The tunnel was to be 3 miles 66 yards long, making it the country's third longest after the Severn and Totley bores. It was also to be rather different from its predecessors. Instead of a rising gradient from the western portal almost to the eastern end, it would rise for roughly 2 miles at 1 in 129 before a new summit produced a fall of 1 in 1187 towards Dunford Bridge. The two rising planes were connected by a vertical curve of 800 yards diameter. The thinking behind this change was that, should any future decision be taken on increasing line capacity by allowing two trains (on the same track) into the tunnel simultaneously, the track geometry would be no bar and all that would be required would be alterations to the signalling system.

The new bore was to be 27 feet wide at its widest point and 20ft 7¼ in high. Internally, it would be quite unlike any traditional tunnel built with steam power in mind. For a start, there would be just one, centrally placed, ventilation shaft. The new tunnel would be barred to steam traction completely, so ventilation would be an almost non-existent issue. It would also look different: instead of the usual brick or stone, the plan was to line it with Portland cement, 21 inches thick. This would give it an off-white appearance. If that was not enough, lighting was to be fitted along both walls, though with only the down side normally switched on. Finally, with operational issues in mind, it would be signalled to allow single-track working for maintenance and repair work.

Work began by boring a 12-foot-high pilot tunnel, working from both ends and outwards from the base of the central ventilation shaft. This phase went almost without incident and the bores met and handshakes were exchanged in May 1951. But the project was not without its problems. A plan to use a new drilling technique had to be abandoned – with the realisation that conventional methods would allow only half the required rate of progress to meet the schedule.

As the engineers were grappling with this problem, a 72-foot section of enlarged tunnel – ie the full cross-section – collapsed without warning at the Woodhead end, sealing off the heading. A haulage road was dug around the obstacle and this allowed two new faces to be started. And here was the solution to the original problem: more 'bypass' tunnels were dug alongside the pilot bore, allowing more working faces to be started up at intervals along the line of route. Eventually nine were in operation.

In many ways, a Victorian navvy would not have felt out of place on the site. Lorries and dumper trucks had replaced horses, but in other ways little had changed since the first two tunnels were dug. The rock was drilled, blasted out and the spoil loaded into skips on narrow-gauge tracks laid to serve each working face. True, gunpowder had given way to gelignite, but

Work on the new Woodhead Tunnel began much earlier in the project, and in this 1951 view work is already well advanced. *IAL*

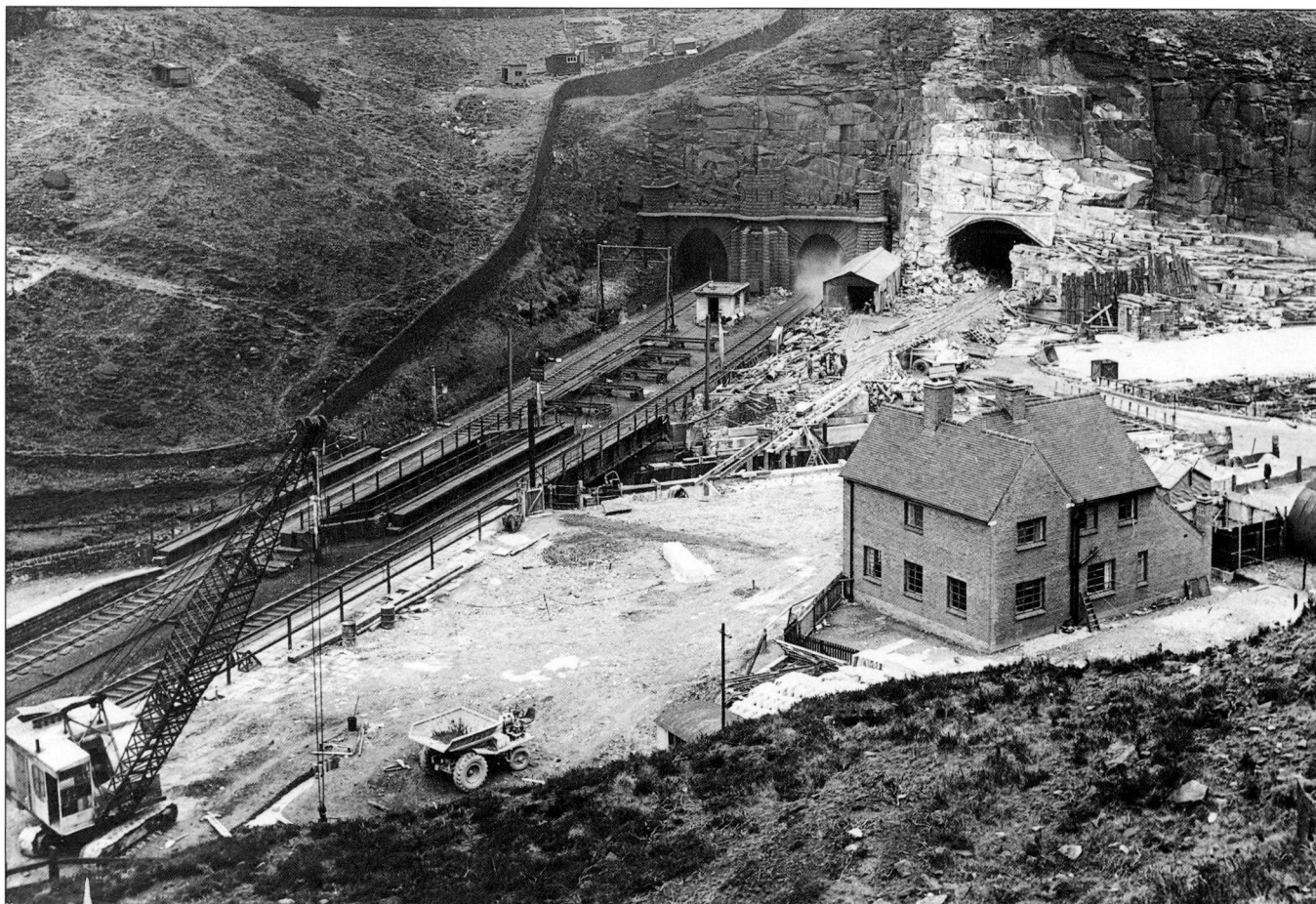

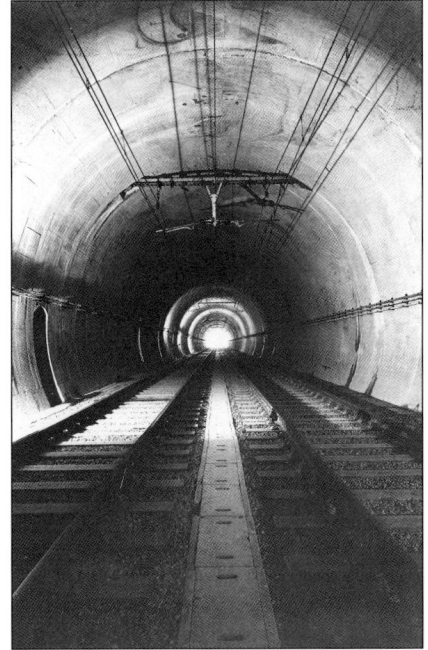

the technique remained essentially the same. The only new issue was having a working railway in operation just 100 feet away through the rock. What if a blast caused one of the two existing tunnels to collapse?

British Railways took no chances and observers were posted in the running tunnels approximately level with the working faces. When a gelignite charge was detonated, they had to report in to Dunford Bridge that all was clear before more trains were allowed through.

If the work was familiar, then so were the lives of the 1,100 or so people building the new tunnel. The remoteness of the site meant that there was no option but to set up a construction camp, though this time it was at Dunford Bridge, rather than Woodhead. It was also rather more comfortable than the Victorian equivalent. In addition to dormitory huts, there was a shop, a cinema – where the programme changed three times a week – a recreation hall, both 'dry' and 'wet' canteens, a sick bay and even a Post Office, which had its own letter frank: Dunford Bridge Camp.

Considering the scale of the project there were remarkably few setbacks and, despite a further rockfall in late May 1953, just three weeks before the last of the cement lining was due to be poured, it was completed only two weeks behind schedule. Six men had died in the 4½ years it had taken to build it.

In October the camp was dismantled and its contents and surplus materials auctioned off. Now it was time to transform the tunnel from a hole under the hills into the centrepiece of the MSW project. Track and overhead line equipment was laid in, and signalling was installed, controlled from two new signal boxes at Dunford Bridge and Woodhead. These formed part of two new stations, all finished in a modern style. Neat courses of local stone were used, and while the little stations – the platforms were just two coach lengths – were of an unmistakeably modern design, they did not jar and, as they weathered, fitted in remarkably well with the Pennine landscape.

By the time the new tunnel was finished, Stage I of the project had been complete for more than a year and trains were being electrically worked between Wath and Dunford Bridge. Test running had also taken place on Stage II, between Manchester and Woodhead. A pair of locomotives, Nos 26001 and 26016, made a trial trip through the new tunnel. It would take only the snip of a ceremonial tape to link the two together.

That snip was provided by the Rt Hon Alan Lennox-Boyd, Minister of Transport, on 3 June 1954 with a little help from EM1 locomotive No 26020, suitably bulled up for the occasion and wearing the bright stainless steel handrails produced for her appearance at the Festival of Britain exhibition three years earlier.

Above left: **Two years later, track-laying teams are at work.** *IAL*

Above right: **All is now complete and this official view shows how different the new tunnel, with its Portland cement lining, appeared compared with a traditional tunnel.** *IAL*

Left: **Both Woodhead and Dunford Bridge got new stations together with the new tunnel. This is Woodhead, showing the ticket office/waiting room and signal box.** *John Quick collection*

The changed appearance of Dunford Bridge station is evident in this 1962 view of an unidentified Bo-Bo heading west. By this time the locomotive is wearing green livery. *Peter Sunderland*

The following day Wath–Mottram traffic began working with electric traction throughout. Passenger services were electrically hauled between Manchester and Penistone. Stage III of the project, from Penistone to Sheffield Victoria, then Rotherwood Sidings, was just months away from completion. The work was over by the end of January 1955.

Above: **Soon it was time for the old tunnels' swansong; 'J39' No 64740 enters the up tunnel on the last day of steam working, 12 June 1954.** *Kenneth Field*

Right: **Opening the new tunnel was left to the Festival of Britain locomotive, No 26020, which broke a tape stretched across the running lines at the Woodhead end.** *IAL*

But it had come at a price. The cost of the project ballooned to almost £12 million, and cutbacks were ordered even as the work was going on. The planned electrified link from Fairfield around to Manchester Central and Trafford Park was abandoned, something that would arguably affect the long-term viability of the route. And the number of locomotives was cut.

Still, it was a time for celebration. On 14 September 1954 another ceremony was held, this time to inaugurate the new electrically-hauled passenger service between Sheffield and Manchester. Much was made of the fact that this was Britain's first all-electric main line, with all types of traffic handled by just two classes of locomotive.

British Railways was sufficiently pleased with the results to publish a commemorative booklet giving details of the project. It ended with this passage:

'In concluding this short and necessarily abridged account of a great work, so long in contemplation, and for so long delayed and even suspended by the hazards and shortages of war, we had almost compared the railway to a sleeping giant awakened. But if there is one railway in Great Britain which has never been dormant, it is this great main line through the backbone of England. Rather, in its new form, it presents itself as a giant refreshed.'

Stirring words indeed.

Above: **One of the new suburban three-car EMUs provided guests with a shuttle service through the new tunnel. In the background, a 'B1' steam locomotive waits to return to Sheffield with the special opening train.** *IAL*

Below: **A commemorative ticket issued for the opening day of the Woodhead New Tunnel.** *Howard Turner collection*

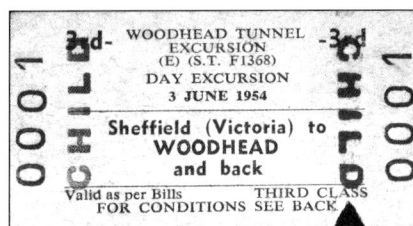

Above: **An EM1 rumbles through Penistone station, with the Huddersfield lines off to the left, on a down freight. Although the marker lights were lit during daylight hours, the headcode had to be 'validated' (the term used in the working instructions) by placing a white disc around each illuminated lamp. By the late 1960s the discs had been dispensed with.** *Peter Sunderland*

Right: **Victoria station looks neat and tidy in this 1959 view as a block load of coal for Liverpool's Clarence Dock Power Station rumbles through behind EM1 No 26015. The loco has already swapped its all-over black for lined green livery.** *P. J. Lynch/IAL*

Manchester–Sheffield–Wath electrification track plans — Stage 2, Section 2

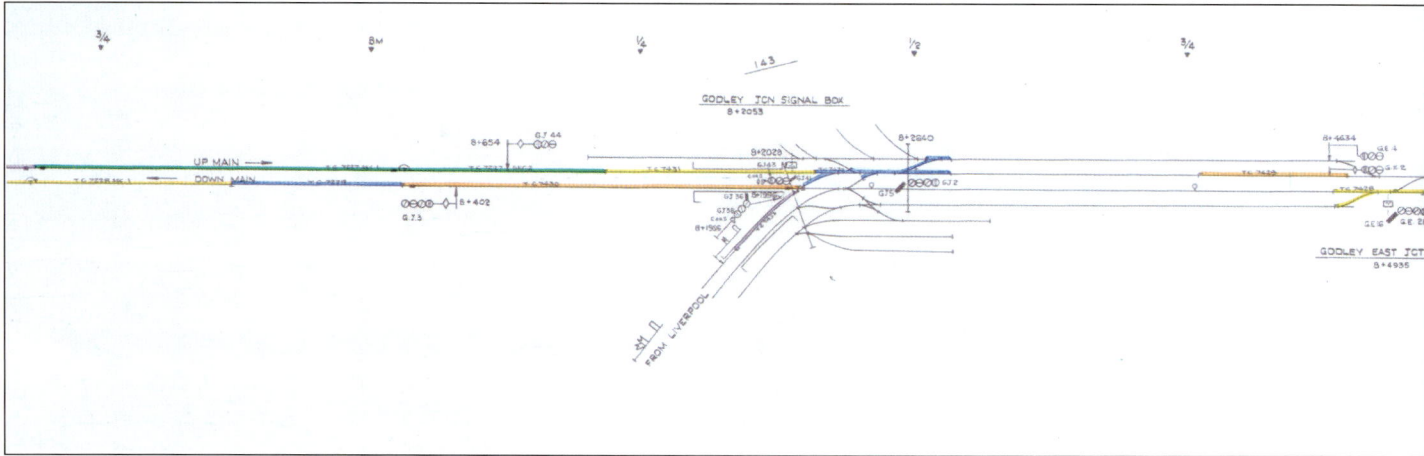

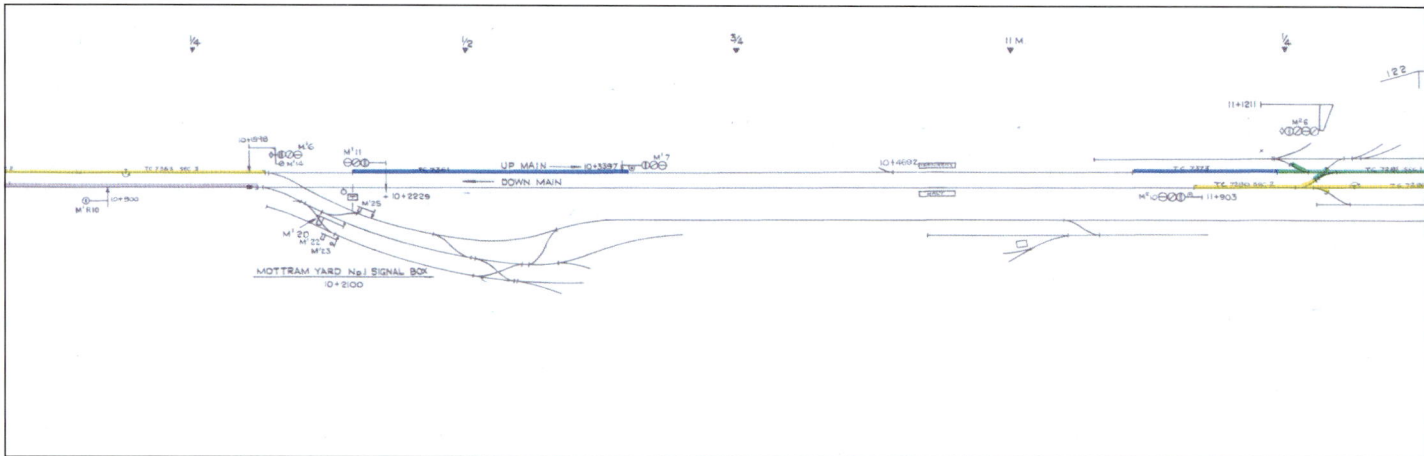

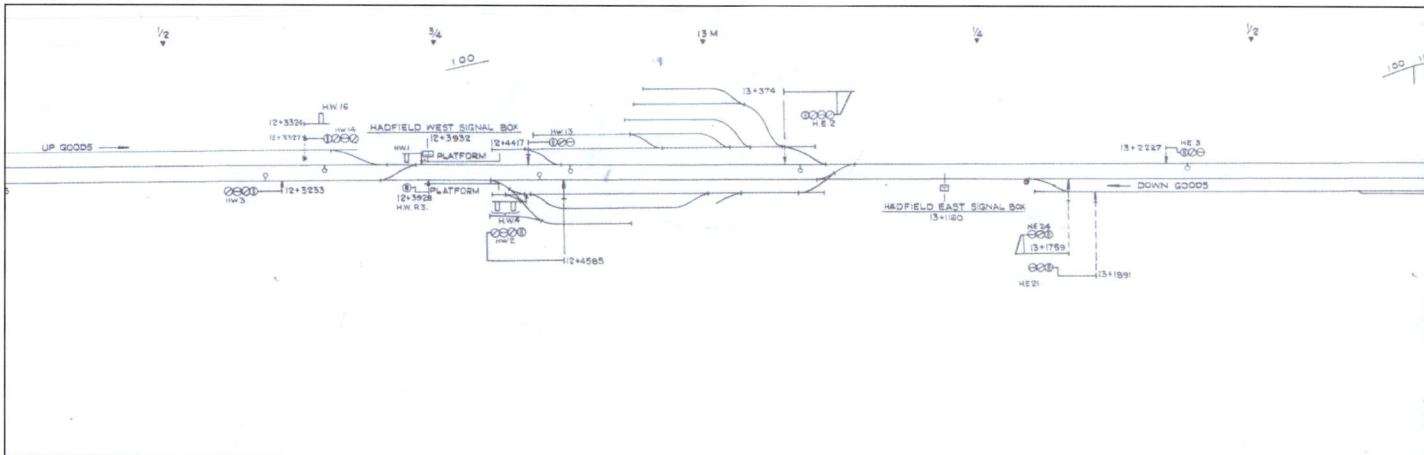

GODLEY JCN SIGNAL BOX
8+2053

UP MAIN →
DOWN MAIN

8+654

8+402

8+2029

8+2840

8+4634

GODLEY EAST JCT
8+4935

FROM LIVERPOOL

MOTTRAM YARD No.1 SIGNAL BOX
10+2100

UP MAIN — 10+3397
DOWN MAIN

10+2229

11+903

11+1211

HADFIELD WEST SIGNAL BOX
12+3932

UP GOODS —

12+3324
12+3271

12+4417

13+374

13+2227

13+3253

12+3928

12+4585

HADFIELD EAST SIGNAL BOX
13+1180

13+1759

13+1891

DOWN GOODS →

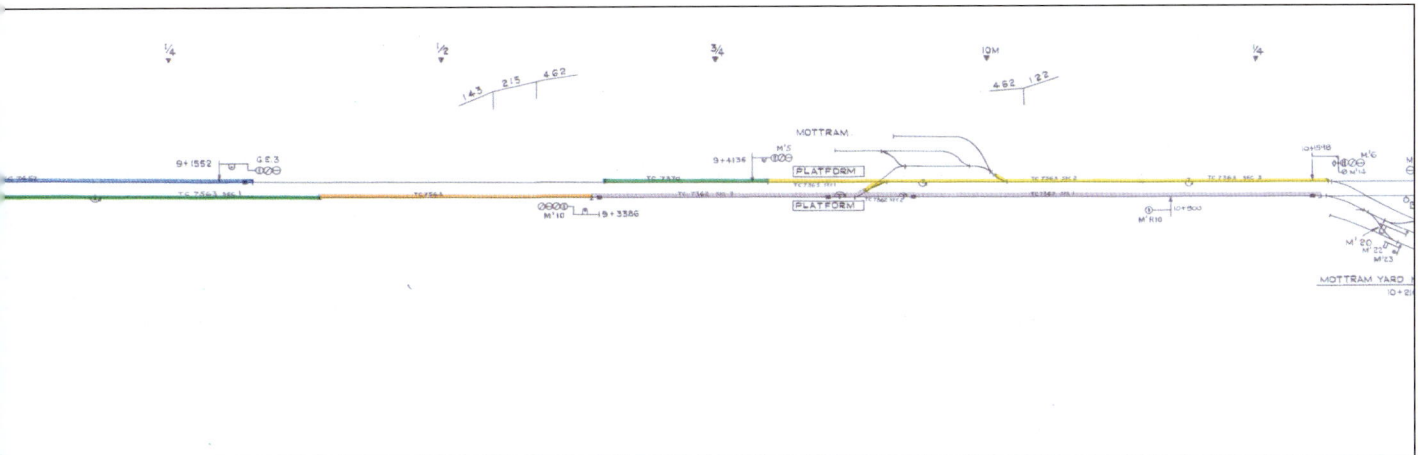

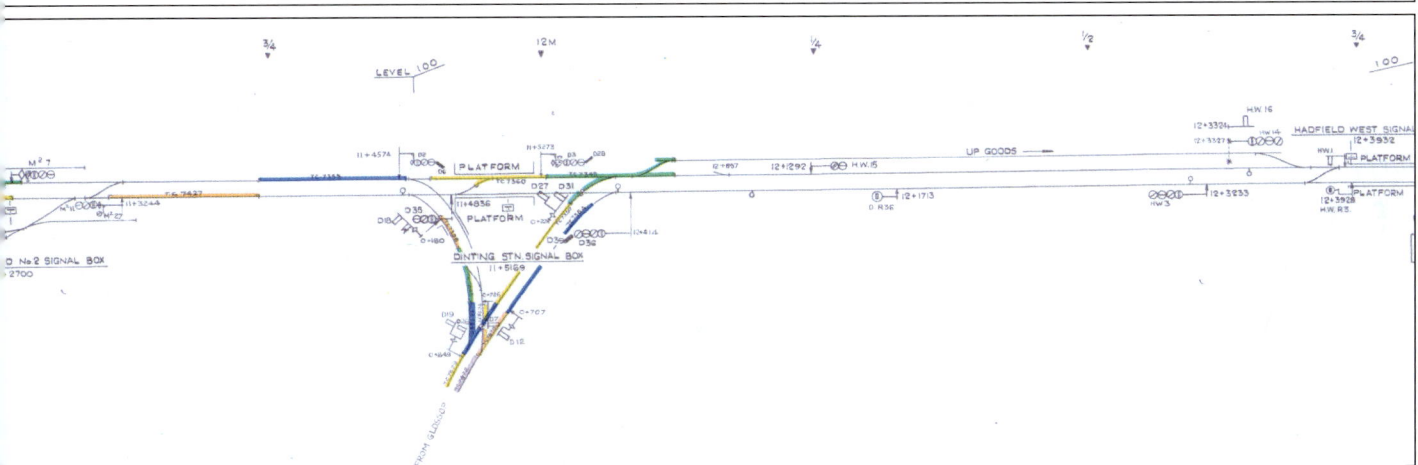

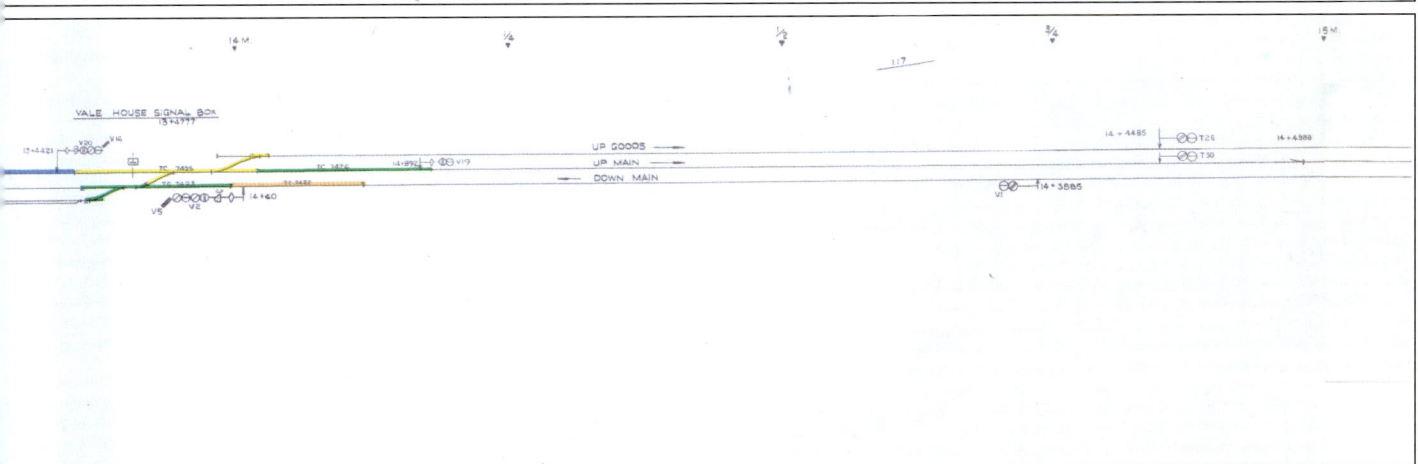

73

Right: **The classic British Railways publicity shot of EM2 class leader No 27000 on a lengthy test train in Longdendale. The train is almost as interesting as the locomotive!** *BR/IAL*

Above: **As the EM2 fleet came on stream, they were sometimes paired with EM1s as an 'insurance policy' against failure until they were considered to be run-in. EM2 No 27003 and an unidentified EM1 share the work of the 2.22pm Manchester–Sheffield service at Milepost 33 between Wortley and Deepcar.**
BR/John Quick collection

Right: **EM2 No 27004 shunts out onto the Wicker Arch at the west end of Sheffield Victoria station at some time in the early 1950s.** *Peter Cookson*

Above: **EM1 No 26020, powers through Dinting on a five-coach Sheffield–Manchester express soon after the full electric service began.** *P. R. Vickers*

Middle: **EM2 No 27001 is at the head of a Sheffield–Manchester express in the first full year of electric operation.** *Peter Sunderland*

Left: **Heading in the opposite direction on the same July day, No 27006 pauses at Penistone.** *Peter Sunderland*

Above: **Initially, trains were operated with electric locomotives simply attached to the front of a complete steam-hauled service. A nearly new No 26007 performs this task with an 'O4' and train of mineral empties in tow near Godley Junction. Judging by the safety valves, the 'O4' fireman is having an easy time of it.** *N. Fields/IAL*

Below: **No 27003 stands proudly at the head of an eastbound express about to leave London Road. The locomotive may be new, but the rolling stock surrounding it certainly is not.** *P. R. Vickers*

Left: When the first electric train service began on the Wath–Dunford section, the EM1s took over completely. This picture shows a typical early train with No 26039 on a Cudworth–Mottram coal train. The banking loco can just be seen at the rear. The train has just left Wombwell Main Exchange Sidings where steam power would have been swapped for electric. *C. Ord/IAL*

Middle: The banking loco was never coupled to unfitted trains, simply buffering up behind the brake-van as in steam days. This called for some skilled driving over a route that, despite the ruling gradient, undulated. EM1 No 26014 gives a hefty shove at Oxspring Junction, in the days when bankers went all the way to Dunford Bridge. *Kenneth Field/IAL*

Below: Initially, all traffic through the new tunnel was electrically worked. But operational convenience began to make itself felt and certain trains became diesel-hauled, including what was once the 'North Country Continental' between Harwich and Liverpool. A traction change would have been needed at both Sheffield and Guide Bridge, so EE Type 3 No D6803 has charge of the train at Penistone in July 1963. *Peter Sunderland*

Above and right: **The line – and its locomotives – were quickly in demand for enthusiast and other specials. On 12 May 1956 No 27002 operated an Ian Allan Pullman special, pictured here leaving the new tunnel and a little further west, cruising down Longdendale.**
Peter Sunderland, N. Fields/IAL

Below: **It was the same story on the normally freight-only Wath branch. Here, 'D11' 'Director' class No 62667 *Somme* stands at Wombwell Main Junction, waiting to take over from EM1 No 26013 on an RCTS special.** *J. F. Henton/IAL*

The locomotive fleet

The locomotive fleet stood at the heart of the Manchester, Sheffield and Wath electrification scheme, and all the evidence is that design work for the largest single class of locomotives – which evolved into the EM1 Class – was heavily influenced by the North Eastern Railway's experience with the Newport–Shildon project.

Plans for the locomotive fleet went through several revisions as the scheme progressed. As already mentioned, there were initially to be 88 locomotives – nine express passenger engines, 69 mixed-traffic locos and ten bankers, which were to be converted from the Newport–Shildon engines.

Work began by looking at a design for the mixed-traffic locos and converting one of the Newport–Shildon locomotives into a banking engine. No 11 was selected and the work was done at Darlington. The 1-hour traction rating was increased from 1,100 horsepower to 1,250; additional sanders were fitted; the twin pantographs were replaced by a single, centrally fitted one; and the cabs were rebuilt, with the doors repositioned. The result was a smart, functional-looking locomotive that was placed back in storage to await the outcome of the war and – hopefully – a resumption of the MSW project.

Prof Tuplin remarked in *Great Central Steam* that as a locomotive designer you could hardly go wrong if you turned out a new class that was a straightforward enlargement of something that had gone before: bigger, heavier and with more pulling power would generally fit the bill. Something similar appears to have happened with the design of the MSW mixed-traffic type.

Starting at ground level, it is hard to escape the conclusion that the design was heavily influenced by NER practice and the Shildon engines. Indeed, one former Doncaster drawing office source describes the loco as 'pure Darlington below the bodywork'. The same 0-4-4-0 twin bogie arrangement was used, once again with the drawgear and buffers mounted on the bogies, which took all the traction and braking forces, the body simply sitting atop them. Once again, the bogies were articulated, coupled together in the belief that this aided 'steering' through curves, reducing track wear and the tractive effort needed to overcome flange resistance.

Like the Shildon locos, the bogies had a long wheelbase, but with the bogie centres set close together. The result was that the axles were almost equidistantly spaced under the body. The new design was considerably larger and more powerful, with a 1,868hp 1-hour rating against the Newport–Shildon locos' 1,100hp. The length was a shade over 50 feet as opposed to a little over 39 feet, while the new loco weighed in at around 87 tons compared with 74.

The body itself appeared to have been largely derived from earlier locomotives built by Metropolitan Vickers for export; one batch, for a South African mineral railway, bears a marked resemblance. Sir Nigel Gresley himself visited South Africa to see several classes of both 8- and 12-wheeled engines in use. One result was that he returned home convinced of the benefits of regenerative braking, the equipment for which was built into No 6701. The adoption of this technology may well have been one of the wisest decisions made in the whole MSW project, bringing huge savings in time and maintenance costs.

The first locomotive was built at Doncaster, numbered 6701, and referred to as an 0-4-4-0 type. Initial trials involved not electricity but steam: No 6701 was coupled to a 'J39' class loco and towed up and down the East Coast main line between Doncaster and Retford to test its riding capabilities. It was a far from instant success, as the Railway Travel & Correspondence Society's *Locomotives of the LNER* records:

'It was found that the natural period of oscillation was around 20mph when the vertical movement was severe and riding in the cab was extremely uncomfortable. Various forms of alternative springing were tried out at speeds up to 60mph until better riding conditions were obtained. It was in this condition that 6701 was put into stock in September 1941.'

The riding tests were quickly followed by tests under power on the Manchester South Junction & Altrincham line. These included hauling a train of 45 loaded wagons and several sets of empty coaching stock. It was found that No 6701 could accelerate a set of bogie stock to 25mph within 25 seconds – as fast as electric suburban trains of the day.

The regenerative braking system was tested by coupling the loco to a pair of 'J39s', which were worked full out while No 6701 was put into 'regen' to slow them. All apparently went well and proved that 6701 actually worked as promised. But *Locomotives of the LNER* concludes that helpful as they were, these tests 'could not forecast the mechanical troubles that lay ahead'. No 6701 was returned to Doncaster and stored until hostilities ended.

When the MSW scheme was revived at the end of the war, thoughts once again turned to the motive power. In a clear indication of their intended use, the entire Newport–Shildon fleet was reclassified EB1 (Electric Banking type 1), in anticipation of further conversion work. But it was not to be. For whatever reason – and it appears not to have been officially recorded – the idea of creating a class of specialist banking engines was abandoned.

One widely held theory is that Mexborough loco crews objected to the use of locomotives with a lengthy bonnet ahead of the cab. Mentally scarred, perhaps, by years of trying to manoeuvre the 'U1' Garratt behind trains ascending the Worsborough Bank, they saw no point in EB1 when a class of flat-fronted locomotives was already on the drawing board. An alternative explanation is that, even after uprating, the EB1 was deemed underpowered for the weight of trains planned for the electrified services.

The truth may never be known, but it is a fact that, just as in steam days, the idea of a banking loco was abandoned and the sole representative of EB1 went not to Wath but to Ilford, to shunt the new electric depot opened there as part of the Great Eastern electrification scheme. It lasted until the route was converted to 25kV AC, and was then withdrawn and broken up in 1964. The remaining Newport–Shildon engines were reclassified EF1 (Electric Freight type 1) – a purely paper exercise, as they remained in store until scrapped a few years later. Remarkably, one retained its original NER oval numberplate.

The story resumes in 1946, with No 6701 being taken out of store, dusted off and sent to the Netherlands for extended trials. Dutch Railways were in a poor state after the war and were grateful to have the use of even a single locomotive. The LNER was keen to see its new engine tested more extensively than would have been possible in Britain, so at the end of August 1947, renumbered 6000, it left for Holland via Harwich. The first test running began in early September and by November it had completed 10,000 miles, working mainly on 330-ton passenger trains and covering 400 miles per day, five days a week.

Goods trains of 1,600 tons were also tackled, with No 6000 accelerating them to 40mph in 5 minutes. Later, 1,750-ton trains were successfully handled. Clearly, No 6000 was a gutsy locomotive.

But the issues with the suspension system would not go away and the riding qualities deteriorated alarmingly. Several minor changes were made, but eventually the complete bogie and body suspension systems were reworked, as was the articulation between the bogies. The results of these trials, and other issues, such as the tendency of the leading axle on each bogie to tilt upwards when starting off under heavy load, were fed into the design process for the production locomotives.

The Dutch themselves certainly took to No 6000. Crews nicknamed it 'Tommy', after the generic name for British Army infantrymen, and the nickname became official when it returned home, with a naming ceremony at Liverpool Street station in 1952. This included the presentation of a splendid Delft plate bearing an illustration of the locomotive, which for many years was on display in the British Railways Eastern Region boardroom at the Railway Headquarters building in York.

Meanwhile, production of the EM1 (Electric Mixed-traffic type 1) fleet had begun. Initial plans to build them at Doncaster, then Darlington, were abandoned in favour of Gorton – an apt choice given that the new locomotives would spend their entire working lives running over a portion of the old Great Central Railway main line.

The body shape closely followed that of No 6000, with cab widths inset from the main body, which itself was divided into five compartments. The main changes were to provide larger windscreens and to rework the cab sides to give narrower doors, but providing the crews with droplight windows next to their seats, as well as a quarterlight.

Bodies and bogies were fabricated and mated up at Gorton. Each loco was then transferred to the former Great Central carriage works at nearby Dukinfield to have its electrical equipment, supplied by Metropolitan Vickers, installed. The locos were then returned to Gorton for completion work, painting and testing. They were also given the wheel arrangement notation of 'Bo+Bo'. The letter 'B' indicated a two-axle bogie, and the suffix 'o' that both axles were individually powered; the '+' sign meant that the bogies were coupled together.

The first batch of ten engines appeared from October 1950 – long before any significant section of the MSW had been energised. They were therefore sent south for trials on the Great Eastern suburban lines, where a range of proving tests was conducted, including a better trial of the regenerative braking system. In mid-1951 the first stretch of line from Wath was energised, and the ten locomotives returned north to allow crew training to begin.

A group of hand-picked men were trained first as instructors. They then took on groups of six trainee 'motormen', as they were to be called, and began a course of theory, examinations and practical handling of the locomotives, initially along a siding, then out on the short stretch of line from Wath that had been energised. Skills learned on the footplate had to be translated into abilities in the driving cab. For some, the choice was a hard one to make: George Potts writes of his own internal struggle to decide what was the best course. Sticking with steam meant harsh, dirty working conditions but a wide variety of work – and promotion prospects. Switching to the EM1s meant a comfortable seat in a heated cab, but working only over one route. Potts

Above: **No more than ten years after passenger services began, rumours were starting up about possible closure. By the time this picture of No E26000 *Tommy* was taken at Manchester Piccadilly in August 1969, the rumours were a fact and the pioneer loco – and the train it is hauling – were both heading for withdrawal.** *Peter Hogarth/IAL*

Right: **Another shot of *Tommy*, this time rounding the Bullhouse curve with the 14.45 Sheffield–Manchester express in July 1969.** *Peter Hogarth/IAL*

Left: The summer of 1954 was a busy time with traction changes from steam to electric as the third stage of the MSW scheme was completed into Sheffield. Here a train is triple-headed by a Robinson 'O4' Class and two 'B1' 4-6-0s. A possible explanation is that the three were being worked back to Darnall shed without taking up unnecessary train paths. It is known that an anonymous controller made certain that Great Central steam had a final fling in the last few days before the electrics took over – perhaps this is what is happening here.
J. B. C. McCann

Below: Steam could still be seen under the wires at Penistone in 1966, 15 years after the first electric trains began running! By now it was just one service, the summer Saturdays Bradford–Poole. No 45647 *Sturdee* has the duty on 2 July. *Gavin Morrison*

eventually concluded that going electric was the right thing to do, as did many of his colleagues.

Trial running from Wath Yard to Dunford Bridge began in the autumn of 1951, and the full scheduled service was launched on 4 February 1952 with one electric locomotive hauling and one banking all the way to Dunford. Overnight, Wentworth Junction became a lonely place to be, the steam bankers gone for ever.

On the return journey from Dunford Bridge, two locomotives were used at the head of each train for regenerative braking. This feature quickly began to show its worth. Instead of each loose-coupled train having to stop to pin down wagon brakes to prevent it running away – and then having to stop again to pick them up – the regenerative system proved capable of holding trains completely under control. Indeed, the second locomotive did not need to 'regen' at all, but merely coasted. The only exception to this was on the Worsborough Bank between West Silkstone Junction and Wentworth Junction, where, because of the gradient, both engines went into 'regen', the second locomotive coming out at the bottom of the incline.

But there were problems. It became apparent that building four-axle locomotives for heavy haulage work had been a mistake, probably made because the LNER needed to keep costs down as much as possible. The main issue was with weight transfer, which was first discovered during the Dutch Railways trials. The effect was so severe that the top edge of the bogies could tilt upwards and crash into the underside of the body. In one recorded instance, the impact was so severe that it smashed the glass in the control desk dials. The partial answer was the addition of a 'weight transfer switch' to the control desk, which, when operated, cut the current to the leading axle of each bogie, limiting the amount of work it would do compared with the trailing axle. With this axle taking more of the load, the problem was partly resolved.

There were also issues with the bogie centre pins becoming bent or even fractured under load. Much work went into tracing the causes of and finding cures for these problems. It included modifying two EM1s, Nos 26030 and 26034, for trials with dynamometer cars. The testing was a drawn-out affair, but finally, in 1955, performance tests were carried out to check that the EM1 fleet was fulfilling contract specifications. *Locomotives of the LNER* reveals that the testing was carried out on

'... passenger, partially vacuum-braked goods and loose-coupled goods trains. No 26052 worked passenger trains on 13 March and kept time with 11-coach (380 tons tare) loads. However, the riding in both cabs was most uncomfortable at speeds over 50mph with pronounced vibrations over rail joints and lurching at high speeds. There was less discomfort when No 26052 was working the freight trains as speeds did not exceed 43mph. It was concluded that the EM1 was ideally suited for hauling freight trains but that its riding qualities with passenger trains were not good at speeds over 50mph.'

But the achievements of full electric working when it finally came in 1955 could hardly be overstated. The time taken to work a coal train from Wath to Mottram was cut by almost two-thirds, from 3hr 50min to 1hr 20min. Lodging turns became a thing of the past, and it was not long before the work of the EM1 fleet attracted the attention of the enthusiasts and students of locomotive performance. Peter Semmens was one of the first to record and analyse a footplate trip. Within a month of the Wath–Mottram electric service being launched in 1952, he was on board No 26021, banked by 26022. At this time 850-ton trains were being worked with the banker coming on at Wath and staying with the train to Dunford. Writing again in *The*

Right and below: **The overhead equipment still looks very new in this view of No 26004 at Lewden Crossing in charge of a Wath–Mottram goods in 1958, while an unidentified EM1 brings up the rear as banking loco.** *Both Peter Sunderland*

Right: **The connection to Wentworth Silkstone Colliery is on the extreme left of this picture of Wentworth Junction. The former loco siding and pit can be seen to the left of the running lines, made redundant when the EM1s took over. In steam days the train would have stopped here to pick up wagon brakes, but that's now railway history, as a pair of EM1s 'regen' down the bank on the way back to Wath with a lengthy train of empties.** *Les Nixon*

Locomotive No E26011 will be working at full stretch, banking a freight up the Worsborough Bank between the two Silkstone tunnels in August 1969. The gradient here is 1 in 40 on a curve. Combined with the two tunnels, it had been a steam locomotive crew's nightmare. *Les Nixon*

Railway Magazine, he compares his electrically hauled 47-wagon train with a 56-wagon 960-ton train, which had required no fewer than four steam locomotives to get it up the Worsborough Bank. The comparison is shown here, and provides a graphic illustration of how electric power transformed the way the route was operated. As he remarks:

'Two electric locomotives did the work of four steam ones and there was no need for a stop at Wentworth Junction, which enabled us to start the 1 in 40 at over 15mph.'

The same was true of the return trip with 60 empties and both locomotives available for regenerative braking:

'Instead of stopping at West Silkstone to pin down sufficient brakes to hold the train, our motorman gave two short and one long blast on the horn to signal to the second locomotive and we moved into regeneration… Our descent right through almost to Wombwell was controlled in this way and our time from Barnsley Junction to Wombwell was 37 minutes compared with 57 for a comparable steam-hauled train.'

This puts in a nutshell all the advantages of the new order: fewer locomotives; fewer stops to attach and detach engines; no water stops; and no stops to pin down or take up wagon brakes. For those used to conventional railway operating, this truly was a revolution.

Few MSW motormen have set down their experiences on paper, but there is little doubt that the EM1s were popular locomotives. Peter Howard became a secondman on the route in the early 1960s after being promoted to Wath's 'dual link', in which enginemen could find themselves working on electric, diesel or even steam traction. He recalls:

'When I went in the dual link we had to go on a week's course to Reddish to receive instruction for secondman's duties. Instructions for working the steam heat boiler, using the hand pump to pump up the pantographs if there was no air pressure and using the long wooden pole kept inside each loco in the corridor to pull the pantographs down from the wires if the cab buttons failed.'

Although the driving technique was different from steam, there was clearly an equal degree of expertise needed when working the unfitted, heavy coal trains. Although a secondman, Peter Howard did a lot of driving; just as in steam days it was a semi-official way of gaining the necessary experience for promotion:

'Trains would be worked [with the motors] in series all through the Worsborough branch to Penistone. As we got to the station, if we had got the Distant signal for Penistone Goods we would go into parallel connections and our speed would go up from 16mph to 28mph. It was like another loco had come on behind us.

'If the signals were clear, we would stay in parallel until we were a quarter of the way into Woodhead Tunnel. We would then come out of parallel into series and then into series regen. You needed to come out of the tunnel at 18-20mph and you could work the train for the rest of the journey in regen. You only needed to use the loco air brake for the final stop.'

There was a transformation on the passenger side of the business, too. The time savings were not nearly so dramatic, but even so the standard Manchester–Sheffield time came down from 65 to 59 minutes. Like everyone else, Peter Semmens had

A splendid portrait of No 26028 coasting through Dinting station with a westbound coal train. *P. R. Vickers*

Above: **A fine 1960s view of a busy Mottram Yard with the control tower on the left, an EM1 awaiting its next duty in the centre and the main lines with the platforms for the Mottram staff halt on the right.** *Richard Parkes/IAL*

Middle: **Long strings of empty coal wagons were a hallmark of eastbound hauls and No 26056 *Triton* is a perfect example as the train rolls over the Wicker Arch and into Victoria station en route to Rotherwood.** *Brian Stephenson/IAL*

Right: **Most freight through Victoria was diverted discreetly behind draught screens that effectively partitioned off the passenger platforms from the goods lines. No E26055 *Prometheus* emerges back into view at the east end of the station in October 1969.** *Les Nixon*

Left: It's *Prometheus* again, this time caught by October sunshine in 1969, on the 09.23 arrival from Manchester. *V. Bamford/IAL*

Middle: Newly outshopped in BR Blue with full yellow ends, No E26044 heads west from Sheffield Victoria in June 1968. *V. Bamford/IAL*

Left: Also sporting the new colour scheme, No E26034 heads west with coal in 21-ton hopper wagons, at Darnall. Curiously, the handrails have been painted black. The famous Cravens factory can be seen. *Terry Whitham/IAL*

Right: **No 27006 *Pandora* will not be calling at Hadfield with its Sheffield-bound express. The year is 1966 and the white headcode discs have been dispensed with.** *C. R. Whitfield/IAL*

Below: **No E26052 *Nestor* was one of the boiler-fitted EM1s intended for passenger use, and is seen here at Penistone working a Sheffield–Manchester service in November 1969, less than two months before the axe fell.** *Keith Long*

to wait almost three more years before through electric haulage could be sampled. But he was back on the route in early 1955, this time aboard No 26052, one of the batch of EM1s fitted with train heating boilers. His description of the run in *The Railway Magazine* oozes enthusiasm from the start:

'Motorman W. Garwood of Darnall had us notched up to the fourth stage of weak field in parallel within 2min 15sec of starting, with a speed of 46mph. A single yellow then necessitated power being cut off and our brakes applied, but we quickly got going again and were back to 37mph by Wadsley Bridge. At Oughty Bridge we were up to 51 and up the 1 in 120 speed varied between 49 and 53 as the effects of the curves made themselves felt. Just after Wadsley Bridge we were taking 500 amps from the overhead line through each pair of motors (which are permanently coupled in series) at 43mph.

'We took 17min 33sec to Penistone, a minute and a half less than the booked time in the Public Timetable.

'Restarting from Penistone was equally as effortless, and speed rose to 54mph by Dunford Bridge as we entered the portal of the new tunnel. Compared with steam journeys it was an amazing contrast to be able to see the white concrete arch ahead, spanning the pair of tracks. Along the left-hand wall was the line of electric lights stretching into the distance where they arched downwards, indicating the point, about a mile from the Dunford Bridge portal, where the rising gradient of 1 in 1186 changes to a fall of 1 in 129 for the remainder of the new tunnel.

'We quickly accelerated to 60mph and, as we crossed over the "divide", Motorman Garwood put the locomotive into regenerative braking with the motors in parallel. There is a separate controller for this system and the drill is to move it round the quadrant until the voltage being produced by the motors is equal to that over the overhead line. Once the voltage has been "balanced" in this way the controller is opened fully and the regenerative brake is in action. Regardless of gradient, the locomotive then continues at that particular speed, within a very small margin, the motors returning current to the wires or, on easier stretches, taking power and motoring. The speed can be readily controlled at the desired figure by notching up or down on the "regen" controller.

One exception made to the 'no-steam' rule through the new Woodhead Tunnel was *Flying Scotsman*, hauling a rail tour in April 1964. It was permitted to pass, but only with the fire damped down and hauled by the first production EM1, No 26001. The train is about to enter the tunnel. *Gavin Morrison*

86

'Britain's First All-Electric Main Line': on the core MSW, electric traction ruled supreme on all classes of traffic. Two Class EM1 locomotives on very different duties are caught on film on the moors above Penistone. *Howard Turner*

'Our time to the Dinting stop was 2 seconds over the booked 20 minutes, but the concluding sections of my Woodhead electric journey were beset with signal checks and stops, although we still kept the booked time to Guide Bridge.'

For all their teething troubles (and other problems that would continue almost until final closure and withdrawal), the EM1s were clearly proving themselves to be the universal mixed-traffic power units of which railway operating officers had dreamed. This image was reinforced by a paper given to the Institution of Locomotive Engineers, compiled after September 1957 when the fleet had run more than 11 million miles. It describes a system of operating that feels roughly 11 million miles from the traditional steam environment: instead of a filthy running shed here is a light, clean airy building; instead of make do and mend, here is a carefully regulated system of component exchange and repair to keep each locomotive available as much as possible; instead of a cursory wipe over the number with a cleaner's oily rag, here is an electric mop – a mop! – for polishing the bodywork.

Not that problems were entirely absent. The paper also lists a number of permanent and trial modifications, several of them aimed at curing the riding issues. In addition, extra cab heaters were fitted and, by 1959, all the EM1 fleet had been equipped with rheostatic brakes to complement the regenerative braking system. The latter could operate only down to 16mph, whereas the rheostatic brake operated down to about 3mph. But the current generated could not be returned to the overhead line and was dissipated as heat from resistors instead. It did, though, save considerable wear on the brake blocks.

There was also one major problem out on the road. Like many steam designs

before them, the EM1s proved better at starting heavy trains than stopping them. On the long descent from Woodhead there were incidents of runaway trains, where drivers handling heavy loose-coupled workings simply could not retain control. Several of these ran through the stop-blocks at the end of the Down Slow line at Torside, and there were other close shaves. Ultimately, the solution was to reduce train weights, which led to operational changes. Instead of going all the way to Dunford Bridge, banking locos on loose-coupled trains came off at West Silkstone Junction, where they waited for a suitable up train to assist down the incline with regenerative braking. The operating instructions list the section between West Silkstone and Wentworth Junctions as one of very few places where two locomotives were allowed to use the regenerative brake at the same time; elsewhere, only the leading locomotive was permitted to use the technique.

The rules were different for fully fitted trains. Loose-coupled workings had a banker at the rear partly as a safety feature to guard against runaways. There were no catchpoints on the incline other than a trailing connection from the siding at Wentworth Junction, whose 'normal' position was what would usually be regarded as 'reversed' – ie turning runaways off the main line and into the siding. With six (five after the closure of Strafford Crossing in the 1950s) level crossings just down the line, the prospect of a runaway was not an attractive one.

With fully fitted workings, this was not a consideration, and on the few fitted workings that used the branch the assisting engine was coupled onto the front and worked through to Oxspring Junction, the next box after West Silkstone. By 1969, immediately before the advent of 'merry-go-round' (MGR) coal train operation, which is dealt with later, there was only one regular fully fitted working, a Wath–Mottram steel train.

No E26019 passes West Silkstone Junction with 8M78, a mixed freight for Mottram, in March 1969. This loco was seen as something of an unlucky one; it was involved in one of the several runaways in the early days before train weights were reduced, and was withdrawn early. *Keith Long*

Manchester–Sheffield–Wath electrification track plans —Stage 2, Section 3

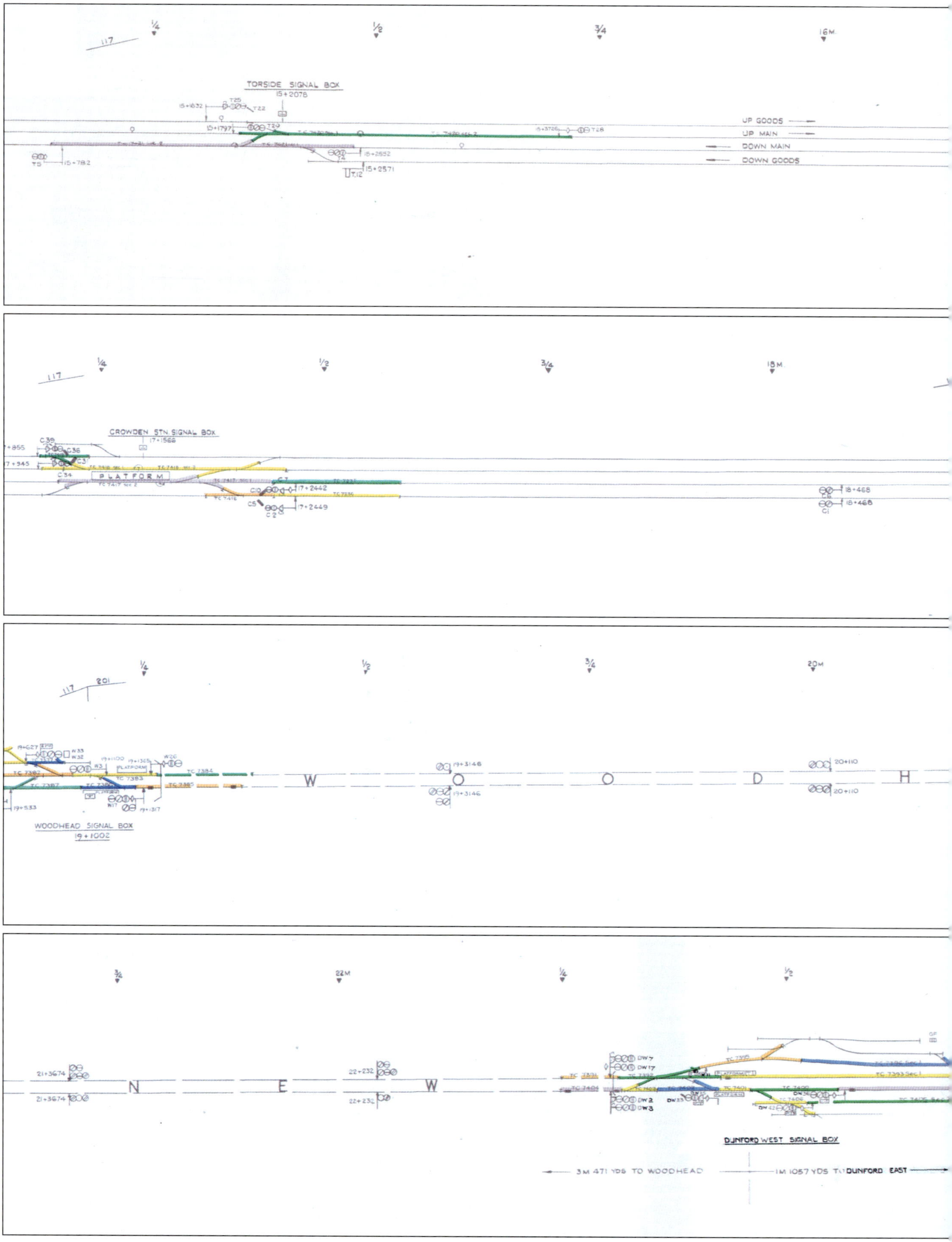

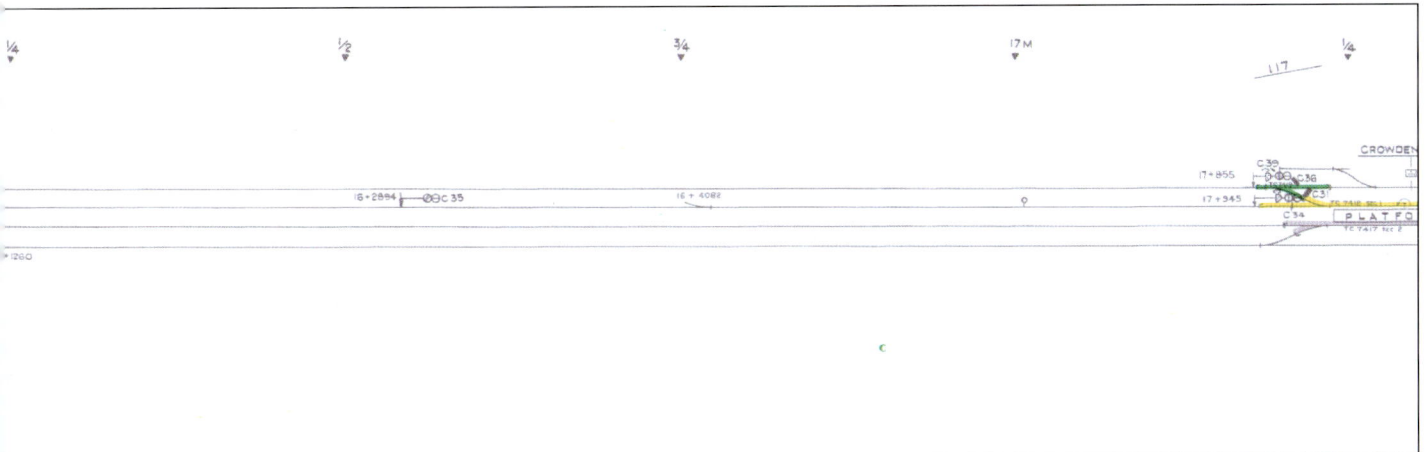

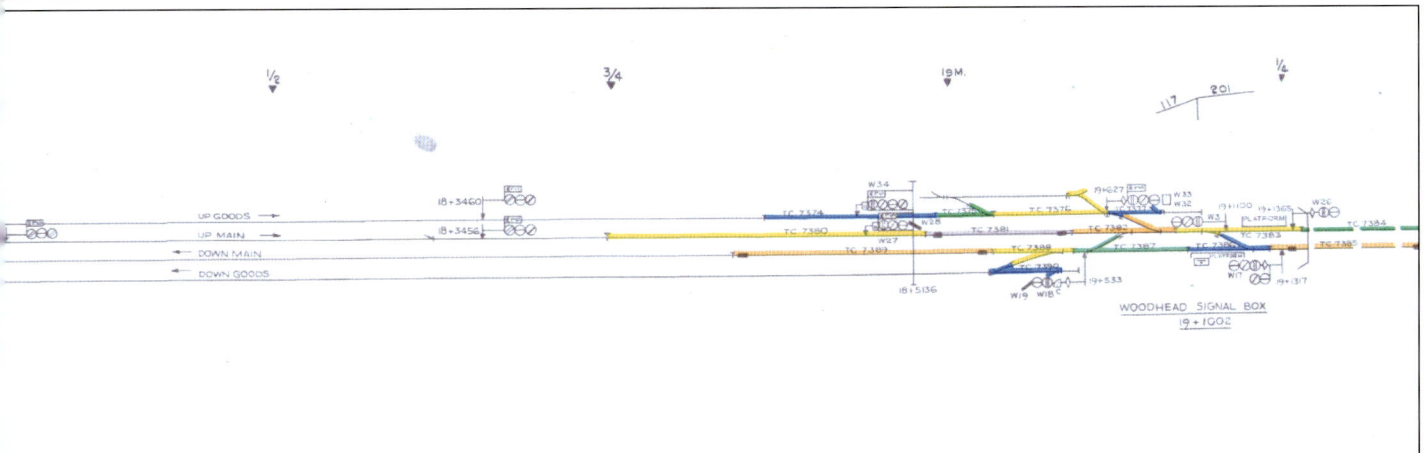

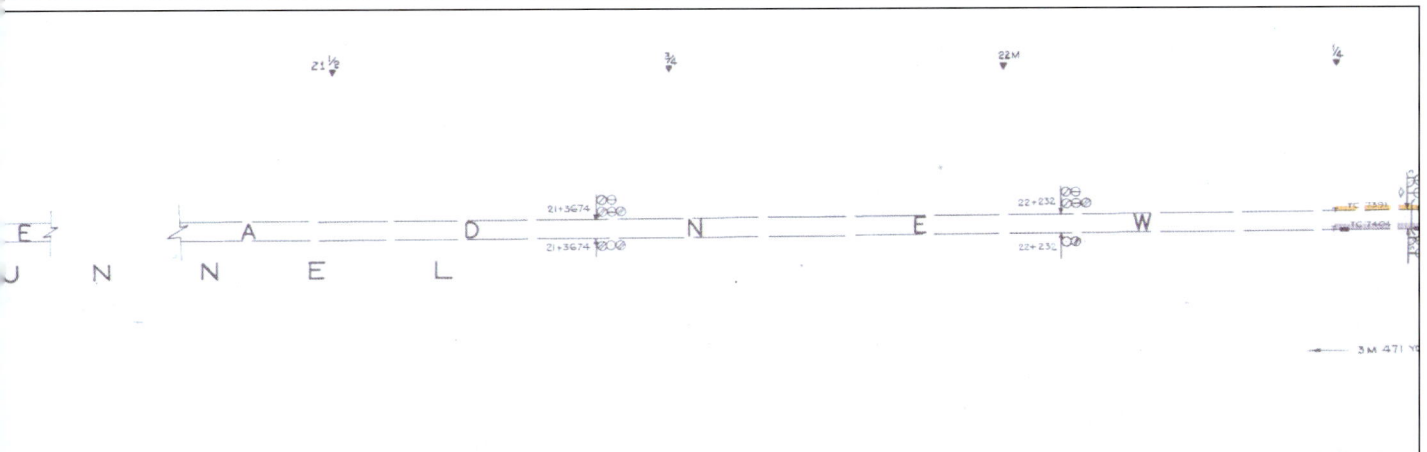

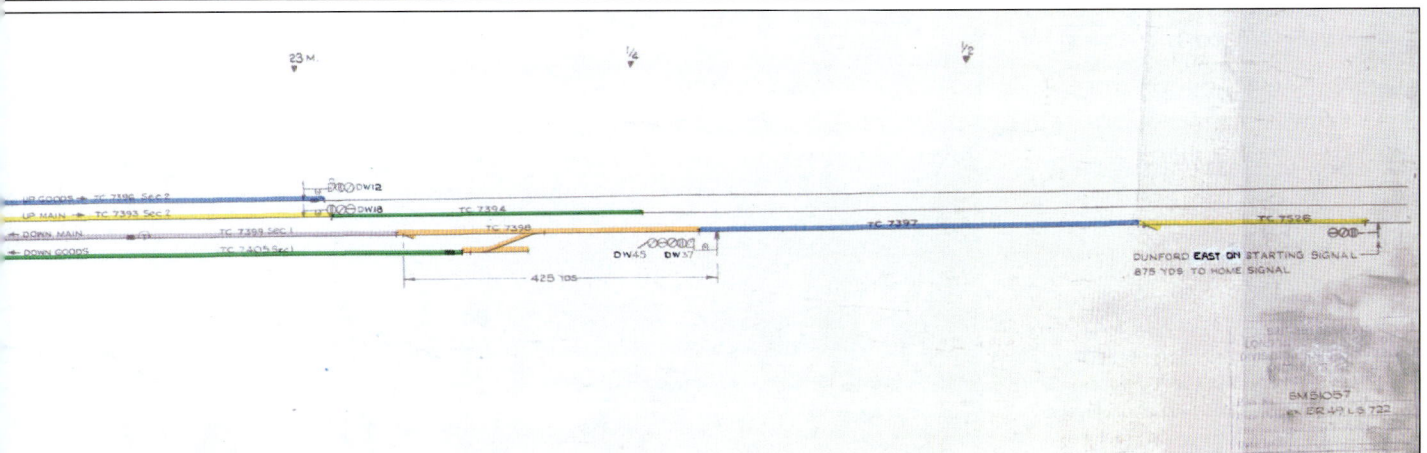

Overall, the original design and the subsequent modifications left the EM1 as a rather complicated locomotive to drive. The motorman had to understand the best combination of motors – series or parallel – according to load and speed, and the combination of full and weak field control notches. Footplate crews recall that a good deal of both experience and intuition were needed to get the best out of the EM1.

The complication extended to the brakes. In their final guise, the EM1s, or Class 76 as they became under the British Rail TOPS renumbering scheme, had six braking systems: straight air for the engine only, train vacuum, train air brake on the locomotives later modified for MGR working, regenerative, rheostatic and a parking brake.

But they were reliable workhorses. The ILE paper records an availability of 93 per cent across the locomotive and multiple unit fleet, a remarkable figure for the time.

And their adaptability is illustrated by the final chapter in the Class 76 story. Between 1968 and 1970 a batch of 21 locomotives were converted to operate in multiple, with the aim of starting a service of 'merry-go-round' coal trains, which, in theory at least, would operate non-stop from pit to power station using fleets of purpose-built wagons with loading and discharge accomplished while on the move.

The Class 76s selected were modified for multiple operation – something the original design team had not seen as necessary – and were fitted with train air-braking equipment. They were also fitted with 'Clear Call' cab-to-cab communication sets, which used the overhead line as a telephone wire. This was to allow the crews of train engines and banking engines to speak to each other; with planned 30-plus wagon MGR trains, the distance between the locomotives would be too great to reliably hear whistle codes.

Although the MGR trains were to operate from both Wath and Rotherwood to Mottram, trials began on the Wath branch where the added complication of banking had to be tackled. Initially, the plan was to operate 37-wagon 1,575-ton trains using two train engines and two bankers, with a stop at Barnsley Junction to detach the latter. The RCTS's *Locomotives of the LNER* gives a comprehensive account of the testing, and at times it reads more like an adventure story than a locomotive history:

'The train was headed by Nos E26025 + E26028 banked from Wath to Penistone by E26011 + E26010. The train was coupled and air-braked throughout, including the banking locomotives, with the driver's brake valves on the leading banking locomotive in the shut-down position.

'A starting test was made just beyond Wentworth Junction on the 1 in 40 rising gradient and a steady speed of 10mph was maintained up the bank. Wheel slipping in the first Silkstone Tunnel (actually Silkstone No 2) causing the leading motorman to reduce power, the banking motorman was forced to reduce power to avoid entering an overload condition, whereupon there was a severe snatch that threw an accompanying inspector against the inner compartment door, shattering the glass panel. The snatch also broke the shackle pin of the screw coupling between the two banking locomotives, though they stayed together because of the multiple control. The final parting came when the rear banking locomotive next developed wheelslip and dropped back. This broke the jumper connections, air pipes and vacuum brake pipes, bringing the entire train rapidly to a state of rest as the air brake was automatically applied throughout. The rear banking locomotive stopped about 15 yards behind the leading one. The banking

Above right and right: **Nos E26016 and E26012, recently converted for multiple operation and air-braking, is at the head of 6Z50, a 'merry-go-round' test train from Wath, on 23 April 1970. The working is pictured emerging from Silkstone No 1 Tunnel, approaching West Silkstone Junction and the end of the 1 in 40 climb. At the rear of the train No E26006 is on banking duty. This test included stopping and restarting on the gradient and it was found that three locomotives had insufficient in reserve to cope with poor rail conditions or other emergencies. After this test, all MGR workings over the Worsborough branch used two train engines and two bankers.** *Keith Long*

Although the line was modernised, many original structures were left in place – including the signal cabins. This is Blackmoor Crossing, an MS&LR design that lasted until closure. *Howard Turner*

locomotives were recoupled with the sound coupling and resumed banking the train to Penistone, now working independently with a relief motorman on the second banker.'

The train reached Guide Bridge with no further incident, but the lesson learned was that a 37-wagon train was simply too ambitious; if problems developed the four locomotives had too little in reserve to cope. A second test was arranged, this time with 30 MGR wagons weighing 1,300 tons, two train engines and a single banker.

'A starting test was made on the 1 in 40 rising gradient just beyond Wentworth. It was raining at the time and three attempts were needed to restart the train. The train locomotives slipped, causing the current in the motors of the banking locomotive to soar to 835 amps so that it too slipped. To finally get under way, currents up to the limit of 800 amps were necessary on the train locomotives, while the resistor banks became very hot and almost up to their temperature limits. It was recommended that the load should be reduced in future or two banking locomotives be provided.'

In the end, the second course of action was decided on and the standard Woodhead line MGR train became 30 wagons with two train engines from Rotherwood and two train engines plus two bankers on the Wath branch. Banking duties were modified so that all bankers, both MGR and loose-coupled single bankers, were stationed at Wombwell, and banked their trains as far as West Silkstone Junction – a partial reversion to steam practice. MGR services had to pause for uncoupling, but the single bankers merely shut off power and coasted to a standstill before being turned onto a spur track to await the next descending train for regenerative braking duties. As noted above, fully fitted single bankers were attached as assisting engines at the front of the train and worked through to Oxspring Junction. In later years these banking duties were designated as trip workings, with the single banker being Wath Trip T80 and the MGR bankers T81.

The MGR workings brought one other oddity to the Wath branch. The overhead line system had not been designed to cope with the use of four locomotives, all working flat out, on one train. Therefore a system had to be devised that kept all other down line traffic away from an MGR working while it was ascending the Worsborough Bank. The system adopted harked back to the LNER 'double block' working on the East Coast main line in the streamline era of the 1930s, where two block sections had to be cleared ahead of each train to give an adequate margin for braking from high speed.

The Wath branch operation was, if anything, even more complex and was designed to prevent any other train entering the section between Aldam Junction electrical substation and Strafford Crossing substation when an MGR train was moving up the incline. It worked as follows.

The signaller at Wombwell Main Junction would offer an MGR working to the next box, Lewden Crossing, using the special bell code 3-4-2. Instead of accepting the train, Lewden offered it to the next box, Worsborough Dale Crossing, which also offered it on to Glasshouse Crossing, and so on, all the way up the line to Wentworth Junction, the first box beyond Strafford Crossing substation. Wentworth Junction then accepted the train by repeating the 3-4-2 bell code in the usual way. The accept code was passed back down the line from box to box until Wombwell Main Junction received it. The MGR train with its four locomotives could then be signalled away.

As it made its way up the incline, signallers were not allowed to 'clear out' as it left their section. Instead, although signals were replaced and crossing gates opened to road traffic, the block instruments were left set at 'Line Occupied' until the MGR working reached Wentworth Junction. The signaller there cleared out by sending the 2-1 (Train out of Section) signal, which was repeated back down the branch to Wombwell Main Junction. At this point, the next train could be offered on. After Wentworth Junction, the bell code reverted to the normal five beats for a fully fitted Class 6 train.

There was one final signalling oddity: when the Train on Line bell signal was sent and acknowledged, the presence of a banking engine required a follow-up 2-2 code to be sent. So far, so normal. But for whatever reason, even though they were operating in multiple under the control of one crew, these workings were always signalled with a 2-2, 2-2 bell signal, leaving no one in any doubt that there were two assisting engines at the rear of the train.

This system, which became a daily feature of the route from October 1970, effectively set the pattern for the final decade of the line's existence. The MGR workings came to dominate the working timetable and, in the mid-1970s, another nine Class 76s were converted to multiple operation and air braking, though this batch, in recognition of the decline of the vacuum brake, had their vacuum braking equipment removed.

By now, with the passenger services gone – an issue we will look at in the next chapter – the MGR workings had become the staple traffic, out from Rotherwood or Wath to Mottram for a change of traction, then on to Fiddlers Ferry Power Station in Cheshire.

Above: **For a decade after electrification, electric and steam traction rubbed shoulders at Rotherwood where the overhead line ended. Here a 'J11', No 64292, passes through with an ordinary, but lengthy, passenger train.**
Howard Turner collection

Middle: **At Mottram Yard in 1969 the driver of No E26043 climbs down from his cab after stabling the locomotive. Alongside, Class 40 No D231 waits with a westbound train whose leading vehicles are a pair of ferry vans.** *David Birch/IAL*

Right: **During the miners' strike of 1971 electric working was suspended on the MSW system, and what little traffic remained was worked by diesel traction. Because of the westbound gradients, MGR trains were operated in two halves to Dunford Bridge, where they were combined and sent forward as one train. This remarkable picture shows two Class 47s, No 1794 at the front and No 1988 banking, with 15 MGR wagons passing Dunford East box on 24 November.** *Keith Long*

Left: **Problems with water seeping into Totley Tunnel on the Hope Valley line caused a stream of diversions over Woodhead even before it lost its own passenger service. That is why 'Peak' No D163 *Leicestershire and Derbyshire Yeomanry* is off its home ground and waiting at Sheffield Victoria to take over a diverted St Pancras–Manchester service. E26050 *Stentor* stands in the background.** *V. Bamford/IAL*

Below: **The final Woodhead line passenger service to run beyond the limits of the electrification was the Harwich boat train – the former 'North Country Continental'. Latterly it was diesel-hauled throughout, and Class 37 No 6968 is displaying the pre-TOPS headcode 1E78 as it passes Mottram.** *David Birch/IAL*

Now it was possible to see locomotives built in the early 1950s to what was essentially a 1930s design still in complete command of trains whose weight and speed could not have been foreseen by their designers – a real tribute to a locomotive that, while not flawless, was nevertheless hugely successful.

Only one EM1/Class 76 made it into preservation, No 26020. Its outing to the Festival of Britain and its role in officially opening the new Woodhead Tunnel ensured it a place in the National Collection and, withdrawn in 1977, it was returned to something approaching original condition and is today housed at the National Railway Museum in York.

The EM1s, with 57 examples, became a sizeable class of locomotive – at least in diesel and electric terms. But its companion, the EM2, was certainly one of the smallest, possibly the smallest class ever built, if one-off, modified and prototype locomotives are excluded.

The class remains something of an enigma: it is hard to discover any concrete reason for it being designed and built in the first place. True, the initial pre-war electrification scheme had made provision for a class of nine express passenger locomotives. There are few details of how these engines were intended to turn out,

other than they would have shared some similarities with the North Eastern Railway's solitary express locomotive No 13, with six driving wheels in the centre and a four-wheel bogie at each end.

When the scheme was revived and revised at the end of the war, the idea of having any specialist express loco had been rejected in favour of a single class of 88 mixed-traffic engines. Then, at a moment that is difficult to pinpoint, the thinking changed again and express engines were back on the agenda – this time as a class of 27 locomotives, which were ordered in 1949.

Even a casual glance suggests that 27 locomotives for a main line of just over 40 miles was a little excessive. What where they thinking of?

The first clue comes with the date of the order: July 1949. By this time the prototype Bo+Bo locomotive had been on trial in the Netherlands for very nearly two years and the full extent of the problems with its riding qualities were apparent. The conclusion was rapidly being drawn that

Left: **With the electric control centre in the background, No 26020, now shorn of its stainless steel handrails and exhibition finish, coasts down the gradient with eastbound empties.** *V. Bamford/IAL*

The skyline of Sheffield has seen many changes since this 1969 view was taken of EM1 E26054 *Pluto* with a Manchester-bound express. *D. L. Percival/IAL*

the Bo+Bo design was good for speeds up to around 50mph, but not much use for anything faster.

What to do? The answer seems to have been to get a new design out PDQ. And the EM2 design does have something of a 'lash-up' feel to it. The cabs were made from the same jigs as the EM1. The body followed the same segmented design based around the compartments needed to house the various items of equipment. The bogies were based very closely on those fitted to the pioneering LMS diesel locomotives Nos 10000 and 10001.

There is almost a sense that the design team, under pressure to deliver, had raided the spares bins to see what could be put together: cabs from here, bogies from there, and so on.

There were, of course, major changes. The main one was the six-wheel bogie, giving a Co-Co-type locomotive. And, as the hyphen indicates, the bogies were to be completely independent of each other with no articulation or coupling. The second major difference was to move the buffing gear to the body rather than having it on the bogie headstocks. This would give a smoother ride.

The locomotive that resulted was an impressive beast: about the length of a contemporary carriage, it generated 2,760 horsepower – roughly the same as the Brush Type 4/Class 47 diesel locomotive that appeared about a decade later – with a top speed of 90mph. And this is the second mystery: why build a locomotive that was so obviously over-powered for the only line over which it would be able to operate? As *Locomotives of the LNER* remarks:

'No justification has so far emerged for ordering so many high-speed electric locomotives for a passenger line only 41½ miles long with no foreseeable hope of their use elsewhere.'

And yet there is evidence that the EM2 was being seen as a key plank of British Railways' electrification ambitions. In 1953, the year before the first EM2 appeared, the eminent steam locomotive engineer, R. C. Bond – by then the British Transport Commission's Chief Officer, locomotive construction and maintenance – spoke of the need for widespread electrification and told his audience that the EM2 class would be used 'over a wide area'.

This is an intriguing idea for such an enigmatic class of locomotives: that they were designed not in a panic to compensate for the perceived shortcomings of the EM1 class, but instead as a potential standard electric express passenger type – indeed, the first BR non-steam standard locomotive – designed to be used almost anywhere just as quickly as the overhead line could be reeled out. Couple this thought with the large number of overhead line structure designs already mentioned, and the idea that major expansion plans were being mulled over is hard to reject.

In those heady days there was no shortage of proposals about where to go next. British Railways' own commemorative booklet, issued to coincide with the completion of the MSW system in 1955, made a range of suggestions, from the remainder of the Great Central main line to Marylebone, to Liverpool via the Cheshire Lines Committee route, or east to Whitemoor to tap yet more freight traffic.

But it was not to be. The cost of the MSW system had been spiralling out of control, and when it went beyond £11 million (the post-war estimate had been £6 million) economies were ordered. One of those economies was to cut the EM2 order from 27 to just 7 locomotives. In all likelihood, even these 7 were built only because construction was so far advanced.

Nevertheless, the EM2 quickly established itself as an outstanding design. Powerful, smooth-riding and very stable even around Woodhead's curves, it was able to handle with ease the heaviest 11-bogie trains of the Manchester–Marylebone service.

When electric passenger services were started in 1954, a few months ahead of the scheme's final completion, there were 14 passenger trains each way on weekdays. The EM2s handled most but by no means all of them. Some observers claim to have detected a hierarchy in which the EM2 class worked the Manchester–Marylebone trains, leaving the Manchester–Cleethorpes and other east-west services in the hands of the boiler-fitted EM1s, maintaining a Gorton tradition of using the best locomotives on the London service.

Remarkably little has been published about their working lives. Peter Semmens recorded a run made in 1966 on board No 27003, by then named *Diana*, remarkable for an incident in which a signal was put back to danger as the train approached it!

But the truth is that the EM2 fleet need never have been built. The EM1s' high-speed riding qualities might leave a lot to be desired, but they were equal to the task. When the ruling line speed over the route was cut from 65 to 60mph in the mid-1960s, there was no longer any justification for keeping such a small fleet in operation. In 1968, in a move which also clearly presaged the end of the passenger service, the class was withdrawn en bloc and stored at Bury shed together with the MSW pioneer, *Tommy*. But before they were finished, the class almost certainly set a record or two.

Locomotives of the LNER claims a run from Sheffield in which an EM2 lifted eight bogies and a van up the 1 in 120 to Penistone at 60–62mph, arriving in 14min 4sec, a record that has never been beaten. From the same volume comes what must be the definitive

EM2 story: the legendary trip undertaken for the benefit of Dutch Railways, which had just bought the fleet from BR. The tale is worth telling in full:

'What was clearly the swansong of the class on the MSW took place on Wednesday 20 August 1969, ten months after they had been withdrawn from service in Britain and four weeks before they were dispatched to Holland. No E27002 with five coaches worked 1Z36, the 11.00am Reddish Depot to Sheffield (Victoria), arrival time 11.57, and the return 12.18pm Sheffield (Victoria) to Reddish Depot, arrival time 13.14. Authority was given to exceed the line speed as follows:

Up direction:
Torside (mp 15¼) to Woodhead (mp 19): 75mph

Down direction:
Dunford (mp 22) to Woodhead Tunnel West (mp 19¼): 75mph

Woodhead Tunnel West (mp 19¼) to Woodhead (mp 19): 70mph Woodhead (mp 19) to Crowden (mp 17¼): 75mph

The locomotive was single-manned with Guide Bridge motorman Bert Wagstaff, who put up a good performance. On the return run, speed through Woodhead Tunnel was 75mph, dropping to 60 over the points at the signal box. Accelerating again on the 1 in 117 gradient down to Crowden, speed just about touched 80mph whereupon Wagstaff turned round to the accompanying technical representative and exclaimed "How's that!"'

There is an unproven story that Motorman Wagstaff's feat was even more impressive: it claims that a missing milepost on that run down Longdendale resulted in a huge underestimate of No 27002's speed. Did it really touch 100mph? Alas, we shall never know.

The EM2 fleet went to Holland a few weeks later and remained in service until 1986, each engine covering around 2½ million miles with a best recorded run that saw one of the class touch 86mph. Three of them survive: one in Manchester Museum of Science & Industry, one in preservation in Holland, and the third, No 27000 herself, in preservation in England.

What, then, of the almost equally small fleet of EMUs that took over the Manchester–Hadfield–Glossop service? There is little to say – indeed, little that can be said – because suburban passenger work, even in steam days, was so humdrum and predictable as not to merit the attention of train timers or students of locomotive performance.

The 8 three-car units were closely modelled on the Liverpool Street–Shenfield fleet, with a single roof-mounted pantograph and compressed-air-operated doors. Like the Shenfield units, they were designed for short journeys and many standing passengers at peak times.

Each one comprised a Driving Motor Coach, with the pantograph mounted above the adjacent guard's compartment, a Trailer Coach and a Driving Trailer Coach. Two units could be operated in multiple for peak-time services. Each three-car set had seats for 176 passengers, and standing space for around 220.

The EMU sets were unremarkable but, in many ways, unremarkable for all the right reasons. There are no records of any major faults or teething troubles. The 1957 paper given to the Institution of Locomotive Engineers makes no mention of any issues or the need for modifications, even though by this time the eight sets had between them covered 1¾ million miles.

And they certainly transformed the Manchester–Hadfield–Glossop service. Prior to electrification services had been relatively slow, not particularly punctual and at irregular times. The new electric timetable provided a half-hourly service to and from Glossop. The same level of service operated to and from Hadfield in the peak periods, with an hourly service between peaks. After about 7.00pm the whole service went hourly.

The Glossop–Manchester service was increased from 17 to 31 trains per day and the Hadfield service went from 10 to 23. Perhaps most remarkably of all, the Hadfield–Manchester journey time was cut by 14 minutes, which says more about the trains' abilities than any number of statistics and performance tables. The inevitable result was a 'mini sparks effect', with a surge of new passengers, many of whom tried the railway, liked it and stayed with it.

The units became Class 506 under BR's TOPS classification scheme, finally disappearing in 1984 when what was left of the route was converted to 25kV AC electrification. There was an abortive attempt to preserve one unit.

Above: **Sunday maintenance work often meant switching off the power and using diesels. This Derby Lightweight unit is on a Glossop–Manchester Piccadilly working substituting for the usual EMU, and is pictured at Godley in September 1964.** *John Clarke*

Left: **An EMU approaches Dinting as it comes off the Glossop branch in 1969. Rationalisation soon afterwards reduced the track here to a single line.** *J. S. Hancock/IAL*

6

Decline and fall

The year 1955 must have felt like a good one for anyone working on the Manchester–Sheffield–Wath system. Loco crews had the best that post-war technology could provide – engines that performed reliably and consistently, and no more worries over poor condition, bad coal or any of the other variables.

Operating the line was easier. Transit times through the new Woodhead Tunnel were quicker, which increased the capacity – and therefore the whole route's capacity – at a stroke. As we have already seen, the Wath–Mottram timings had been cut by almost two-thirds, giving far better locomotive and crew utilisation. Passenger trains between Manchester and Sheffield completed the journey in just under the hour, an important marketing tool and one that worked – takings rose by well over a third in the six months following the introduction of the all-electric passenger service.

And for anyone connected with the system at all – station porter to running superintendent, track ganger to overhead line technician – there was a mix of pride and satisfaction that here you were, working on what had become one of the country's premier railway routes, at the cutting edge of railway technology. The British Railways Board was sufficiently satisfied to commission a Vic Welch painting depicting an EM2-hauled express crossing with an EM1-hauled coal train in Longdendale. It became a publicity poster. 'Britain's First All-Electric Main Line' shouted the accompanying slogan. What could be better?

But hovering right on the horizon of this otherwise flawless blue sky was a small cloud – a cloud that would grow and darken. Within a few years the line would have gone through what amounted to not one but two closures, seeing its passenger services run down, then withdrawn, followed by another downward spiral that ate away the freight services that were meant to keep the route open and healthy. From national showcase to unwanted liability in just 29 years. How did this come about?

The reasons are many and varied, and the story of the MSW's decline really begins even as the inaugural DC electric services, Co-Co electrics at their head, were speeding between Manchester and Sheffield. Trials with a new generation of AC electric trains were taking place not too far away, between Morecambe and Heysham, on the North West coast.

AC electric traction was not a new idea. Indeed, the Morecambe–Heysham line had used it from the turn of the century. But the French had pioneered a new set of technical standards, building on the idea that AC equipment was potentially cheaper and simpler to install and maintain. There were some technical issues to be overcome, including rectifying the AC current fed to the locomotives for use by DC traction motors. But the prize was significant, and the French had shown that by applying industrial specifications to railway electrification, significant cost savings could be made. AC would come in cheaper because it needed less infrastructure – such as substations – than conventional DC systems. On the MSW, for example, there was a substation every 8 miles or so.

And so it turned out. In 1956 the Weir standards for DC electrification were abandoned in favour of a new set of standards for AC current. By 1958 the first stretch of new AC electrification had been energised – the Styal line into Manchester. At London Road station – soon to be renamed Manchester Piccadilly to mark the completion of the electrification to Euston – the two rivals sat side by side. At the same time, the decision was taken to re-electrify the Liverpool Street–Shenfield route, converting it to the new AC standards because of the maintenance savings that would result.

The writing was now clearly on the wall. Electrification at 1,500v DC was outmoded and the MSW system was becoming a 40-odd-mile island of obsolescence. Any thoughts of large-scale expansion as expressed just a couple of years earlier in British Railways' commemorative booklet could be forgotten unless the route was also converted to AC.

Other changes were also taking place. Regional boundary changes meant that control of the Great Central main line from Nottingham to Marylebone was transferred from the Eastern to the London Midland Region. What happened next is still a matter of furious debate, but in 1960 the line was stripped of its expresses to Sheffield and Manchester, becoming a secondary route with little more than a skeleton service of stopping trains between London and Nottingham. Six years later it would close completely. The politics of the decision are still hotly disputed: was this Derby taking its revenge on the upstart GCR at last? What was the sense of abandoning a line capable of taking continental vehicles to the industrial heart of England? In the end it mattered little. The Woodhead route became even more of a self-contained island of railway operation, with a basically hourly service linking the two cities.

Apart from the psychological importance of all this, it also meant that one end of the route – Sheffield Victoria – became a much less important place. As other services were either closed or diverted into the Midland station, it became more run-down and less useful to passengers travelling anywhere other than Manchester.

As early as 1964 rumours began to circulate that British Railways wanted to axe the Woodhead passenger service completely, replacing it with a diesel railcar service running via the Hope Valley line – which would add to the journey time.

There was a deep irony in all this. The Beeching Report of 1963, far from recommending closure, had actually come down in favour of long-term investment and development of the route as an example of 'the future of good railway operation in Britain'. Beeching envisaged a route carrying a mix of inter-city trains between Lancashire and South Yorkshire/Nottinghamshire and freight trains. With investment, the route might handle up to 200 trains per day. The price would be an end to all local services, including the Manchester–Hadfield–Glossop trains.

But British Railways itself appeared not to be listening. Rumours about the fate of the passenger service continued and, in late 1964, a BR public relations official was compelled to deny them, with an assurance that there were 'no plans' to close Victoria station in the near future. Alas, within months the same official had to admit that plans were in place to close Victoria, but only after a new link to allow Woodhead line trains into Sheffield Midland station had been completed. True enough, a link was being created by upgrading an existing chord line between Nunnery and Bernard Road. But it would never be suitable for main-line passenger services because it faced the wrong way; to reach Sheffield Midland station from the Manchester direction required a reversal at Sheffield Victoria No 4, just east of the station, down the steeply graded chord line to Nunnery main line Junction and thence to Sheffield Midland.

The official pointed to the £250,000 then being spent on an electrified connection into the new Tinsley Marshalling Yard as evidence of British Railways' commitment to Woodhead's future. In fairness, this was a positive development. Tinsley – although it turned out to be a huge white elephant – was then the modern face of rail freight, one of a chain of 'super yards' being built to streamline wagonload traffic previously dealt with by many smaller yards and sidings. Plugging the MSW system directly into it was a vote of confidence. And, intriguingly, the overhead equipment used was intended to allow easy conversion to 6.25kV AC, should this become necessary. It is one of very few indications that BR ever took the idea of converting the MSW to AC at all seriously.

Along the route itself, stations, sidings and loops were still being closed, and the air of general rundown was hard to ignore. Woodhead station itself closed in July 1964. Wortley station had been axed as early as May 1955, with Crowden following two years later. Deepcar, Oughty Bridge and Wadsley Bridge stations put up the shutters in 1959 with the withdrawal of the Sheffield–Penistone local service. Apart from the Manchester–Hadfield–Glossop stations, these closures left only two intermediate stations: Penistone and Dunford Bridge.

But the real watershed came in 1967 when British Railways finally broke cover and admitted that it now wanted to abandon Woodhead as a passenger route and concentrate all passenger services on the Hope Valley line running into Sheffield Midland station. A plan to chop the purely local passenger service via the Hope Valley had to be abandoned after BR was refused consent to withdraw it on the grounds of hardship to villages such as Hope and Edale if their stations were closed.

What followed was a classic 1960s railway closure saga: a string of objections were registered, triggering public hearings by the Transport Users' Consultative Committees for Yorkshire and the North West. These were the official rail passenger 'watchdogs'. But their terms of reference were severely limited. They were not allowed, for example, to question either British Railways' economic case for closing a service or the commercial judgment that lay behind it. All they were allowed to do was to consider issues of 'hardship'. In practice this consisted of listening to passengers' stories of how the loss of their rail service would inconvenience them and translating this into a report to the transport minister. In the cases where the TUCC recommended retention of the rail service, its comments were almost always overridden by a 'consent to closure' decision from the minister. Only rarely were services reprieved.

But the objectors piled in with stories of changed lives, inconvenience and hardship. Many objectors – and local politicians – suspected a hidden agenda, and it is easy to see why British Railways would to want abandon the Woodhead line – it would also permit Sheffield Victoria to be closed. Victoria was by now used for little other than the Sheffield–Woodhead–Manchester service. The new chord line allowed trains to and from Lincoln to run into Midland station. With no local services left, no trains to London and an alternative route from Midland station via the Hope Valley to Manchester, Victoria must have appeared little more than a cash-guzzling nuisance to local and regional managers. The way the plans were announced, after months of official denial, also fed the conspiracy theories.

The then chairman of Penistone's local council, Councillor Wilf Gledhill, certainly thought he smelled a rat. As he said at the time:

'For months the railway officials have denied all knowledge of closure proposals and promised we would have advanced notice of any plans affecting Penistone. This is typical of the underhand way in which railway politics operate.'

BR also put forward an unusual case for withdrawing the passenger trains. The Woodhead route, officials said, made far more sense as a freight route across the Pennines. In a reversal of the usual order of things, the suggestion was that the passenger services were actually getting in the way of a more efficient freight service. Concentrating passengers on the Hope Valley route would allow freight to be concentrated on the Woodhead route. It struck a chord with the politicians of the day for, two years later and despite a national commitment to paying the running costs of socially useful railways, the transport minister, Richard Marsh MP, gave consent to closure of the passenger service.

A pair of multiple-working examples passes through a decaying Victoria station. *S. R. Batty*

Right: **One of the eight EMUs built for the line, now known as Class 506, brakes to a halt at Godley station. In the background can be seen the rather empty-looking exchange sidings.**
David Clough/IAL

Below: **Looking back towards Manchester, another 506 unit rolls to a stop in the bare and deserted platforms. Godley was not a welcoming place and this 1980 view conveys some of the bleakness.**
Keith Smith/IAL

However, the citizens of Penistone had played the same card of isolation and hardship as the citizens of the Hope Valley had a few years earlier, and to avoid the town becoming an isolated community, the diesel multiple unit service from Huddersfield, which terminated at Penistone, would be extended into Sheffield. It would run through the empty shell of Victoria station, pause, and then reverse down the chord line into Sheffield Midland.

The decision had the hallmarks of a classic political fudge: of the 42 miles of route that saw passenger trains, around 26 miles would still be carrying passenger traffic – only the central section between Penistone and Hadfield would lose all services. And even here there was a proposal, backed with actual trials, to extend the Manchester–Hadfield (MHG) EMU service on to Penistone to connect with the new Huddersfield–Penistone–Sheffield DMUs.

But this idea was abandoned. The precise reasons are now difficult to determine. At the time there was a story that the Woodhead Tunnel had 'insufficient clearance' to allow the EMUs through. This is an implausible theory, not least because the new tunnel was built to more generous clearances. The MHG units also operated a shuttle service through it when the new tunnel was officially opened. But they may have struggled with a 15-mile non-

stop run with about half on a rising gradient – their traction motors were geared for stop-start running for short distances. There may also have been an issue of diagramming just eight units to do the extra work. For whatever reason, the idea – if it was ever seriously considered – was not taken forward.

At around the same time the line had featured in a BBC documentary, *Engines Must Not Enter the Potato Siding*, an obscure title arising from a warning notice at the Bridgehouses Goods Depot, which was being demolished when the film was being made. Subtitled 'A film about railways and railwaymen', it contrasted life on the Woodhead route with the sparkling new Euston–Manchester service.

The choice of backing music told its own story: The Euston–Manchester commentary was underlaid with the tune from a contemporary pop song, *Good Morning Starshine*. The Woodhead line story was accompanied by piano music that could easily have come from a silent movie. The subliminal message was clear.

The end finally came on 5 January 1970, and in the weeks leading up to it enthusiast traffic was so heavy that many trains were strengthened from what had become the normal five bogies. For example, on the last weekday service, Saturday 3 January, the 11.45 departure from Sheffield loaded to seven vehicles with many compartments reserved for specific railway groups and societies.

Locomotive No E26053 *Perseus* gave a convincing demonstration that the Woodhead electrics were still on top of their game: despite two permanent way slacks and the heavier load, she reached Penistone in just over 17½ minutes. By Dunford Bridge the train was moving at 57mph on the 1 in 135 gradient. More slacks beyond the tunnel did not prevent an on-time arrival at Piccadilly.

But on the final day of scheduled services, Sunday 4 January, events turned almost farcical. The final passenger train through the tunnel before the end of scheduled services was meant to be the 22.15 departure from Sheffield Victoria. It left,

Above: **The weeks leading up to withdrawal of the passenger service in 1970 were cold and wintry. Just looking at this view of a train strengthened from five to seven vehicles is enough to make one shiver!** *Bernard Mettam*

Middle: **The Pennines saw plenty of wintry weather and for three months of the year it was not unusual to find lying snow. No E26008 plods its lonely way through the snow at Hazlehead in February 1970.** *Keith Long*

Left: **As the 1970s wore on and the threat of total closure became more real, the Woodhead route was in greater demand for charters, both for the line itself and its unique traction. Enthusiasts make a huge fuss of No 76006 as it heads an eastbound charter.** *Author*

Right: **On the last day of Woodhead's regular passenger service No E26054 *Pluto* has just arrived at Victoria with the 14.10 from Manchester Piccadilly.** *I. S. Carr/IAL*

Below: **A small group of EM1 locos handled services on the final day. Among them was No E26056 *Triton*, seen here waiting to depart from Sheffield Victoria with 1M26, the 22.15 service to Manchester, the final westbound working. The crew appear to have thrown open their cab to enthusiasts before they embark upon their final trip.** *Keith Long*

15 minutes late, hauled by No E26056 *Triton*, to the accompaniment of cheers, flashing cameras and the crack of three detonators. One commentator described it as 'something of an anti-climax', highlighting how run-down and little-used Victoria station had become.

Triton was in a poor external condition with one nameplate missing. In the train behind, many passengers thought they were to be the last scheduled passengers through Woodhead Tunnel. But events had already turned: at about 20.00 that evening a freight had become derailed at Valehouse, blocking the up line. This caused what should have been the final eastbound departure from Manchester Piccadilly to be diverted via the Hope Valley line to Sheffield Midland, operated by a DMU.

This left a substantial number of enthusiasts disappointed and angry. In the spirit of the times, they staged a 'sit-in' at the Piccadilly Station Manager's office. Eventually the pressure persuaded operating staff to lay on a special via Woodhead. A set of coaches that had just arrived as the 19.30 departure from Sheffield – which had also been delayed by the derailment – was commandeered and E26054 *Pluto* put on the front. This left Piccadilly at 23.10. The train reversed at Hadfield, ran 'wrong line' to Torside, bypassing the derailed freight, and then went on to Victoria, calling at Dunford Bridge and Penistone, arriving at 00.44 on Monday morning, 5 January.

But even this 'accidental' last train was not the final chance to ride over Woodhead. The Manchester–Grimsby newspaper train had still to depart at 01.17. Although primarily a newspaper train, it always carried passenger accommodation. This night it loaded to 12 bogies, and was hauled by a diesel locomotive (the newspaper trains left from the 'AC' side of Piccadilly) as far as Guide Bridge, where No E26056 *Triton* took over. It arrived at Penistone at 02.20, where 6 minutes was allowed to split the train. *Triton* and the first four vehicles left for Grimsby via Sheffield, while a Class 37 diesel locomotive, with three coaches, backed onto the remaining newspaper vans. It ran to Grimsby via Barnsley and Doncaster, making it the final scheduled passenger service between Penistone and Doncaster.

Thus ended a 129-year chapter in the Woodhead line's history. With the benefit of hindsight, it is easy to see that, in an anti-railway climate where every service was being called upon to justify its existence, having two competing rail routes between Manchester and Sheffield was simply not sustainable. As British Rail had been effectively told that the Hope Valley line passenger service was there to stay, Woodhead was the only obvious target.

And, in truth, the Woodhead passenger service had become steadily more isolated since the run-down of the Great Central main line. The Nunnery chord allowed more services from the east to run into Sheffield Midland, undermining the reason for having a station at Victoria. In the end, Victoria was only there because of the Woodhead passenger service. A subtle combination of railway politics, geography and money – the cost of building a facing connection to link services from Manchester to the Midland station – had completely undermined it. In an age when BR was trying to group services into one station per town or city whenever possible, being able to shed responsibility for Sheffield Victoria must have appeared a logical next step.

It is also worth recalling that BR was under significant government pressure during this period. To take an example from

Above: **Woodhead's last link with its passenger service was the final Class 1 service to use the route, 1E62, the Manchester Piccadilly-Grimsby news. When daytime passenger services ended, the Brake 2nd coach that carried occasional travellers was removed. It is seen here waiting to depart from Piccadilly in the late 1970s behind No 40050.** *Author*

Middle: **E26022 moves through Dunford Bridge at a smart pace with 1M21, the empty newspaper vans for Manchester Piccadilly, on 11 August 1969.** *Keith Long*

Left: **After regular passenger work finished, even the named and boiler-fitted examples found themselves on humbler duties. Here No E26054 approaches Dunford East with 8M48, an unfitted Wath–Mottram working, in February 1970. The** *Pluto* **nameplates soon disappeared but the boilers, though unused, lasted rather longer. No 54, for example, was still equipped with one at withdrawal in July 1981.** *Keith Long*

A clutch of Class 76s were always stabled at Guide Bridge at the weekends. In this February 1979 view a good mix of unmodified 'vacuum only' locos and the multiple-working and air-braked examples are on show. *Gavin Morrison*

elsewhere on the network, at the same moment that passenger trains were disappearing from Woodhead, the Ministry of Transport was publishing a study into the costs and benefits of retaining or closing the Cambrian Coast line to Barmouth and Pwllheli. The figures were not encouraging and led to yet another appraisal of the worth of the secondary railway system. Sure enough, the decade saw another crop of branch-line closures: the Cambrian Coast line survived, though others – Bridport and Alston for example – did not. Politically and economically, this was not a good time for anything other than trunk, mainstream railway passenger services, and what happened on the Woodhead line was a symptom of these external pressures.

All this was overlaid by the operating inconveniences of the line. What had been its greatest strength – electrification – was now becoming a great weakness. A 40-odd-mile electrified line is too short to be efficient, and trains travelling beyond Sheffield needed to change traction. The abandonment of the 1500v DC electrification standards meant that Woodhead's overhead wires were never going to stretch any further.

But economic and operating conveniences are not usually what is best for the passenger, and so it proved to be. The replacement Hope Valley line service was slower than the Woodhead electrics, and the Huddersfield–Penistone–Sheffield

DMU had to reverse at the Nunnery chord, almost doubling the previous Penistone–Sheffield journey time.

However, all was not lost. The promise from British Rail was that Woodhead would be better utilised as a freight route across the Pennines, and it began its new role on 5 January 1970. Investment had been made both in the shape of the electrified connection to Tinsley Yard, and the 21 locomotives converted to work in multiple on the 'merry-go-round' coal services that were on the verge of being introduced. The line might not be its old self, but it would be there still, performing a useful role.

And it was not finished with passenger traffic by a long chalk. The route was still cleared to handle passenger trains and, just ten weeks after the end of scheduled services, the familiar 'four beats' rang out on block bells along the line as a string of six football excursions made their way from Manchester to Wadsley Bridge, taking supporters to a match at Sheffield Wednesday's Hillsborough ground. It was followed over the next two or three months with more excursions and diversions from the Hope Valley route, including a three-day period caused by a derailment when the Woodhead line handled 88 passenger and around a dozen parcels trains.

Woodhead became an established diversionary route and, even in its final few years, regularly carried the Hope Valley's

Nos E26019 and E26033 begin a cautious descent of the Worsborough Bank from West Silkstone Junction with a train of steel empties for Wath in March 1969. The leading loco is not the train engine, but a banker. Banking locos came off westbound (loaded) trains at West Silkstone, then waited to assist eastbound workings with regenerative braking. *Keith Long*

Above: **Passenger services had only just been axed when this shot of a westbound mixed freight was taken in March 1970. But already Woodhead is becoming a basic railway. The loops are gone, the signalling simplified. The locomotives are Nos E26008 and E26027.** *Gavin Morrison*

Left: **No E26047, formerly *Diomedes*, passes Hazlehead with 8M06 on 15 March 1970.** *Keith Long*

103

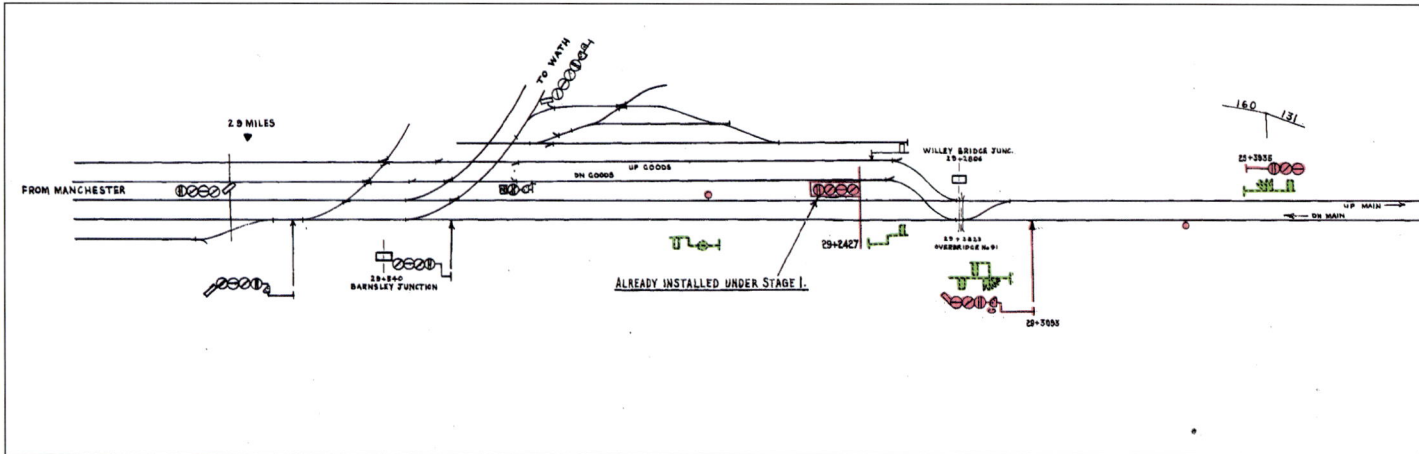

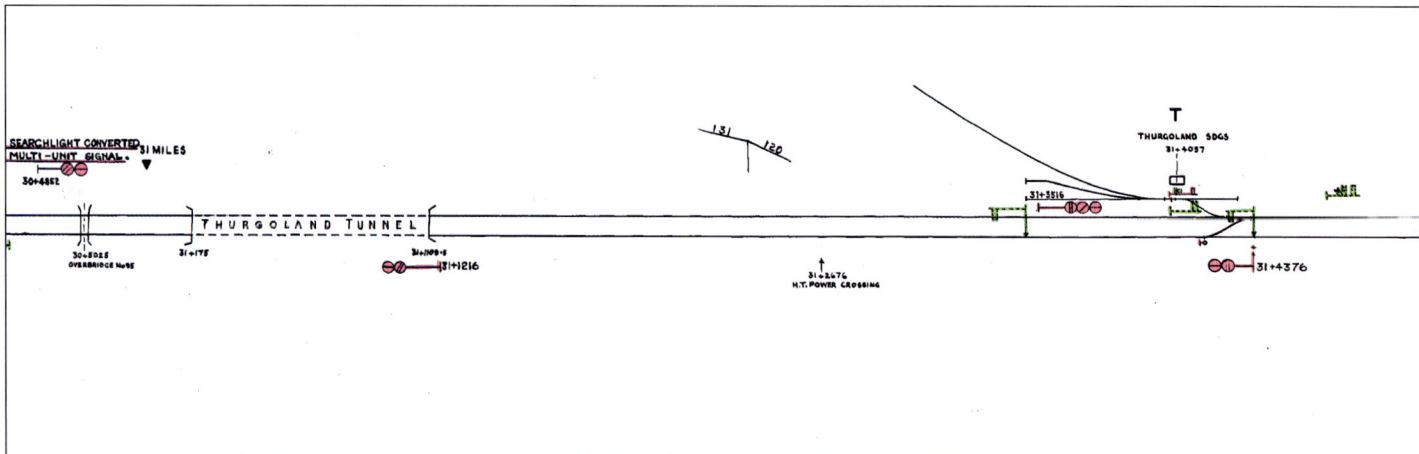

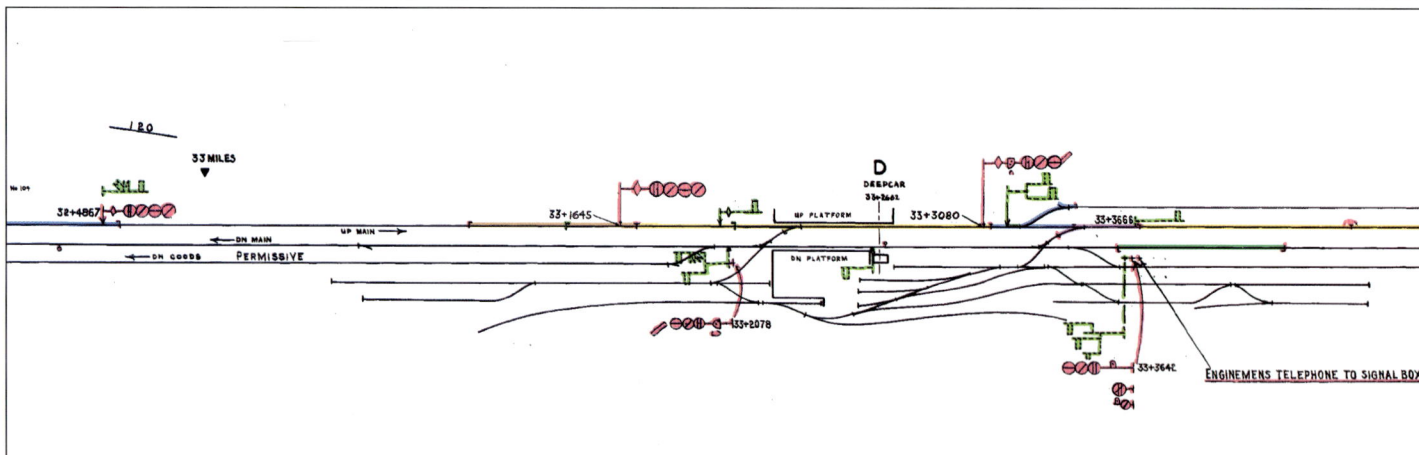

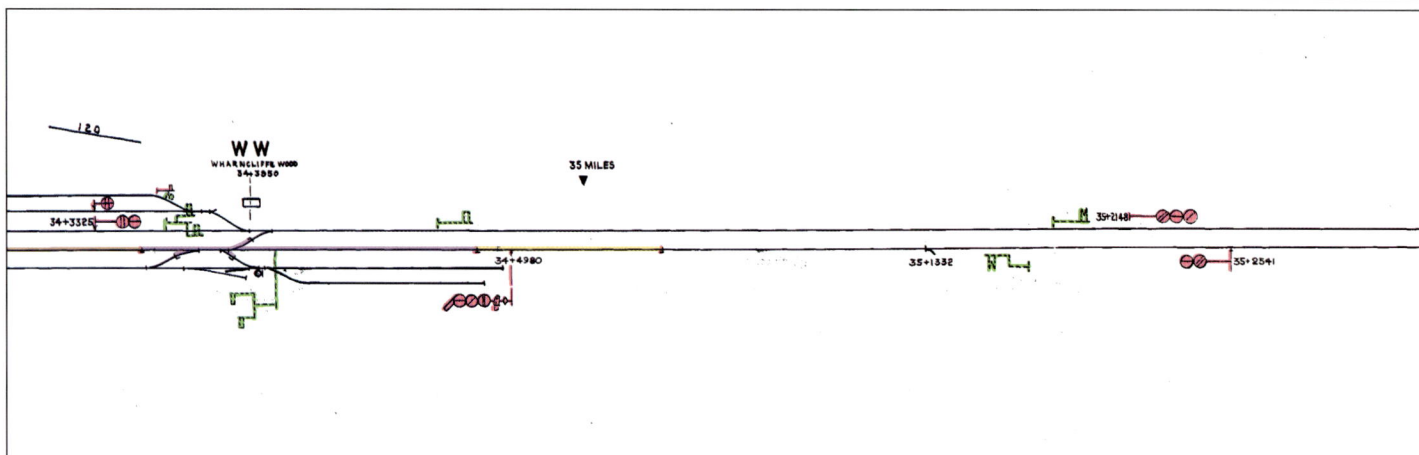

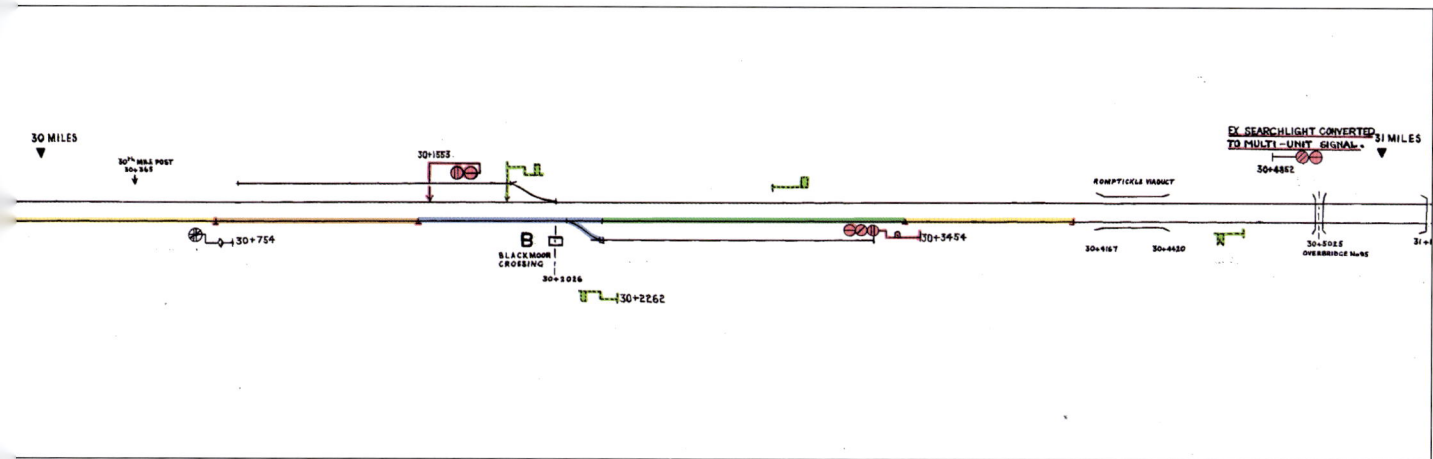

30 MILES ▼

30ᵀᴴ MILE POST
30+345

30+1553

EX SEARCHLIGHT CONVERTED
TO MULTI-UNIT SIGNAL.
30+4852

31 MILES ▼

30+754

B
BLACKMOOR
CROSSING

30+2016

30+2262

30+3454

ROMPTICKLE VIADUCT

30+4167   30+4420

30+5025
OVERBRIDGE No.95

31+

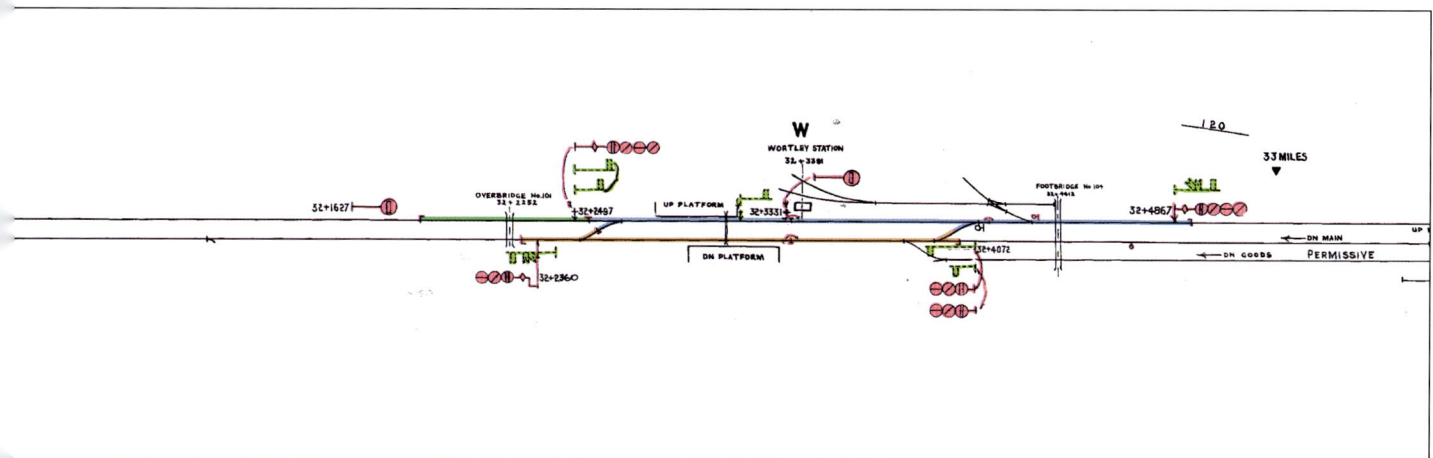

120

33 MILES ▼

W
WORTLEY STATION
32+3381

32+1627

OVERBRIDGE No.101
32+2252

32+2497

UP PLATFORM

32+3331

FOOTBRIDGE No.104
32+4413

32+4867

32+2360

DN PLATFORM

32+4072

DN GOODS

DN MAIN   UP

PERMISSIVE

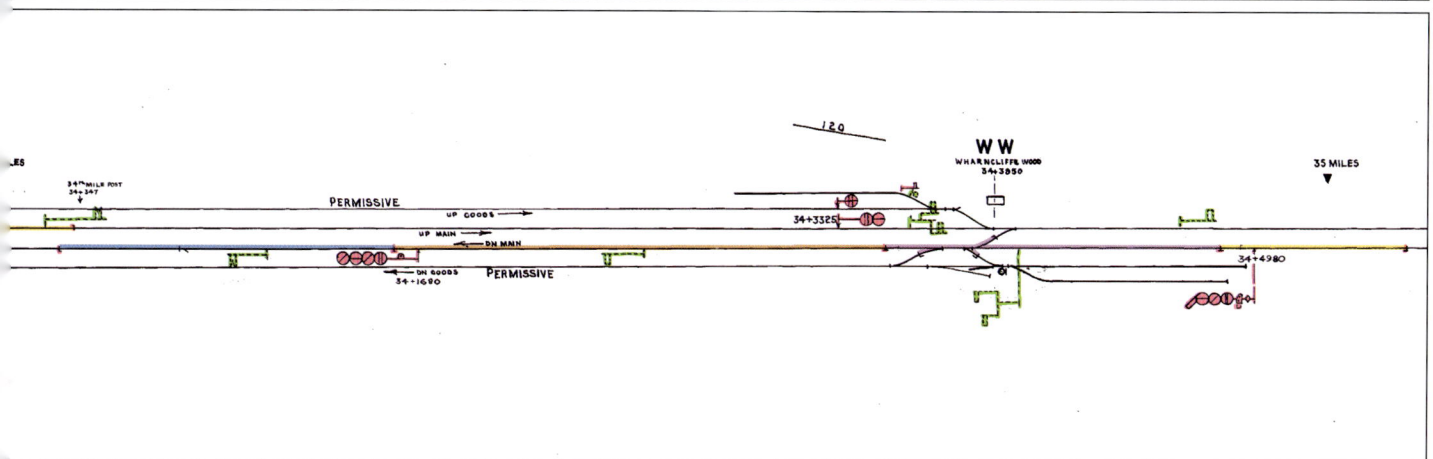

120

WW
WHARNCLIFFE WOOD
34+3850

35 MILES ▼

34ᵀᴴ MILE POST
34+347

PERMISSIVE

UP GOODS

UP MAIN

34+3325

DN MAIN

34+1690   DN GOODS   PERMISSIVE

34+4980

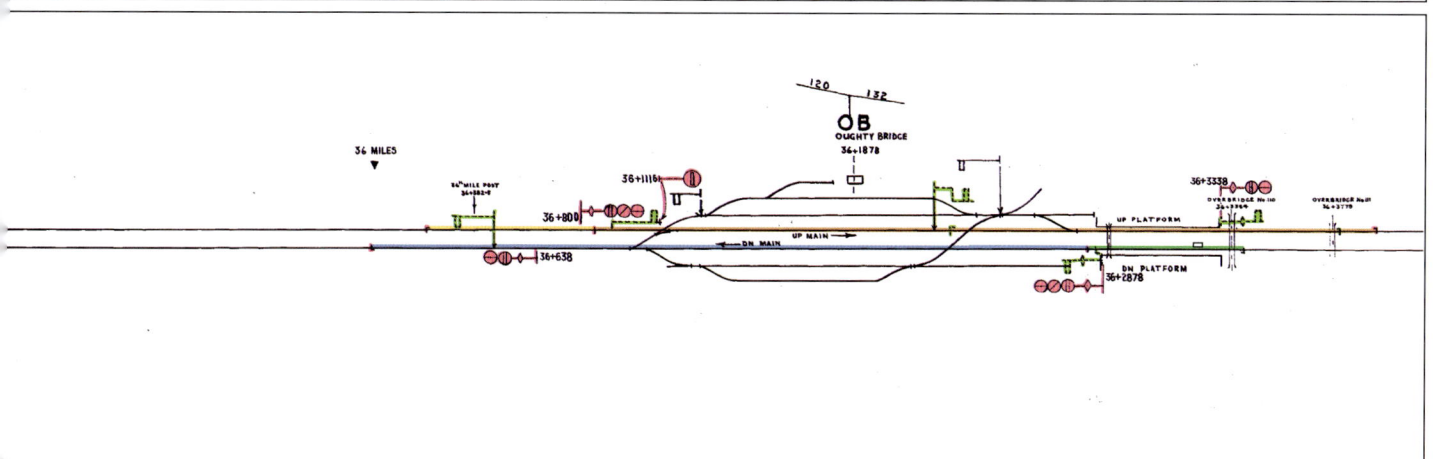

120   132

OB
OUGHTY BRIDGE
36+1878

36 MILES ▼

36ᵀᴴ MILE POST
36+582-9

36+800

36+1116

UP MAIN

UP PLATFORM

36+3338

OVERBRIDGE No.110
36+3964

OVERBRIDGE No.111
36+3779

36+638

DN MAIN

DN PLATFORM

36+2878

105

Above: **A tank train headed by No E26026 and a sister engine, newly modified for multiple working, is seen here at Woodburn Junction, east of Victoria, in February 1971.** *Howard Turner*

Right: **The line was used for a wide variety of diverted passenger trains right up to closure. Here, a Barnsley–Southport excursion exits Woodhead Tunnel behind No 47276 in August 1978.** *Les Nixon/IAL*

Left: **Almost until final closure a steady stream of planned and emergency diversions kept the 'four bells' signals coming. Here a Class 45 passes Dunford East with 1M32, a St Pancras-Manchester express, in June 1971.** *Keith Long*

Below: **A contentious aspect of the route's closure was BR's willingness to use it repeatedly for passenger services diverted away from the Hope Valley route on winter Sundays. Here a former trans-Pennine DMU, reformed into a hybrid four-car set, thunders over Thurlstone Crossing on a Liverpool–Sheffield service in February 1980.** *J. S. Rinder/IAL*

Sunday services to allow engineering work to be carried out under total line possessions.

Indeed, Victoria station itself reopened for a final day of glory early in 1974 when the new Sheffield power box and its associated colour light signalling was commissioned. Platforms 3 and 4 were the only ones with tracks remaining and they took their old numbers for the day. Ticket offices and buffets were cleaned out and reopened – sometimes with the aid of hurricane lamps – while station announcements were made with a portable loud-hailer.

But the most unusual passenger working, post-1970, is recorded in *Locomotives of the LNER*, which recounts an incident in which one of the power cars of the 07.45 Sheffield–Huddersfield DMU became defective, leaving one powered unit to move three cars. It was quickly realised that the unit would not be able to reach Penistone and an unidentified Class 76 was coupled on at Sheffield No 4 signal box and banked the DMU up to Penistone.

Regular passenger trains were now a part of the line's history, and a useful snapshot of the route in its final guise comes from B. K. Cooper, writing in *Railway World* in 1974. He describes a line stripped down to the minimum with most of the loops and sidings of a mixed-traffic railway gone. From Woodhead westwards, most of the route had been reduced from four tracks to two; just one up loop remained at Valehouse as a way of clearing trains from Godley.

Mottram Yard, showpiece of the 1930s, closed in 1972, apart from six of the reception roads, which found a new use for traction changes on MGR trains from pairs of Class 76 electrics to a Class 47 diesel for the onward run to Fiddlers Ferry Power Station. The empties worked back under diesel power to Godley Junction – the yard there reduced to five roads – where a pair of 76s would take over for the run back to Wath or Rotherwood.

The effects had been less obvious at the eastern end of the route, although the sidings at Dunford Bridge had closed, leaving only a couple of roads for recessing MGR trains. Later, this was reduced further to a simple up goods line between Dunford West and Dunford East. The exchange sidings at

Wombwell Main Junction also fell into disuse in 1973 when the chord that allowed access from the Barnsley and Cudworth (Midland main line) direction was closed. The final service to use this line and the exchange sidings is believed to have been the Monckton–Northwich coke train, 8M17, which subsequently was tripped into Wath for reversal back towards Wombwell and Penistone under electric power.

This was not necessarily bad news. The way coal traffic was handled had been long overdue for modernisation and rationalisation, and this is precisely what was happening. As Mr Cooper remarked:

'Traffic patterns on the line have changed considerably since its early days when the basic function was to work coal traffic from east to west. Basic differences today are the reduction of marshalling and of intermediate traffic and of the number of transfer trips.'

Many of the changes were a direct result of the launch of the MGR pit-to-power-station concept in which the train is never remarshalled. This requires fewer railway facilities – and also fewer trains, because each MGR working carried more

Above: **Mottram Yard stood at the foot of the Pennine hills, a situation emphasised by this panoramic view. A pair of multiple-working Class 76s tackles the climb with an eastbound haul of MGR empties, while loaded trains of more conventional stock wait in the exchange sidings.** *M. Dunnett/IAL*

Middle: **Although the line became synonymous with MGR trains, there were still some traditional workings that persisted to the final day. Here Nos 76015 and 76024 approach Penistone Goods on a short and very mixed train in April 1981.** *Vaughan Hellam*

Right: **By the mid-1970s Mottram Yard was a shadow of its former self, being reduced to half a dozen roads for traction changing. The swap was almost always from Class 76 to Class 47 for the onward MGR trip to Fiddlers Ferry Power Station. Here No 47340 powers away with 30 loaded wagons.** *Author*

A hint of the full desolation at Mottram can be seen here as a Class 506 EMU approaches the staff halt platforms. The only other operational track is the exit line from the exchange sidings. A 'cripple' MGR wagon has been knocked out of a train at some point and awaits the fitters' attention. The office block is still in use, but all else is dereliction.
D. A. Flitcroft/IAL

coal more quickly than a corresponding 'traditional' coal train. B. K. Cooper again:

'Twelve trains a day are dealt with at present, conveying 42,000 tons of coal a week, but the plan allows for a maximum of 19. One train starts from Barnsley Junction. The others come from Wath or Rotherwood as convenient. Local trips to the departure points are planned by Sheffield on the basis of data supplied by the NCB.'

When other traffic was added in – steel plate and billets from Scunthorpe to Manchester and Warrington, domestic coal traffic, usually in 21-ton hoppers for Ardwick Yard, British Oxygen Company tanker trains of compressed oxygen, a daily train of ferry wagons to and from Harwich and Europe – the picture was far from bleak. Around 50 of the original fleet of 57 Class 76s were still serviceable and were operating about 54 down trains and between 45 and 50 up trains every day. But already there were the first glimmerings of uncertainty.

British Rail was beginning yet another capacity review, and Mr Cooper hit the nail on the head when he remarked:

'One cannot speak with certainty of the future. Already the line has seen a fundamental change in its traffic, but its equipment, both fixed and mobile, has shown itself to be as adaptable as it is reliable.'

In fact, the Woodhead line had become a conveyor belt for power station coal with an intensely tidal traffic pattern: loaded trains westward, empties back. All now depended on that coal traffic building and providing the line with sufficient reason for existing. For a time the strategy appeared to be paying off. More and more collieries in South Yorkshire, North Derbyshire and Nottinghamshire were equipped with MGR rapid-loading coal bunkers. Another batch of nine Class 76s was earmarked for conversion to air-braking and multiple operation.

But times were changing, and coal, the reason why the MSW system had been built at all, was changing with them. Peter Semmens, in a change from chronicling locomotive performance, put his finger on what was happening in the Stephenson Locomotive Society Journal in 1976, in an article entitled 'Where Have all the Coal Trains Gone?'

No E26022 at Dunford East with 6Z51, a special working of liquid oxygen tanks from Sheffield's Broughton Lane to Ditton in November 1970. This was normally a longer train hauled by a pair of locos, but on this day problems at the Broughton Lane sidings led to an emergency working. *Keith Long*

Brush Type 2 No D5543 arrives at Dunford East with a train of spent ballast for the engineers' tip that occupied part of the former sorting sidings. The train is 9G11 from Beighton, seen on 4 February 1970. *Keith Long*

Middle: **An unidentified Class 40 sweeps through Dunford East with 1Z36, a Liverpool–Sheffield track recording train, on 4 February 1970.** *Keith Long*

Right: **If diesels were uncommon on the main line, they were – colliery trip workings aside – decidedly rare on the Wath branch, but in this 1972 view two-tone-green Class 47 No 1970 hustles MGR empties through Wentworth Junction.** *Author*

Left: **A driver's-eye view from the cab of No E26004 as it meets a loaded steel train at Wentworth Junction. The loco is on T80 (banker) trip duty and is returning light to Wombwell Main in July 1971.** *Author*

Left: **Wombwell Exchange Sidings fell into disuse from 1973, but remained the attaching/detaching point for banking engines. Here a loose-coupled train has arrived on the up main line; the single banker has assisted with regenerative braking down the incline and is now drawing forward to reach the bankers' siding. A pair of multiple-working Class 76s stands waiting for the next MGR working up the incline.** *S. R. Batty*

Left: **A picture that sums up the Wath branch at the end of its life: a 'merry-go-round' train being worked by four electric locomotives, under the control of semaphore signalling. The location is Kendall Green Crossing.** *Paul Salveson*

Right: **Driver Wynn is at the controls of a pair of bankers on a westbound MGR working near Worsborough Bridge Crossing in the summer of 1980.** *Author*

Above: **Bad weather was not confined to the main line. In the winter of 1979 a pair of electric locos head 8M17, the Monckton–Northwich coke, past Glasshouse Crossing and into the teeth of a snowstorm.** *Adrian Gilmartin*

Right: **A striking view of Dunford East box in semi-darkness. This was a remote and inaccessible location that saw few photographers.** *Keith Long*

Left: **Reddish remained the Class 76 home base to the end. Here an unidentified member of the class waits to enter the maintenance area in 1979.** *Author*

Below: **The depot had a siding for stored and unserviceable, but not yet withdrawn, locomotives. Here, 'live' class member No 76051 – which survived to the very end – is parked at the head of stopped locos.** *Gavin Morrison*

He outlined a simple issue. In 1949 Britain produced 215 million tons of coal. It all needed shifting from pithead to a variety of customers from power stations and factories to schools and domestic hearths. By the mid-1970s, production was running at something like 130 million tons per year. Those customers that were left had also changed their energy consumption habits: the wool and cotton mills were more likely to use electric-powered equipment instead of firing their own boilers, while domestic consumers were more likely to switch to (natural) gas fires or central heating systems than face the daily chore of cleaning up ashes and lighting a fresh fire. He remarked: 'Of course, there are ways of moving energy from its source to the consumer, other than humping it in 16-ton coal wagons.'

He went on to describe the effect of the two trans-Pennine natural gas pipelines on the energy market:

'Calculating the capacity of a pipeline in proportion to the square of its diameter, we find that these two links are capable of transferring the equivalent of 220 and 1,030 tons of coal respectively per hour. However, the bulk of the Manchester area's natural gas does not come across the Pennines, but by a 36-inch main from the south. On the same basis, this pipeline is capable of carrying the equivalent of 1,470 tons of coal per hour, making a total potential energy input into Lancashire of some 2,700 tons of coal per hour.'

Based on hauling coal in 16-ton mineral wagons, he reckoned that the three gas pipelines represented four to six trains per hour, based on trains made up of 30 or 50 wagons. He added:

'Mention of the Woodhead route is a reminder that one of the old tunnels was opened up a few years ago to permit the installation of an electric power cable with a normal rating of 900 megawatts.'

Another burst of maths reveals that this translates into another 30-wagon train of 16-tonners every hour, 24 hours per day. Taken together, natural gas and this electricity cable accounted for seven trains per hour. And, as he pointed out, this ignores completely the contribution made by nuclear-fired power stations, which all made a huge difference to the railway landscape:

'If we assume, for the sake or argument, that the average speed of coal trains over the Woodhead route was 10mph and that there were, on average, three per hour in each direction, this would have meant that over the 30 or so miles between Wombwell sidings and Guide Bridge there were at any one time no fewer than 18 coal trains, tying up something like 27 locomotives (including bankers), 720 wagons and 72 crew.'

But it was not just the nature of the traffic that was changing. British Rail was in the grip of important political changes too. The Ministry of Transport document on the costs and benefits of retaining the Cambrian Coast line was the tip of a bigger iceberg – a change in policy that was going to require the railways to support themselves more and rely on subsidies less. For the Woodhead line the key change here was a government requirement that, from 1977, the rail freight business would be allowed no subsidies. Everything the freight division did would either have to pay its way, cut its costs or face the axe. It would concentrate minds wonderfully.

As Woodhead was now a freight railway, it came under the spotlight, and stories about its future – or the lack of it – began appearing in the specialist railway press. In 1976 yet another

The mid-1970s saw some workings associated with BR's emerging air-braked wagonload network – later known as Speedlink – operating over the line. Here Nos 76008 and 76024 pass Hattersley with a lightweight load of one ferry van and a string of empty car transporters. The date is June 1976. *David Flitcroft/IAL*

line could not be closed because the former had been earmarked for passenger service developments and, although it was now 12 years since, the government had ruled against the closure of the Hope Valley local stations on the grounds of hardship. The Hebden Bridge, or Calder Valley, route had a 'slight case' for closure, but carried passenger traffic supported by the passenger transport executives of Greater Manchester and West Yorkshire.

This left the Woodhead line, and the report made it plain that this was the favoured option. BR could realise a once-only windfall by selling assets – such as the copper wire overhead line and the redundant electric locomotives – for scrap. It would also save £1.3 million per year in running costs, mostly by eliminating the traction changes at each end of the route. There were two realistic options: convert it to 25kV AC – but that would cost £23 million – or close it.

With the alarm bells sounding, local MPs began lobbying the ministerial team at the Department for Transport, and as BR's financial case for closing the line began to leak out, other agencies mounted their own challenges. The Peak Park Planning Board produced its own assessment, which claimed that the Woodhead line, far from losing money, was actually breaking even.

This report also claimed that British Rail had four realistic options, not two, for the future of the line. It could be de-electrified and worked with diesels, or it could be singled, with radio signalling, and be used as a lower-volume coal route using the existing electrification assets until they actually wore out.

The official BR and government line that 'no decision' had been taken was held until 21 October 1979 when, at simultaneous press conferences in Sheffield and Manchester, the closure plan for the MSW – and the thinking behind it – was revealed.

For its time, this was a sophisticated production with both an audio-visual presentation – essentially a slide show with commentary – and a glossy folder containing copies of the images in the presentation and a detailed summary of the case for closure.

It came down to this: British Rail had a huge over-capacity on the four trans-Pennine routes with a capacity of 360 trains per day against a requirement of 154. Only 39 trains per day used the Woodhead route, giving it the greatest amount of spare capacity. Changing locomotives at each end of a short electrified railway was inefficient and costly. If the MGR trains ran via Diggle, transit times would fall by a third, only one Class 56 locomotive would be needed on each train and two fewer sets of MGR wagons could operate the same number of trains.

BR claimed an annual saving of more than £1.6 million in addition to the one-off 'windfall' of £1.2 million – slightly less than the estimate given in the 1978 review.

BR also claimed that existing traffic over Woodhead would decline – not through any fault of the railway industry, but

review of trans-Pennine routes began. The fruit of this took almost two years to emerge, but in 1978 the review was complete – and was one of BR's top secrets.

But not for long. A copy was obtained by a researcher working for the Trades Union Congress. Its contents were leaked to a local newspaper and the cat was out of the bag. The review compared four trans-Pennine routes: via Hebden Bridge, via Diggle, via Woodhead and via the Hope Valley. Predictably, it made the point that Woodhead carried no passenger service across its central section and would therefore be easier to close – there would be no need for an expensive and time-consuming public hearing.

But it also made the point that all four routes carried freight to a greater or lesser extent. In addition both the Diggle (Leeds–Huddersfield–Manchester) route and the Hope Valley

Both main line and branch were sought out for rail tours as it became obvious that the route was doomed. Nos 76012 and 76015 glide through Hazlehead with 1Z81, an Axminster–York rail tour, on 31 March 1979. *Keith Long*

Left: **No 76049 passes Bullhouse with a Paddington–Manchester Piccadilly rail tour on 31 March 1979. The GWR stock made a remarkable sight.** *Keith Long*

Below: **One of the most unusual specials to use the route ran in October 1978, with an itinerary that took in Tinsley Yard as well as the main line. Nos 76023 and 76010 pass Broughton Sidings, east of Sheffield Victoria.** *Gavin Morrison*

Bottom: **A pair of Tinsley Yard 'master and slave' units, No 13003, hauls the same train in the opposite direction. Both Class 76 and Class 13 are now part of railway history.** *Gavin Morrison*

The Pennine weather could turn quickly and dramatically in the winter months. Nos 76034 and 76039 prove the point with a train of tankers at Penistone Huddersfield Junction in March 1979. The snow fell within 5 minutes.
S. R. Batty

because the National Coal Board was reorganising the way it produced and loaded coal. Instead of coming out of many smaller pits and loading bunkers, new underground roads were being driven to concentrate coal loading at three centres: Woolley, Grimethorpe and Houghton Main. All but Houghton Main were better placed to send their coal via Diggle than Woodhead, and even from Houghton there was no overwhelming case for using a route via Wath.

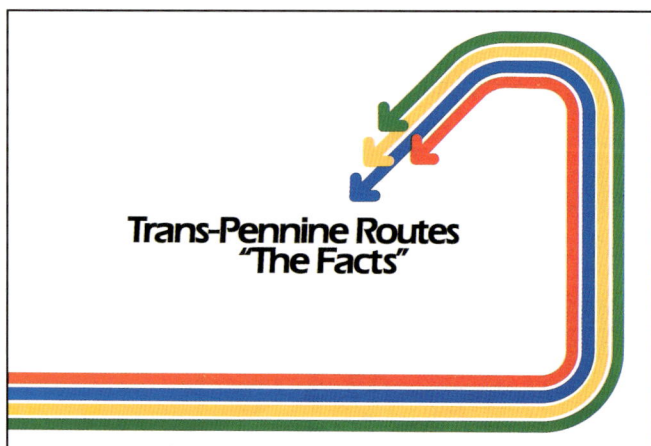

British Rail set out its closure case in a glossy booklet and audio-visual presentation. It came down to two main issues: the four trans-Pennine main lines had vastly more capacity than was needed, and the Woodhead line was inefficient to operate and would need many millions spending on it to keep it running.
Author's collection

What is now known is that well before the press conferences took place and the closure plan was confirmed, BR had been working towards closing the Woodhead line for months. Earlier that year Malcolm Morris, newly returned from a consultancy job overseas, was called in by the Eastern Region General Manager, Frank Paterson, and his deputy, Brian Driver.

'I was told it was a highly confidential project. We knew that announcing closure of the MSW would cause a furore.

But he is still insistent that BR had to do something. And he is equally insistent that the MSW system was facing some big problems that fell, broadly, into two camps.

'I had been Area Manager at Wath from 1974 to 1977. There were then about 40 coal mines in the Wath area. When I left, about half of them had ceased to function as pitheads. It was starting to have a big effect on what was required from the railway because more traffic had been turned over to MGR trains and the way coal was blended for power station use meant changes to traffic patterns.

'And the equipment was obsolete and becoming unreliable. I remember walking a section of line with a technician. He said to me, "Look at this," and pointed to a section of the 33kV feeder cable. The insulation was just crumbling away. It could have blown at any time. I've no doubt he chose one of the worst places, but it still showed the scale of the problems.'

Meanwhile, the Woodhead line found itself in the grip of external political and economic forces that reinforced its own local issues. The Central Electricity Generating Board switched its requirements for coal at Fiddlers Ferry from 3 million tons per annum to 1.25 million, cutting the number of MGR workings needed over the MSW system.

The national steelworkers' strike meant more lost traffic, partly through lost steel production but also because the National Union of Railwaymen 'blacked' any remaining traffic. It went by road instead. And under pressure from a new and hard-line Conservative government, British Rail was being compelled to face huge restructuring and cost-cutting. Details were contained in a report called *The Challenge of the Eighties*. According to a report in *The Times* newspaper, it would involve shedding 30,000 railway jobs.

This was the background against which Malcolm Morris found himself working. But, true to his remit, he did look at every option, including investment in the route.

'For example, just manning all those level crossings on the Worsborough branch cost a fantastic amount. They all had to be manned 24 hours. It was phenomenally expensive and it was becoming difficult to recruit enough signalmen. So I looked at a scheme to take out all those boxes using half-barriers and CCTV, keeping just one box to monitor them. I submitted the idea. But while it looked good on paper, in the real world it didn't stack up. It would have meant other renewals and replacements too.'

He says that there were other expenses associated with the route that received no publicity at the time. For example, taking a Class 76 off the MSW for overhaul – at Crewe in later years – was another huge expense because it could not make its way there under power, but had to be towed, tying up another loco.

As his analysis progressed, he became struck by the inflexibility that a relatively short stretch of electrified railway imposed.

'You couldn't do anything different with it. You couldn't go anywhere else without changing traction. If it had been electrified at 25kV AC or had been capable of expansion, you might have had a chance. But you couldn't do much with it. Those locomotives plodded back and forth and that's all you could use it for. It was one little isolated system. And the line was fragile. Very fragile. It was beyond its useful life and there was the potential for a major failure.'

These were devastating findings for the MSW's future because they turned on their head all the perceived advantages that had been trumpeted in the 1950s; electrification was only truly beneficial when it spread its tentacles to create a network. That did not happen with the MSW through a combination of economies (not extending the system to Manchester Central and Trafford Park) and the almost instant obsolescence suffered by the system when 25kV AC electrification was adopted.

This obsolescence also made repairs and maintenance more expensive, which also tilted the balance away from investment towards run-down and closure.

Finally, the changing traffic requirements were slowly draining away the coal traffic that had become Woodhead's lifeblood. Although the phrase would not be coined until long after the line closed, this amounted to a 'triple whammy'.

Nonetheless, Malcolm Morris's findings were not simply accepted by Eastern Region's General Manager and his staff. When he presented his findings, he was crisply told, 'Prove it!' Proving it entailed more detailed analysis and it was this work that formed the basis of the presentation in October 1979.

It did not prevent the arguments raging. Sheffield City Council joined the Peak Park Planning Board with its own review and reached the conclusion that not only was the MSW system breaking even, it was actually – in 1980 – profitable, costing around £4 million a year to operate while making £5 million in income. In one particularly telling remark, the council said that it was 'a pity' that BR had not used the profits the line had earned in the good years to invest in its future.

And the council had a point: Sheffield Division, although the smallest on the network, was BR's biggest freight division in terms of both tonnage and value. Down the years it had generated a lot of revenue for the national network.

The council suggested that one long-term solution would be to re-electrify the Woodhead line at 25kV AC and use it as the springboard for a northwest–southeast high-speed route from Glasgow to Manchester, Sheffield, Nottingham and London, operated by the emerging Advanced Passenger Train. It was a rallying cry taken up by the broad alliance that had formed around the railway unions to fight the closure.

The main accusation here – apart from the years of neglect and under-investment alleged by the city council – was that BR had deliberately inflated the costs of saving the line to make a better case for closure. Even today it is difficult to judge how much that argument holds water because of the lack of information about the true costs of operating the MSW.

But with the benefit of hindsight, two of the main planks of British Rail's argument certainly do not stand a great deal of scrutiny. The cost of converting the line to 25kV was put at £23 million by none other than the BR Board chairman himself, Sir Peter Parker. Yet five years later the Manchester–Hadfield section – about 14 route miles, or a third of the Manchester–Rotherwood route, was re-electrified at a cost of just £680,000. This suggests that the entire route could have been converted for around £3 million – allowing for the complexities of the overhead line equipment at exchange sidings, etc.

Moreover, the cost of replacement locomotives was also almost certainly inflated. BR put a price of £20 million on replacing stock. If this had all been spent on new electric locomotives, at prevailing prices, it would have bought more than 20. Yet BR's case was that only ten new diesel locomotives would do the work of the MSW electric fleet. At the time, about 15 units were needed to maintain Woodhead's daily service – mostly pairs of Class 76s.

These figures were challenged at the time by, among others, a serving BR employee, Peter Fox, who came up with a cost of £8.5 million to re-electrify. But the arguments could be swept aside: British Rail was answerable to no one when it came to closing a freight line. Even when BR officials agreed to take part in a union-sponsored inquiry – the first time there had ever been any kind of inquiry into a freight line closure – they insisted on presenting evidence in private.

The truth is difficult to pinpoint almost 30 years on, but what appears to have happened is that, having been told by the government that things were going to change, BR found its sacrificial lamb and made sure it had an unassailable closure case. And if that meant making the absolute most of the facts and figures to shore it up, then so be it.

Five or six years later the same tactic of inflating operating costs would be applied to the Settle–Carlisle line closure attempt in an instance where, comparing two successive years, the cost of diesel fuel was inflated well beyond the actual price increase, and the number of diesel locomotives and coaches allocated to the service was also increased, even though an identical timetable of two trains per day was operating.

In March 1980 the developing arguments over the future of the MSW system provoked a House of Commons debate. The Penistone MP, Allen McKay, claimed that coal traffic had been deliberately diverted away from the Woodhead route to make the closure case appear more convincing. 'It is no longer good enough for the minister to say it is a matter for BR and the unions,' he said.

But the time for arguments was now almost over. In May 1980 British Rail announced the closure of three passenger services, including the Sheffield–Penistone–Huddersfield route, and its intention to withdraw from the collect and deliver parcels service.

The Huddersfield–Sheffield closure became inextricably linked with the fate of the wider MSW system and provoked a new round of conspiracy theories. Twelve years earlier, when the fate of the passenger service was being decided, plans to use the Woodhead line trackbed as the basis for a second trans-Pennine motorway were publicly aired.

These plans were nothing if not spectacular. The motorway would run along the trackbed up Longdendale. One carriageway would use the Woodhead Tunnel, while the other would be carried on a huge viaduct that would sweep it out of the dale and over the moorland. The present Junction 35A of the M1 was built, but not commissioned, with this in mind.

So this new proposal to end Penistone's rail link with the outside world was treated by some as simply more evidence of a conspiracy to close the route by diverting traffic away, and convert it into a road. It was a believable claim. Within a few years Marylebone itself would be threatened with closure and conversion to a special 'guided bus' terminal in which road coaches would take the place of trains.

But it is difficult to find any hard evidence that Woodhead's fate was directly linked to the road-building plans. Officials involved with the Huddersfield–Penistone–Sheffield closure proposal maintain to this day that this and the wider MSW closure were completely separate affairs. In fact, the Huddersfield–Sheffield closure, far from being directly linked to the MSW outcome, was actually provoked by a long-running argument between BR and the South Yorkshire Passenger Transport Executive.

PTEs had been authorised for metropolitan areas by the 1968 Transport Act. But they were not set up immediately and, even when they were established, it took several years for them to hit their stride. One of their key responsibilities was for their local railway network. Instead of British Rail deciding the social usefulness or economic worth of a particular service, the PTE would do this, paying BR the cost of operating the service.

But in South Yorkshire the cost of the Huddersfield service between Sheffield and Penistone was considered excessive – more than the cost of the other three services the executive did agree to support put together. John Nelson was Leeds Divisional Passenger Officer, then Sheffield Divisional Passenger Manager, so was the obvious choice to oversee the closure proposal. These are his recollections:

'The Huddersfield–Sheffield service had the biggest deficit in West and South Yorkshire. West Yorkshire were prepared to support their portion of the service but South Yorkshire wouldn't play ball. We cooked up a scheme to divert the service from Penistone via Barnsley to make it more attractive, but still they wouldn't support the service.

'We were then seen as attempting to divert traffic away from the MSW, but that was actually a completely separate issue. West Yorkshire signed up to the idea, South Yorkshire would not so we proposed closure to force the issue. It was a tactic. We never expected it to close.'

On a bright May morning in 1976 an unidentified single Class 76 coasts through the site of Thurgoland Sidings with Rotherwood-bound empties. *Author*

He was right. It took until 1983 to sort out, but in a cliff-hanger ending that gave BR just 75 days to upgrade the Penistone–Barnsley line to passenger standards, the service was relaunched and still follows the same route today.

However, on the MSW events were now moving quickly. On 7 October 1980 British Rail formally announced the closure of the MSW system from 1 June 1981. The line would close between Hadfield and Penistone, between West Silkstone Junction and Wombwell Main Junction (the bulk of the Wath branch of the system) and, subject to the future of the Penistone–Sheffield passenger service, between Penistone and Deepcar. From Deepcar to Sheffield a single track would be left in place to service the steelworks.

The protest movement shifted into top gear. Signallers banned overtime to prevent the diversion of Sunday services from the Hope Valley line over Woodhead. Guards refused to collect fares on the Hope Valley service. Almost two dozen MPs signed a Commons motion demanding an inquiry. As there was no official framework for a freight closure inquiry, the NUR set up its own. BR eventually agreed to take part. It also postponed the closure to 20 July to give time for the inquiry to report.

The rail tour business benefited as enthusiasts scrambled for a last ride over the line. Peter Semmens, chronicler of the locomotive performance over Woodhead for almost 40 years, got in early, arranging a final trip in the cab of a Class 76. Writing as ever in *The Railway Magazine*, he remarked on the changed fortunes of the MSW system:

'In August 1980, admittedly during a period when some collieries were having their holidays, the biggest problem was actually finding a train on which I could travel!'

He eventually found himself on a loose-coupled coal train from Rotherwood, bound for Garston Docks. He recounts seeing only one other train as he crossed the Pennines. Speed restrictions and having two sections reduced to single-track working to allow tamping machines to operate meant that his trip was not even worth logging.

His return, from Godley Junction, was better, and Driver Wiltshire soon had their train of loose-coupled empties bowling along at the maximum speed of 35mph. A 10mph restriction over a worn-out crossover at Dunford Bridge still had them bouncing

Left: **By the late 1970s the Wath branch saw very little other than MGR traffic. With fully fitted trains, banking engines had to be coupled and braked to the main train. This meant a stop at West Silkstone Junction to detach the assisting engines; the working timetable allowed 5 minutes for this. The crew of Nos 76023 and 76027 have just completed the move and are about to begin the trip back to Wombwell Main.** *S. R. Batty*

Below: **At the foot of the bank, at the former Wentworth Junction, a pair of bankers give a hefty shove to the 30 loaded MGR wagons as they enter the 1 in 40 incline. Wentworth Junction closed in 1978 with the closure of Wentworth Silkstone Colliery. The truncated line to the pit can be seen on the left.** *S. R. Batty*

around, but the train coasted down to Sheffield, using regenerative braking all the way. Alas, there was no other traffic to make use of the electricity being generated and it would have been dissipated as heat from the substation resistances. He concluded:

'Clearly the Class 76 locomotives still provide an efficient means of hauling and controlling trains, and it is the changed traffic pattern rather than any failings in the locomotives that is necessitating the closure of the Woodhead route.'

Many people, even within the ranks of BR management, would probably have seconded that remark, but the trap of geography, technology and politics was closing around the MSW. Traffic was still — deliberately or not — trickling away from the line, and when the final working timetable for the route was published in June 1981 it showed just six return MGR workings on the Wath branch, with two 'traditional' loose-coupled workings — 8M17 Monckton–Northwich, whose empties returned via Diggle, and 8E00 Ashburys–Wath empties, whose loaded working ran via the main line from Rotherwood.

But the same timetable also showed a profusion of light engine workings as ancient demarcations between locomotive depots and old working practices continued to hold sway. The locomotive off the 8E00 working could have been used to work 8M17 back across the Pennines. But no. In each case, a locomotive worked light engine from one end of the line to the other to collect its train. The MSW system was no different from the rest of the BR network in this respect, but it was still shockingly inefficient and must have contributed to the system's downfall.

The union-sponsored inquiry reported on 10 June. Predictably, it saw no need for closure and suggested plenty of alternatives. Equally predictably, BR said the closure would go ahead regardless.

And it did. A landslip closed the line two weeks before the closure date, but BR, obviously determined to be seen to be playing fair, reinstated damaged track and the route reopened.

Although closure was to take place from 20 July, for all practical purposes the last day would be Friday the 17th. The procedure put in place by Control was that Class 76s at the eastern ends of the network would work services as required, then would move to Guide Bridge to be sent 'out and back' as remaining traffic demanded.

So, in the late morning, the final MGR working, 6M51, headed by Nos 76032 and 76034, made its way from Wath Yard to Wombwell Main. Bankers Nos 76007 and 76012 were hooked on and the ensemble rumbled up the bank to West Silkstone Junction, pausing to detach the bankers, then on to Barnsley Junction and onto the main line to Mottram. In the opposite direction, a rare diesel working, with No 37070 at the

119

Manchester–Sheffield–Wath electrification track plans — Stage 3, Section 2

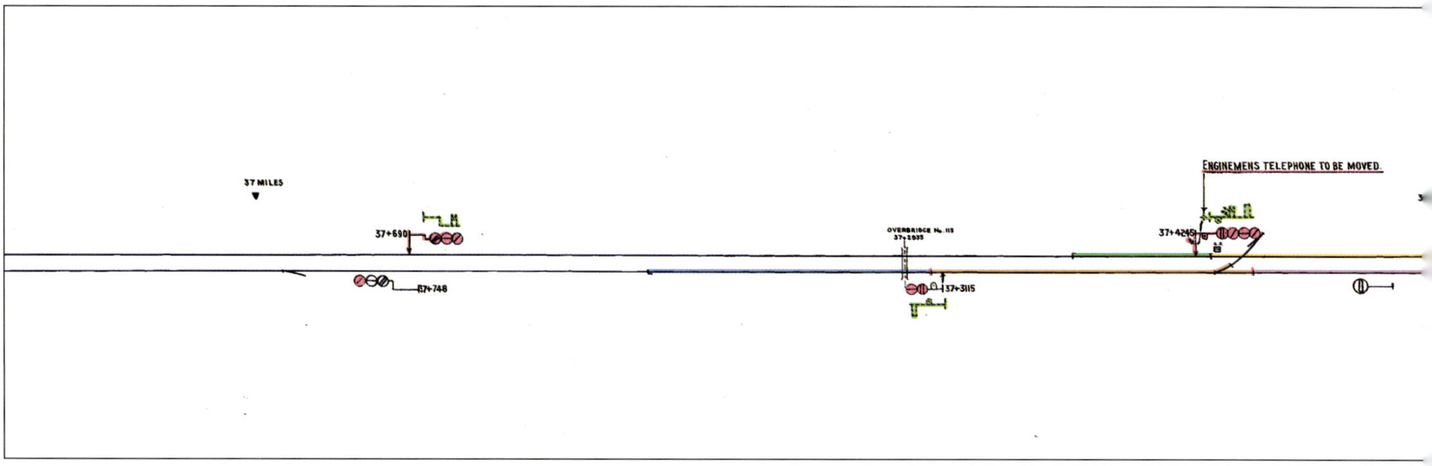

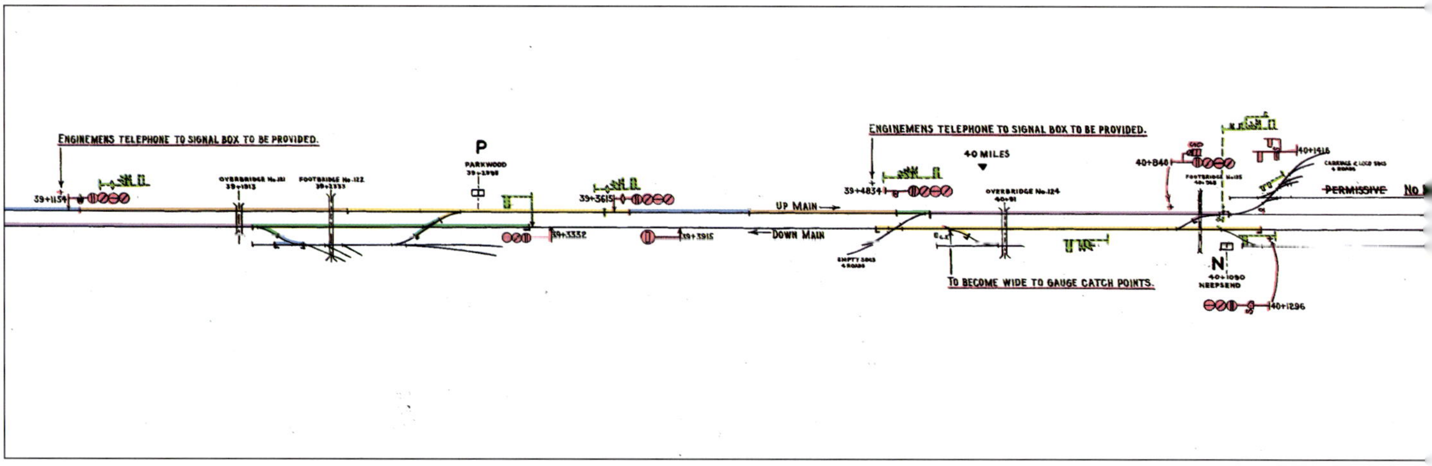

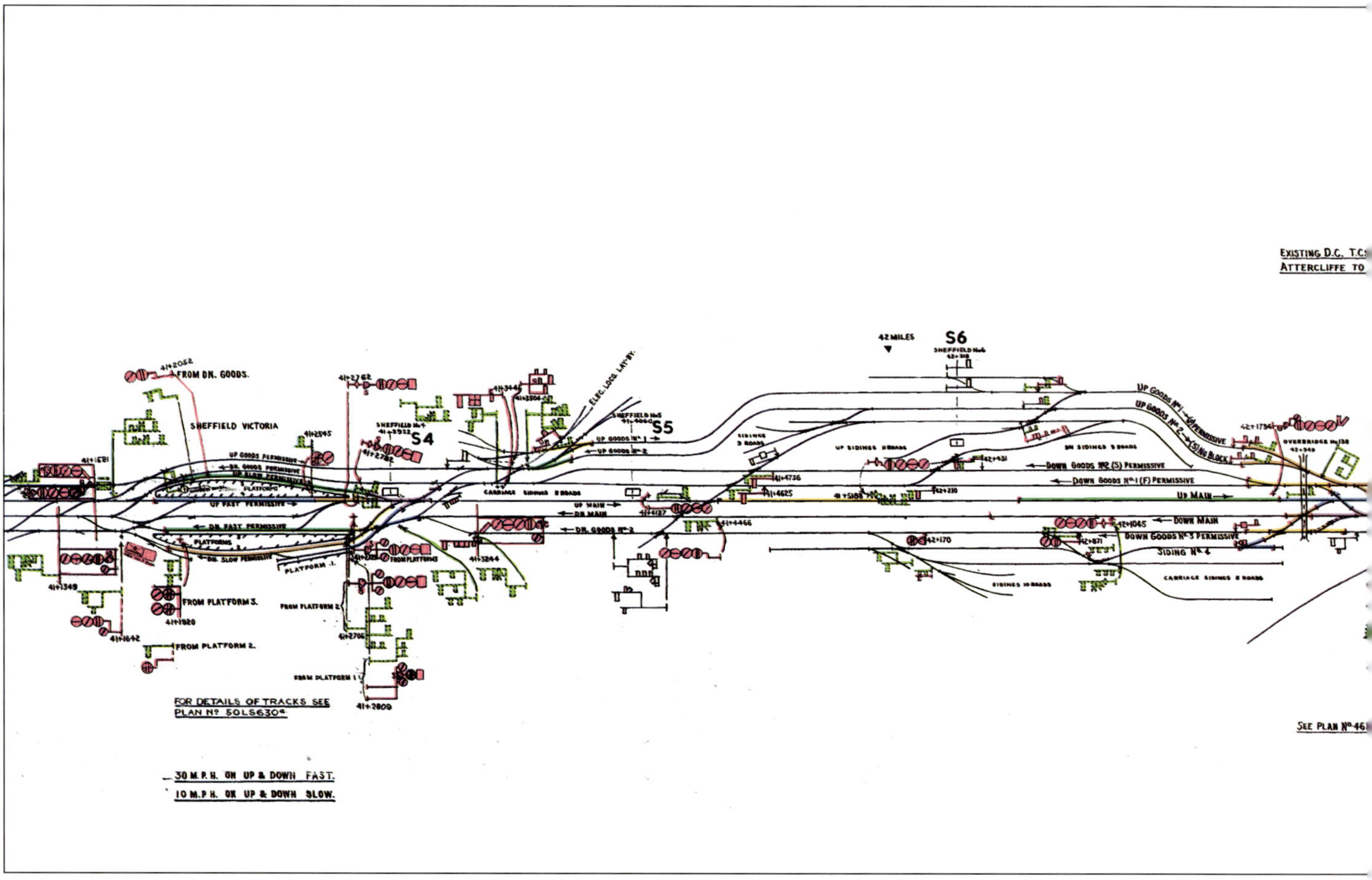

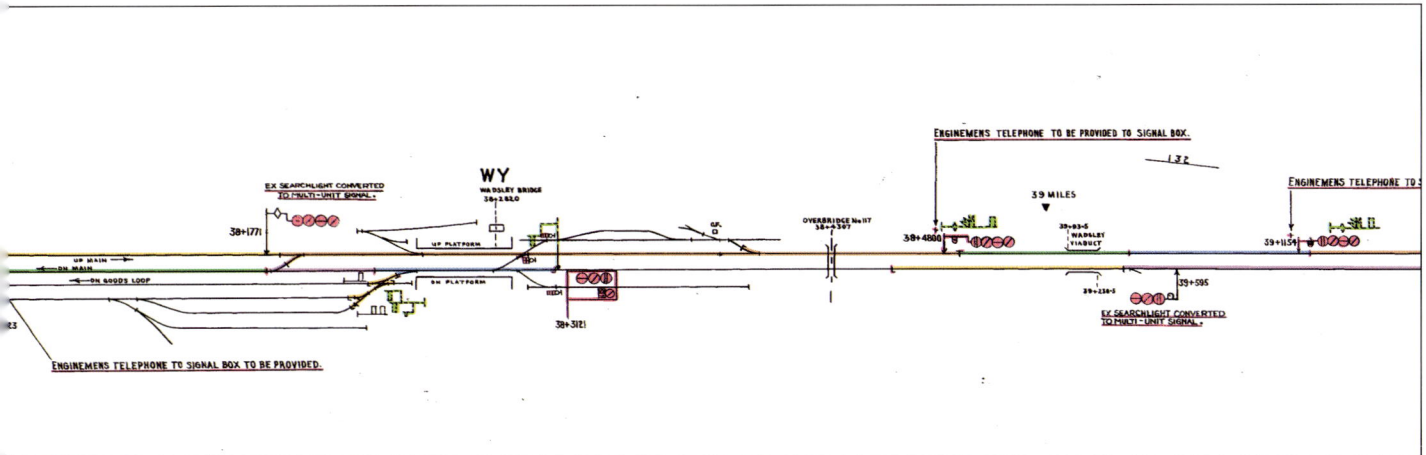

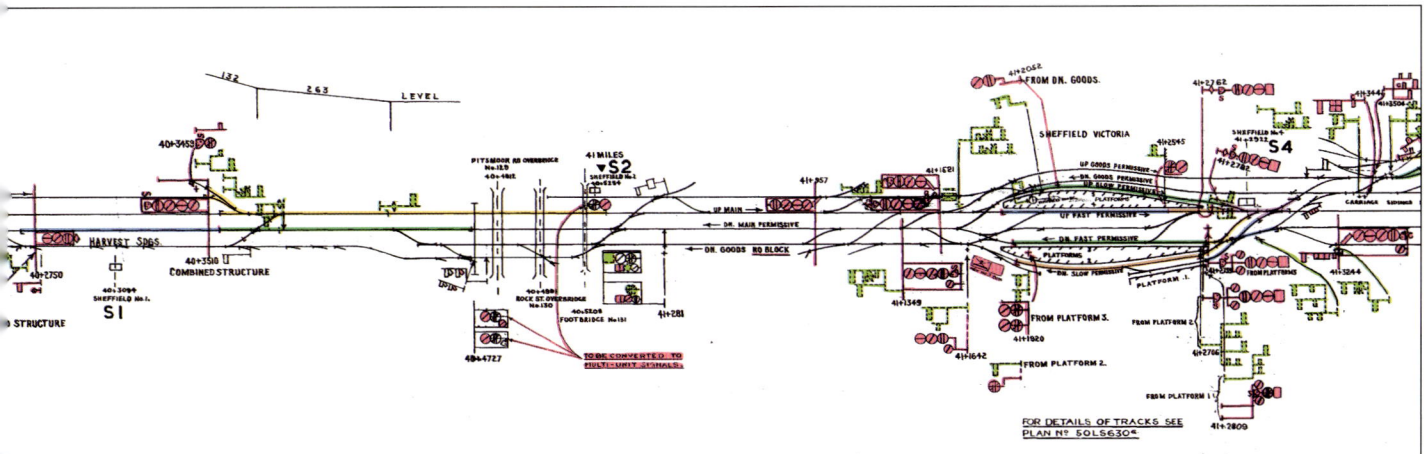

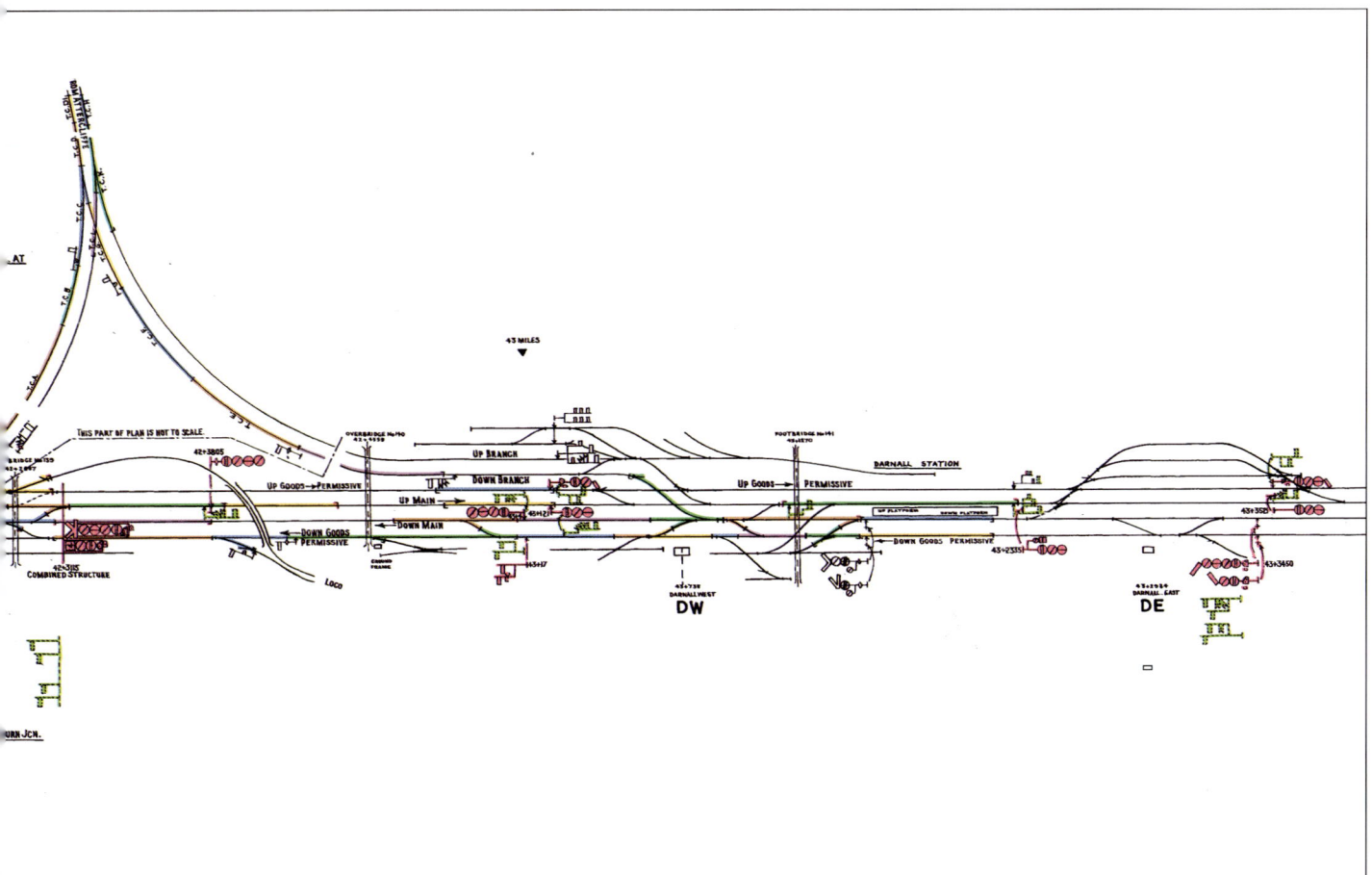

121

head, brought a single 16-ton mineral wagon and brake-van down the branch from Penistone Goods to Wath. The bankers returned, then left Wath for the final time, forming the last train over the branch.

By mid-afternoon the Worsborough branch was no longer an operational railway. Every signal box between West Silkstone Junction and Wombwell Main Junction had block instruments removed and level crossing gates padlocked. West Silkstone Junction itself was switched out. All that remained now were the demolition trains.

Out on the main line, the Class 76s plodded to and fro all afternoon working a variety of traffic from MGR services to a loose-coupled scrap metal train. But the line was slowly but surely winding down. At about 10.00pm the final MGR working left Barnsley Junction, the loaded wagons having been tripped up from Dodworth Colliery on the Barnsley line by No 45007. Class 76s Nos 76006 and 76014 arrived light from Guide Bridge, coupled on, paused for a few moments, then, with a blast of that familiar, mournful single-tone horn, wound their way out onto the main line and into the darkness. Barnsley Junction box was immediately closed and switched out, never to reopen.

A number of hardy enthusiasts were determined to stick it out to the end. Their vigil was brought to a close at around 5 am on 18 July, when 6M10, the Harwich–Trafford Park Speedlink working, passed through Woodhead New Tunnel running more than an hour late. It was hauled by Nos 76010 and 76016. By an uncanny coincidence, No 76016, one of the first pair of engines through the new tunnel, was also one of the last…

Top: **Nos 76007 and 76012 bring up the rear as bankers, and are seen here disappearing into Silkstone No 1 Tunnel on the last leg of the climb to West Silkstone Junction.** *Author*

Middle: **The last trains on the Wath branch had run by midday on the last day. Nos 76032 and 76034 head the final MGR train, 6M51, over Kendall Green Crossing.** *Andrew Walker*

Right: **The last MGR working of all, train 6M31, left Barnsley Junction at approximately 11.00pm, headed by Nos 76006 and 76014. The load had been worked from Dodworth Colliery, as 6T70, by No 45007 before being handed over to electric traction.** *Author*

7

The end?

When the signalmen at Dunford West, Torside and Valehouse exchanged the 7-5-5 bell signal and closed their boxes for the last time it was the end of an era, but not the end of the story. The line was officially closed – staff moved in immediately to fence off tunnel portals and the entry to railway land at Torside Crossing – but the unions and other protesters had put up such a spirited fight that they won from BR the concession that the line would not be demolished for at least 12 months, in case the wrong decision had been reached.

So the line between Hadfield and Penistone mouldered. Between Penistone and Sheffield it would remain in use for the next two years until the Huddersfield–Sheffield passenger service was diverted via Barnsley, and trains to and from the Stocksbridge steelworks continued running.

The Worsborough branch, however, suffered a more immediate fate; not covered by the agreement reached over the main line, demolition work began almost immediately with the removal of the overhead line. Track removal quickly followed and after that signal boxes, crossing gates and electrification portals were removed.

The line from Wath to Wombwell Main Junction remained in place to serve Barrow Colliery at Dovecliffe on the former Great Central line to Sheffield. Coal was tripped into Wath as before from Barrow and Darfield Main collieries, but was moved eastwards.

When the 12-month moratorium expired, British Rail began work on the main line itself, again by removing the overhead line. There was still union resistance to removing the running lines themselves, so they stayed a little longer, but between 1984 and 1986 first one running line then the other was recovered. Many of the concrete sleeper track panels were in good condition and were reused elsewhere. This had been part of BR's justification for closing the line, the one-off 'windfall' savings.

What of the locomotives themselves? When the line closed there were about 30 serviceable units, which were gathered at Guide Bridge and Reddish. Others needed only minor attention to bring them back into use. Some were beyond economic repair while a few were no more than grounded bodyshells, stripped for spares.

Part of BR's closure case was that they had reached the end of their working lives, but there is evidence that this was not the case. At the time David Ward was working for Dutch Railways (NS). He has an intriguing story to tell:

'At the beginning of the 1980s plans were being drawn up for the partial electrification of the 26-mile Europoort Harbour

Left and below left: **The first of these two views taken following closure is looking from the mouth of Silkstone No 2 Tunnel up the Worsborough Bank towards West Silkstone in January 1983. The branch was demolished very quickly after closure – even the unions saw no future for it. However, the main line was a different proposition, with the unions refusing cooperation to remove any running lines at all. Later one was lifted, but the unions still refused to remove the other. The second view is looking towards Dunford Bridge from the tunnel portal in January 1984.** *Keith Long*

Below: **Lewden Crossing, on the branch, is seen here after the removal of the up line and all overhead line equipment.** *Andrew Walker*

Right: A pair of Class 20 locomotives runs into Wath Yard with the T62 trip working from Dovecliffe via Wombwell Main Junction. The overhead line has been taken down, but the portals themselves are still in place. *Andrew Walker*

Below: A Manchester–Hadfield–Glossop Class 506 EMU crosses Dinting Viaduct on 27 April 1984, just a few days before work began on re-electrifying the route to 25kV AC. *Gavin Morrison*

line to Kijfhoek Goods yard at 1500v DC, hence the Dutch interest in a short-haul freight loco. The experience and running of the EM2s made the prospect [of buying some redundant Class 76s] financially very interesting to NS.

'Some many months later – I think about June 1981 – I was invited to attend an informal meeting at which a Derby-based BR representative was present and at which the possibility of purchasing some if not all of the 76s fitted for multiple working was discussed. The meeting ended with the Purchasing Manager [of NS] saying that he would send an official request (Tendering papers) to Derby for a formal meeting and for provisional quotes for locomotives and spares to be arranged.

'The letter was duly sent to the Derby CM&E Officer and a copy to our contact. Three months passed and there was no reply, not even an acknowledgement of receipt of the letter. A second letter was sent and a third, this time hand-delivered by myself. No reply was ever received and all knowledge of such a letter or even any meeting with NS officials was denied when contacted by telephone.

'It was in 1989, I think, that I came across a retired Derby engineer who told me that he knew of the 76 saga and that the word had gone out that not one [more] locomotive, or any spares common to EM1/2, was to be sold to NS. It would seem that what NS did to the EM2s had so incensed the Derby

management that the thought of the Class 76s being treated the same way was literally a nightmare for them.'

It is an interesting thought that the multiple-working Class 76s might have seen out another decade ambling around a corner of the Dutch railway system. Moreover, it is easy to see why BR management would find this prospect an embarrassing one – the locomotives were either worn out or they were not. If it turned out that NS could coax more life out of the fleet, it would leave BR looking less than honest – and make the Peak Park Planning Board's proposal that the existing assets could be used to keep a single-track line open in the hope of better times ahead look wise and far-sighted in comparison with BR itself.

In the event, the locomotives stood out of use for about a year. According to an anonymous contribution to 'The Woodhead Site' website, they remained perfectly serviceable. The contributor recalled how, as a Guide Bridge-based secondman, he and his fellows would wander down to the sidings where the Class 76s were stored. Pantographs would be manually pumped up and, as soon as they made contact with the overhead line, the locomotive would spring to life, gauges flickering, compressors whirring. 'But,' he recalled, 'we never dared to move them.'

In fact, two 76s did keep moving during this period. Nos 76003 and 76015, though officially withdrawn, were commandeered as depot shunters at Reddish, which found a second, if short-lived, lease of life servicing diesel traction.

The pair also occasionally made short forays beyond the shed boundaries, and there is a story, impossible now to prove or disprove, that an attempt was made to run the two locomotives, coupled together, to the buffers at Manchester Piccadilly! The tale goes that Control got wind of what was happening and stamped on it.

Immediately after closure there was a widespread feeling that closing the main line had been a mistake – one that would be regretted and perhaps even reversed in better times. But would those better times ever materialise? To date, the answer is no. The route now forms part of the Trans-Pennine Trail, a long-distance footpath and cycleway, but there have been three quite distinct and different proposals to reopen it. First off the blocks was the

Left: **Demolition of the main line was delayed because of the agreement struck between BR and the rail unions, but in this July 1983 view the overhead line has been removed and a Class 25 and Class 40 have been paired on a track recovery train pictured at Torside Crossing.** *Gavin Morrison*

Below left: **In 1984 DC traction finally came to an end on the MSW with the conversion of the MHG section. Here an AC Class 304 unit heads towards Glossop in December 1992.** *Gavin Morrison*

Below: **In the same year a classmate stands at the new end of the line – Hadfield.** *John Glover*

Central Railways proposal to use both the Woodhead line and the remains of the Great Central main line as part of the Berne Gauge freight route linking Liverpool with Lille in Northern France. The plan rode a wave of optimism about the prospects for international rail freight following the opening of the Channel Tunnel. Central Railways still has a telephone number and it is answered, but a request for information about the current status of the organisation brought no response.

bypass being two major examples – there was fundamentally nothing to prevent the line being reopened. A new two-platform station on the site of Sheffield Victoria and a fleet of Class 180 'Adelante'-type diesel multiple-units would allow a 15-minute-interval service that would link Sheffield with Manchester in 35 minutes. Penistone–Sheffield would be just 13 minutes, encouraging road commuters to switch to trains. If necessary, Woodhead Tunnel could be force-ventilated to get around the

Arriva Trains planned the rebirth of the Woodhead line as part of its bid for the Trans-Pennine Express franchise, using diesel-powered multiple-units. This illustration of a Class 180 'Adelante' train in house colours was produced as part of the bid. *Author's collection, courtesy of Arriva*

The second proposal came from the transport group Arriva, which in 2002/3 was bidding for the Trans-Pennine Express rail franchise. During the brief reign of the Strategic Rail Authority, franchise bidders were encouraged to think both big and long-term. Arriva did, suggesting that reopening the Woodhead line was the most sensible long-term solution to relieving congestion on the Hope Valley route.

This was more than just a back-of-an-envelope scheme. An engineering assessment of the route was made and reached the conclusion that, although parts of the formation had been breached – reservoir works at Crowden and the Stocksbridge

problem of diesel fumes. In the event Arriva lost the contest for Trans-Pennine Express and, shortly afterwards, the SRA itself ran out of money, suggesting that the plans would never have come to fruition anyway.

The most recent proposal is in some ways also the most interesting. Transrail UK is a small organisation set up to lobby for the idea of turning the route into something approaching an inland version of the Channel Tunnel shuttle, with trains of flat wagons carrying lorries from a purpose-built interchange near Hattersley – at the end of the M67 motorway, and close to the M60 motorway ring around Manchester   to Tinsley Yard, within sight of the M1 motorway.

Transrail claims that the scheme is a commercially viable one, needing no subsidy. It would attract heavy traffic off the A628/A616 trunk road that parallels the Woodhead line trackbed by allowing lorry drivers to take their rest breaks during the shuttle transit. This and the savings in fuel and wear

Manchester–Sheffield–Wath electrification track plans — Stage 3, Section 3

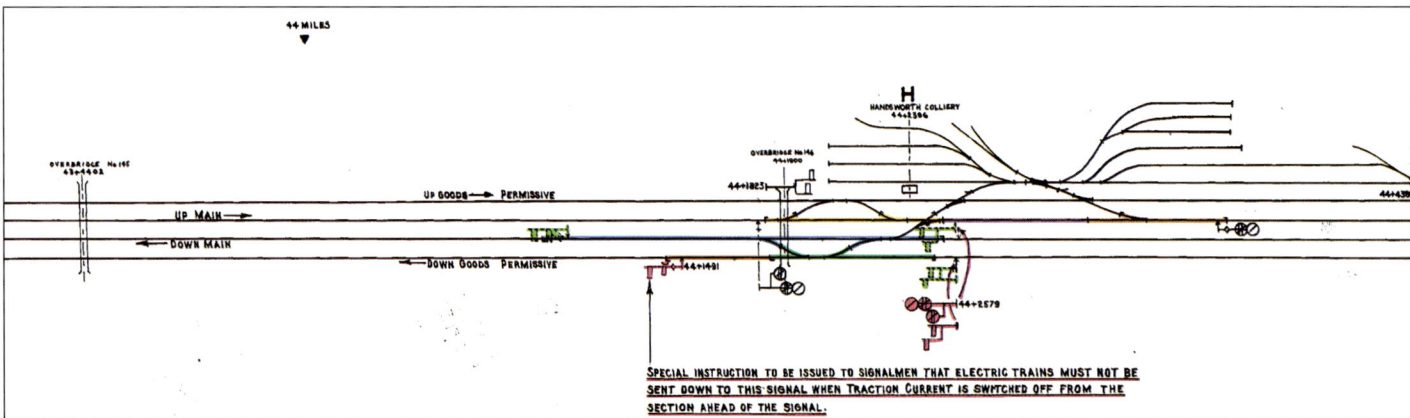

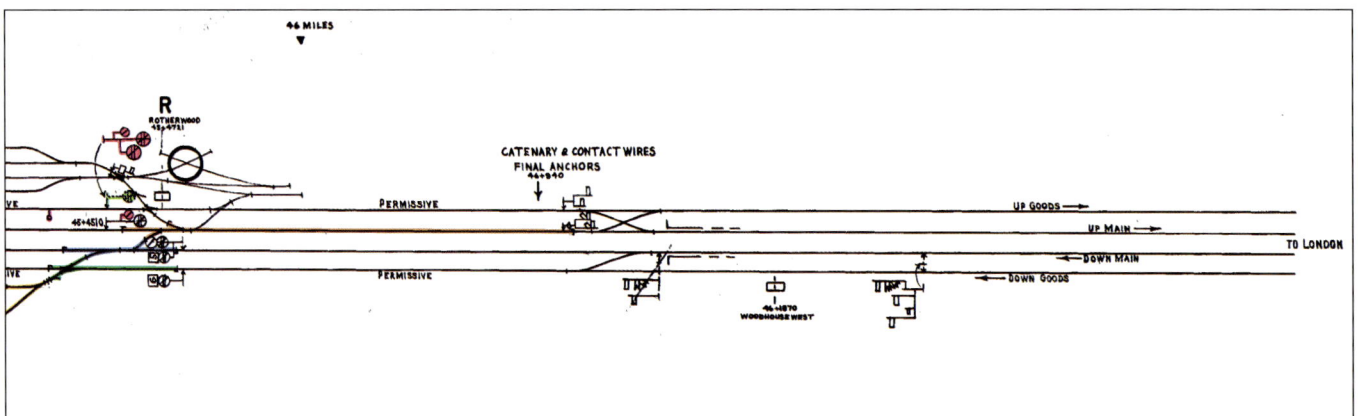

and tear would be sufficient to make it pay its way. It could be seen as a direct replacement for the Manchester–Sheffield motorway proposals of the 1960s and '70s.

The idea attracted support and opposition in equal measure, with critics deriding it as hare-brained. Supporters countered that the same idea has worked well for years in mainland Europe – lorries are banned on certain trans-Alpine routes, being compelled to use a rail shuttle instead. And it is also worth remembering that the only in-depth study of trans-Pennine freight movements ever carried out – conducted in the late 1980s – concluded that Woodhead had little future as a conventional freight route, but would make sense as a 'rolling road'-style shuttle, particularly if the environmental benefits of removing heavy traffic from an environmentally sensitive area – the Peak National Park – were taken into account.

Transrail UK was pushing its scheme at the same time as the Highways Agency was bringing forward plans for a new bypass for Mottram, Hollingworth and Tintwistle, an idea that horrified both the Peak Park Authority and local authorities on the eastern side of the Pennines, fearful of the additional traffic a better road would generate.

The M67 motorway plan, even after the closure of the railway, never came to anything. A bypass around Stocksbridge was constructed, but only as a single-carriageway road with crawler lanes. But even this decanted a substantial amount of extra traffic onto the A628, causing congestion and quality of life issues in the villages. The Mottram–Hollingworth–Tintwistle bypass plan was a complex one, recognising that giving better access to the central section of the A628 would simply generate even more traffic. So a plan to install traffic lights whose only function would be to deliberately delay traffic was drawn up. The idea was that making the A628 journey time slower would encourage some road users to find alternative routes. This somewhat startling plan was officially shelved in 2008 until at least 2016 because of the rising cost of building it. Does this give the Woodhead line a glimmer of hope?

Possibly. Economic forecasting suggests that another trans-Pennine crossing will be needed by 2030 if the north of England is to maintain its competitive edge. Supporters of the idea of reopening the route say that it would be madness to ignore the presence of one of the most modern tunnels in the country, which has been standing idle for almost 30 years. In addition, local authorities in Greater Manchester and Barnsley support the idea of safeguarding the route in case it is ever needed again.

But there are two new obstacles. At the time of writing the National Grid is laying new high-tension electricity cables through the new tunnel, claiming that the cables in the old up tunnel are worn out. This act has triggered the formation of a protest group to keep the new tunnel in a state to receive railway tracks. Government ministers have fudged this issue, claiming that there is no reason why the cables could not be removed and reinstated in one of the old tunnels should the new tunnel be needed again for railway use.

The second obstacle is that, even if it became available, it may be that the Woodhead New Tunnel would not be suitable after all. European Union regulations reach into many parts of our lives and railway tunnels have not escaped their attention. Tunnels must now have a continuous walkway to evacuate passengers in an emergency. There are other regulations, too, which the tunnel would struggle to meet.

For many this would be a nonsensical state of affairs. But in the end, it may be that, despite all the attempts to preserve a line of route and to ensure that the tunnel was there for when it might be needed again, the 5.00am Speedlink working on the morning of 18 July 1981 was indeed destined the be the last train of all…

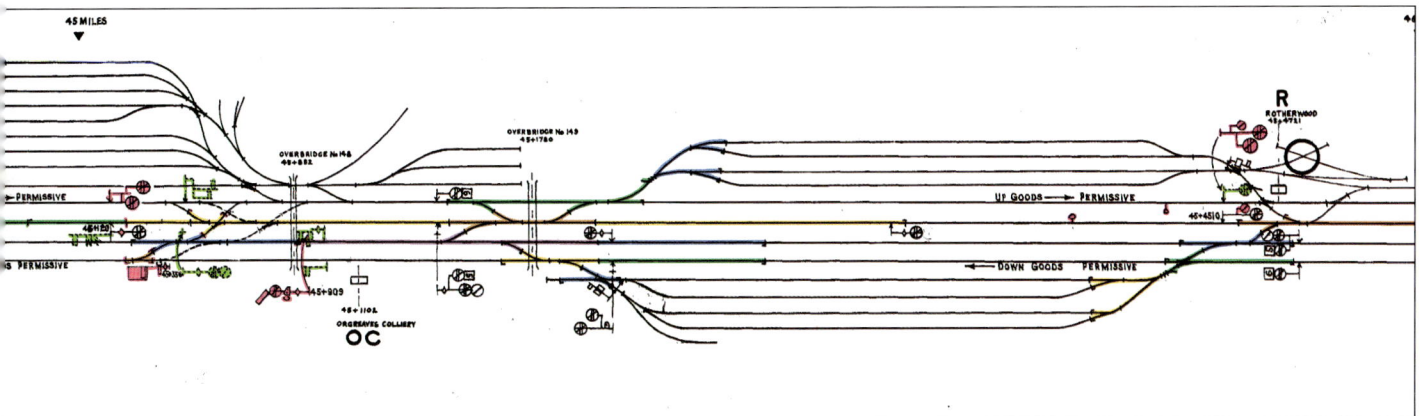

Index